MOVING
FORWARD

JAMES A. JOHNSON METRO SERIES

JAMES A. JOHNSON METRO SERIES

The Metropolitan Policy Program at the Brookings Institution is integrating research and practical experience into a policy agenda for cities and metropolitan areas. By bringing fresh analyses and policy ideas to the public debate, the program hopes to inform key decisionmakers and civic leaders in ways that will spur meaningful change in our nation's communities.

As part of this effort, the James A. Johnson Metro Series aims to introduce new perspectives and policy thinking on current issues and attempts to lay the foundation for longer-term policy reforms. The series examines traditional urban issues, such as neighborhood assets and central city competitiveness, as well as larger metropolitan concerns, such as regional growth, development, and employment patterns. The James A. Johnson Metro Series consists of concise studies and collections of essays designed to appeal to a broad audience. While these studies are formally reviewed, some will not be verified like other research publications. As with all publications, the judgments, conclusions, and recommendations presented in the studies are solely those of the authors and should not be attributed to the trustees, officers, or other staff members of the Institution.

MOVING FORWARD

The Future of Consumer Credit
and Mortgage Finance

NICOLAS P. RETSINAS
AND ERIC S. BELSKY
Editors

JOINT CENTER FOR HOUSING STUDIES
HARVARD UNIVERSITY
Cambridge, Massachusetts

BROOKINGS INSTITUTION PRESS
Washington, D.C.

Library of Congress Cataloging-in-Publication data
Moving forward : the future of consumer credit and mortgage finance / Nicolas P. Retsinas
and Eric S. Belsky, editors.
        p.   cm.
   Includes bibliographical references and index.
   Summary: "Explores what caused the housing and mortgage crisis and provides remedies
to repair the damage to ensure fairness, protect consumers, and guarantee soundness of the
financial system without stifling innovation and overly restricting access to credit and consumer choice"—Provided by publisher.
   ISBN 978-0-8157-0503-1 (pbk. : alk. paper)
   1.   Consumer credit—United States. 2.   Mortgage loans—United States.   I. Retsinas,
Nicolas Paul, 1946–   II. Belsky, Eric S.   III. Title.
   HG3756.U54M688 2011
   332.70973—dc22   2010043334

9 8 7 6 5 4 3 2 1

Printed on acid-free paper

Typeset in Adobe Garamond

Composition by Circle Graphics
Columbia, Maryland

Printed by R. R. Donnelley
Harrisonburg, Virginia

Contents

Acknowledgments

This book is a collection of papers presented at a symposium convened by the Joint Center for Housing Studies in February 2010 on the campus of the Harvard Business School. The purpose of the symposium was to explore the roots of the crisis that caused credit markets to seize up in late 2008 and, more important, to focus on the way forward. The symposium brought business, government, civic, and nonprofit leaders together to consider new research and new ideas about how best to better protect consumers and the safety and soundness of the financial system without overly restricting access to consumer and mortgage credit. Principal funding for the symposium was provided by the Ford Foundation, Freddie Mac, and NeighborWorks® America to whom we are indebted for seeing the value of sponsoring the event.

We would like to offer our special thanks and appreciation to Frank DeGiovanni and George McCarthy. We have long benefited from their experience and wise counsel. In addition, we would like to thank Ken Wade and Edward Golding, who along with George and Frank, helped shaped the research questions addressed in the papers presented at the symposium.

We are blessed with wonderful, hardworking colleagues at the Joint Center for Housing Studies and would like to express our appreciation to them and acknowledge their extraordinary contributions. Daniel McCue, Nela Richardson, Margaret Nipson, and Chris Herbert provided exceptional research support, while Mary Lancaster, Angela Flynn, Laurel Gourd, Jackie Hernandez, and Kerry Donahue organized the event and worked with authors in ways both large and small that ensured the success of the venture. To our longtime colleague and close personal friend, Pamela Baldwin, we thank you once again for the professionalism and excellent judgment you bring to all of our mutual endeavors.

To our wives, Joan Retsinas and Cynthia Wilson, we cannot thank you enough for your many contributions not only to the richness of our personal lives, but also our professional lives.

Introduction: Credit Everywhere, but Not a Drop to Drink

NICOLAS P. RETSINAS AND ERIC S. BELSKY

C redit, credit everywhere, nary a drop to drink." If Coleridge's ancient mariner could time-travel to the United States today, he would empathize. Low-income Americans live in a society lavish with houses, cars, and stuff lining the shelves in retail malls. The problem is money. Most low-wage workers do not have enough to buy what they need, much less what their heart desires.

And credit is scarce, at least for them. Worse, that scarce credit is becoming tighter.

This world of tight credit is not new, but many have forgotten that it ever existed. Until three years ago, we all were awash in credit and had been for some time. Many lenders were eager to extend largesse, regardless of where you worked, and were quick to pay scant attention to what you earned. Credit scoring let lenders, at least in theory, calibrate rates to risk. But since very few lenders said no, borrowers lived in a rarefied world of optimism, where tomorrow would inevitably be better.

In 2007 the cascade started: the subprime market fell, then the prime one; foreclosures followed. Median household income, rising for the past three decades, dipped. In March 2009 median income for households of all ages was $49,882, compared to $52,378 in 2001. For low-income Americans (many moderate-income ones too), "tomorrow" turned grim. Rising unemployment led to more foreclosures, which depressed the revenues coming to cities and towns, which

I

forced cuts in services, which exacerbated the plight of residents. As for the lenders, many tottered.

Uncle Sam came to the bailout rescue, with the Troubled Asset Relief Program, Cash for Clunkers, and the Federal Housing Tax Credit.

Loose credit, particularly subprime loans, emerged as the bogey. The solution: shut off those spigots, particularly to the workers with minimal collateral and shaky credit histories. Taking a page from Coleridge, America's financial gurus saw the subprime market as an albatross, and they wanted to slay it. At least for now, the gurus have stifled the market.

The secondary consequences of this excision have been grim. Low-wage workers desperately need credit to survive, if not to prosper. Try getting to a job without a car; try buying a car—even a rickety second-hand one—without credit. Try renting an apartment without a security deposit or buying a major appliance without a credit card. For many renters, homeownership is still a strategically sound investment, just as it was for generations past. But the would-be buyer needs a mortgage.

Closing the spigots to easy credit "solved" the problem of cascading delinquencies: no credit eventually led to slowing defaults. Yet that strategy has left millions of Americans without any way to leverage their incomes. Just as crucially, the economy depends on consumers—not just wealthy ones—having access to credit. In the past year retail outlets, car manufacturers, and home builders have watched their earnings plummet, their unsold inventories mount.

In February 2010 the Joint Center for Housing Studies of Harvard University convened a national symposium, "Moving Forward: The Future of Consumer Credit and Mortgage Finance." Experts from both the public and private sectors came to ponder ways to open up those spigots responsibly and fairly.

Eugene Ludwig ("Comments: Seven Steps to a Rational Credit Policy"), reflecting on the history of consumer and mortgage credit, offered seven steps that could be taken to ensure decent access to credit for low- and moderate-income people, while protecting consumers and the economy. Most of these suggestions focused on ways to strengthen regulation and macroeconomic policy, but Ludwig also called for placing renewed emphasis on jobs and small businesses in the national conversation on credit, as well as for studying and learning from successes with microcredit in other nations.

Eric Belsky and Nela Richardson ("Rebuilding the Housing Finance System after the Boom and Bust in Nonprime Mortgage Lending") traced the regulatory and lender actions that led up to the fall and proposed measures to maintain a market for low-income borrowers, including greater regulation of the "shadow" banking system, a retooled role for government in guaranteeing debt, and stronger risk-based pricing models.

Rachel Schneider and Melissa Koide ("How Should We Serve the Short-Term Credit Needs of Low-Income Consumers?") zeroed in on short-term credit. Low-income borrowers who need to replace a broken appliance, repair a car, or make up for lost income seek out not just banks and credit unions, but payday lenders, rent-to-own centers, pawnshops, refund anticipation lenders, and family members. The authors decried an "insufficient supply of products that are profitable for the provider yet affordable and responsibly structured." They examined several potential solutions, including credit unions that make small-dollar loans, installment lenders, account advance products (available to borrowers with direct deposit accounts), and workplace loans, often repaid through payroll deductions.

Marsha J. Courchane and Peter Zorn ("A Changing Credit Environment and Its Impact on Low-Income and Minority Borrowers and Communities") focused on the "price of credit risk"—that is, the price that lenders must pay investors to hold additional risk. With risk-based pricing, higher-risk borrowers pay higher rates.

As credit spreads widen and credit tightens, there is greater movement toward risk-based pricing. The reverse holds when credit spreads narrow. Ironically, just as greater risks were being taken at the peak of home prices, there was too little room in spreads to cover the greater risks. The authors explored the impact on low-income and minority borrowers of the flattening of risk-based pricing in 2004–07 and the tightening of credit in 2008.

Before 2008, the U.S. housing finance industry was the envy of the world; post 2008, the system has been marked by foreclosures and defaults. Michael Lea ("Alternative Forms of Mortgage Finance: What Can We Learn from Other Countries?") discussed the Danish model, the European covered bond model, the Australian and U.K. depository model, and the Canadian and Japanese guarantee model. He cautioned, "All models have strengths and weaknesses" and suggested helpful features of each.

Allen Fishbein and Ren Essene ("The Home Mortgage Disclosure Act at Thirty-Five: Past History, Current Issues") spotlighted the Home Mortgage Disclosure Act, enacted in 1975. Initially, the act, with a focus on redlining in inner cities, prompted the compilation of summary statistics on loans in census tracts. In an expansionary period, the act as amended in 1989 shifted to mortgage discrimination at the loan level, adding data on the race and income of mortgage applicants and whether or not their applications were accepted. Now the act has shifted its focus to reverse redlining. Revised in 2001, Regulation C requires lenders to collect pricing information for high-cost loans. The authors discussed the possibilities for expanding reporting under the act.

Howell E. Jackson ("Loan-Level Disclosure in Securitization Transactions: A Problem with Three Dimensions") pointed to the initial problem of disclosure: the tranches of initial securities were merged with the tranches from other offerings into collateralized debt obligations and other complex creations. With no uniform loan-level information, analysts could not distinguish good from bad loans or evaluate the collateralized debt obligations. One call today is for new reporting requirements for securitized loans, including public disclosure.

To date, the U.S. system of consumer finance regulation has been "idiosyncratically fragmented" compared to the systems in other developed countries. John Campbell, Howell E. Jackson, Brigitte Madrian, and Peter Tufano ("The Regulation of Consumer Financial Products: An Introductory Essay with a Case Study on Payday Lending") discussed the administration's proposed Consumer Financial Protection Bureau, including the limits to regulation, the role of measurement, and the types of future research needed.

Before the fall, credit was too loose, the disclosure of risk was minimal, and oversight was fragmented. Over the past three years, analysts have looked back, laboriously probing the agents of "blame."

These panelists looked forward. They recognized the crucial niche of credit in the lives of working Americans. Their challenge was to envision a system that would extend credit to low-income borrowers, while keeping all parties—borrowers, lenders, and investors—solvent. Gone, they hoped, will be today's complex fine-print financial product explanations that baffle even graduates of the finest business schools. (Try reading the terms of conditions for a credit card, which can run as long as eight pages.) The explanations, as well as the products, will be clear and easy to understand.

Financial education will go hand-in-hand with borrowing. Drivers do not need to understand carburetors to buy cars, but they do need some basic financial understanding to borrow for those cars. "Borrower emptor" has been not just cruel to the borrower, but also disastrous to the financial system.

Lenders will profit not from the origination of the loans, but from their performance, giving lenders a genuine incentive to lend to people with a reasonable chance of paying. Again, defaults have wreaked havoc not just on individual borrowers, but also on lenders and investors.

The government will move off the sidelines, no longer trusting "the market" to even out the cyclical dips and rises. The 2008 dip was too deep for the government simply to step aside, with anodyne bromides about short- and long-term cycles working themselves out. The government moved to bail out a collapsed system; from now on, it will remain involved more actively in overseeing that system.

Transparency will be the watchword not just for borrowers, but also for investors. In the past, toxic mortgages infected the financial products, but those mortgages were buried deep in complex securities. No longer will securities obfuscate the toxic loan components.

There will be a more unified regulatory structure for financial institutions. Consumer financial oversight will no longer be an appendage to a bevy of diverse regulators, but it will be centralized in a single authority.

Steps in these directions are already being taken. Revisions to the Truth in Lending Act, the Home Owners Equity Protection Act, and the Real Estate Settlement Procedures Act have been made. The financial reform bill that passed Congress in the summer of 2010 has improved the loan-level disclosures for investors and the disclosures of credit histories in the Home Mortgage Disclosure Act, promised to strengthen consumer protection through creation of a unified bureau within the Federal Reserve, imposed more stringent requirements on underwriting loans that do not meet a narrow "qualified" definition, placed limits on the ways that brokers can be compensated, and improved the disclosure of this compensation. While these steps will bring greater transparency and reduce risk taking, their impacts on access to credit remain to be seen.

Let us return to the ancient mariner: he repented; the albatross lived. So too the nation must reopen the spigots of credit to low- and moderate-income Americans, but those spigots should work more efficiently and fairly for borrowers, lenders, investors, and the nation as a whole.

Comment: Seven Steps to a Rational Credit Policy

EUGENE LUDWIG

While shock waves from the biggest financial crisis since the Great Depression continue to roll through our nation, some experts wonder how we will reconcile extending credit to low- and moderate-wage borrowers, including credit-impaired borrowers, while protecting the economy and consumers. This question is occasioned, of course, by the current mortgage and consumer catastrophe we are living through and by the hue and cry raised by those who claim that the entire financial storm of the past three years was caused by the Community Reinvestment Act and, in their view, benighted programs to make credit available to the low- to moderate-income borrower.

Lending to any consumer was viewed as an unsound—if not unsafe—banking practice until the beginning of the twentieth century. Indeed, prior to that time, banks, including national banks, were prohibited from making mortgage loans to consumers. In the eighteenth century, loans were only made to the wealthiest and most powerful individuals. It was not until the 1920s that national banks entered the business of consumer lending.

The move was sparked by the mayor of New York City, who asked the predecessor of Citibank to start making small loans to consumers. Loans from reputable banking institutions would provide a more acceptable way to deliver much-

These remarks were previously published on February 10, 2010, at www.americanprogress.org/issues/2010/04/extending_credit_fairly.html.

needed credit to strapped consumers than was being provided by pawnshops at that time. Indeed, the lore is that to get into the business of learning how to make the loans safely, Citi hired two former pawnshop operators.

This seminal event by Citi is only one step along a path to the "democratization" of credit. Like all human pathways, it has been neither smooth nor straight. But along the way we have learned many lessons about how to make safe loans to poorer borrowers. These loans can relieve suffering, encourage entrepreneurship, revive neighborhoods, and foment a better future for the borrower.

Whether it is for the promise of homeownership, a college education, or the start of a new business, when made prudently and used responsibly, credit put in the hands of low- and moderate-income borrowers is a powerful tool to better their lives. The successes that Nobel Peace Prize winner Muhammad Yunus, founder of Grameen Bank; Fazle Abed, creator of the Bangladesh Rural Advancement Committee, a sprawling Bangladesh-based microfinancing operation; Ingrid Munro, founder of Jamii Bora, a financing operation that works with the poor in Nairobi, Kenya; and a host of others are a testament to the virtues of this process.

At the same time, just as credit can be a powerful tool for good, it can also be misused. The last 200 years in America and around the world are a testament to the boom and bust of credit cycles, most of which have nothing to do with lending to low- and moderate-income borrowers. Rather, they are proof of both the natural tendency of financial markets to swing to excess and then bust and the fact that innovation often produces an immediate surge when the controls come off, ending in grief.

In the credit arena, low- and moderate-income borrowers not only are affected by the natural volatility of the credit markets, but also are vulnerable to unscrupulous lenders. This group has been preyed upon practically since Adam and Eve. From the company store to loan sharks to pawnbrokers to tin men and unprincipled merchant lenders, quick-buck artists have found ways to make money by taking advantage of the poor.

In this cycle, we had a combustible mixture of a governmental philosophy that allowed for negative savings, high liquidity, minimal regulation, and complex financial instruments that allowed risk to be sliced, diced, and misunderstood. To compound matters, the government maintained a view that housing prices would continue to rise and home values would fill the hole in the consumer's badly weakened financial statements.

And then there were the wolves—in this case, a combination of mortgage brokers and others—who profited from pushing exotic loans to people who could ill afford to make the monthly payments when they readjusted. We could blame the poor for this and deny them credit—some of that is going on now—but that would be a bit like blaming the sheep for the fact that wolves exist.

In addition to the wolves, there were what Nicolas P. Retsinas, director of Harvard University's Joint Center for Housing Studies, referred to in his December

2009 *Boston Globe* op-ed piece as "strategic defaulters."[1] This "new breed of home-owner-economicus," Retsinas wrote, "compounded the problem in the current credit cycle." The strategic defaulters are not the low- to medium-wage-earning borrowers. They are defaulters who are able but unwilling to pay. They would rather default on their mortgage obligations, viewing them as they would a bad investment.

So how do we reconcile making low- and moderate-income credit accessible while at the same time protecting consumers and the economy? Let me give you seven steps to consider:

1. Creating appropriate underwriting practices tailored to the particular credit product; we have learned an enormous amount about lending responsibly and safely to low- and moderate-income borrowers, including the utility of rainy day reserves, credit counseling, lending circles, more traditional income ratios, and some down-payment obligations, among others

2. Insisting on disclosures to borrowers that are honest, simple, and understandable

3. Prohibiting, along with enforcement efforts that have teeth, practices (so prevalent in the past several years) of phony credit applications and real estate appraisals

4. Policing the unregulated and underregulated providers of financial services, or, in other words, the wolves that prey upon the poor

5. Altering our national conversation about credit, placing renewed emphasis on jobs and small businesses rather than homes

6. Engaging in sound macroeconomic and financial regulatory policies (so absent this past decade) to avoid credit spikes and busts that fuel unemployment and force even responsible borrowers into unemployment; in this regard, much of the lending and financial excesses in this cycle were not low- and moderate-income borrowers, but upper-middle-income borrowers who embraced sophisticated yet risky financial products

7. Studying and learning from the successful practices of microcredit and other experts around the world.

I am confident that lending to low- and moderate-income borrowers can be reconciled with sound consumer and economic practices. When done correctly, this kind of lending can be a viable business for financial institutions. What is more, its benefits are sweeping and tangible, with the results clearly seen within households, neighborhoods, cities, and states throughout the country.

---

1. Nicolas P. Retsinas, "When Home Isn't Where the Heart Is." *Boston Globe*, December 21, 2009.

1

Rebuilding the Housing Finance System after the Boom and Bust in Nonprime Mortgage Lending

ERIC S. BELSKY AND NELA RICHARDSON

The cycle of boom and bust in nonprime[1] and nontraditional[2] mortgage lend-ing in the United States is without precedent. The factors that fueled the boom and the way it unfolded sowed the seeds for the bust that, in hindsight,

The authors wish to acknowledge the following individuals for their help in researching this chapter: Daniel McCue, Meg Nipson, Kevin Park, Polina Dekhtiar, and Jordan Roberts. They also wish to thank William C. Apgar for his advice and his work on this project. Lastly, they wish to thank Frank DeGiovanni and George C. McCarthy of the Ford Foundation for their support and keen insights into the operation of mortgage markets. The views presented here are the authors' own and do not represent the views of the Commodity Futures Trading Commission, its commissioners, or staff.

1. "Nonprime" encompasses subprime, Alt-A, and higher-priced lending. Subprime and Alt-A are, however, imprecise terms. Typically, subprime loans are made to borrowers with credit scores below a certain cutoff (commonly a 620 cutoff, although somewhat higher cutoffs may also have been used by some lenders when self-identifying loans). Alt-A mortgages are typically loans to borrowers with near-prime credit scores, loans requiring little or no income documentation, or loans allowing high debt-to-income ratios. All three categories of nonprime loans also include some loans with high loan-to-value ratios. When we refer to federal Home Mortgage Disclosure Act data, the term "higher priced" is used because it has a specific definition. While often used interchangeably, the terms "sub-prime" and "higher-priced loans" are not equivalent. Definitional issues make drawing common con-clusions about nonprime lending difficult.

2. "Nontraditional" encompasses loan products that were rarely used prior to the 2000s, such as interest-only and payment-option loans. Interest-only loans expose borrowers to payment resets when principal payments kick in after a specified period. Payment-option loans can result in negative amor-tization. Balloon loans also fall under the nontraditional heading, as do some adjustable-rate loans such as 2/28 loans with teasers. All these loans expose borrowers to extra risk. There is some overlap between nonprime lending and nontraditional products (and a large overlap if adjustable-rate hybrid loans with teasers are included) because these loan products were extended to some nonprime borrowers.

appears to have been inevitable. The amount of risk in the system ballooned as a result of changes in lending practices. At the same time that credit was opened up to borrowers who previously had been denied loans because of past problems repaying their debts, many other underwriting standards were loosened. In addition, products with heavy payment reset risks proliferated in both the prime and nonprime markets. This layering of risk at or near the peak of an overheated housing market proved very deleterious to loan performance.

Yet few predicted that performance in the nonprime mortgage market and the way these loans were packaged, sold, and referenced in the global capital markets would cause a loss of investor confidence so profound that it would spark a severe global financial crisis.[3] It was not until August 2007 that the Federal Reserve decided that the rapidly eroding performance of subprime mortgage loans—and evaporating demand for the securities they backed—was enough of a threat to the broader economy to warrant easing monetary policy. In an unusual move, the Fed lowered the discount rate for borrowing from the Federal Reserve in between regularly scheduled meetings of the Federal Open Market Committee. Although the committee held the more important federal funds rate target constant until its September meeting, lowering the discount rate signaled both its concern and willingness to take action to contain the damage from the deteriorating subprime residential mortgage market.

These interventions would prove inadequate. A little more than a year later, and within the span of less than two weeks, the government helped to rescue Bear Stearns and Merrill Lynch from collapse, allowed Lehman Brothers to fail, and bailed out insurance giant AIG. Credit markets froze nearly solid in the fall of 2008, the stock market went into a freefall, and job losses accelerated sharply. The interconnectedness of the global financial system became apparent as problems emanating from residential debt in the United States and in the derivatives used to hedge and trade mortgage risk prompted a global credit crisis.

Uncovering the causes of the nonprime boom and bust is essential to formulating effective government and business responses to the crisis. At stake are not only the safety and soundness of the financial system the next time that excess global liquidity creates pressure to relax underwriting standards and raise leverage, but also the access that Americans will have to mortgage credit, on what terms, and at what cost. Access to mortgage credit is vital to building assets through homeownership and opens up avenues to finance consumption and investment on terms that are generally more favorable than those for consumer credit. Government cannot easily back away from it without risking great economic dislocations. Especially at a time when the share of U.S. households with credit problems has soared, how credit-impaired borrowers are treated will shape asset-building oppor-

---

3. Capital markets are the secondary markets where loans with terms of one year or more, and the securities backed by them, are bought and sold.

tunities during the next economic expansion for millions of Americans. And while the recent housing bust has underscored the risky nature of investing in residential real estate, it also has created the conditions—ratios of house price to income in some locations at or near lows not seen since the early 1990s—that could make homeownership very attractive for years to come.

Understanding the boom and bust in nonprime and nontraditional lending first requires a brief discussion of the evolution of the housing finance system in the United States from the 1970s onward.

Evolution of the Modern U.S. Housing Finance System

Throughout the 1970s, 1980s, and 1990s, mortgage lending was conducted with a limited number of mortgage products that dominated the market and were underwritten, with few exceptions, to long-accepted common standards. These relatively stringent underwriting criteria formed the backbone of a single "prime" market in which credit was allocated by adhering to these tight standards and charging all who were able to qualify for mortgages a similar interest rate. Only loans with higher ratios of loan to value commonly incurred the additional payment of a private or government mortgage insurance premium to offset the greater risk associated with lower-down-payment lending. As such, the system of credit allocation was considered a rationing system rather than a risk-based pricing system. This began to change around the early to middle 1990s, when—haltingly at first—individuals with previous problems repaying their debts were allowed to qualify for a loan but were charged a higher interest rate to cover the expected higher risk of default. Thus began a period of pricing for risk in a nonprime market rather than allocating mortgage credit at a common price in a single prime market. Around the same time, the number of mortgage products available to borrowers slowly began to increase, first with more widespread use of "hybrid" adjustable rates (which had an initial adjustment period of more than one year followed by conversion to a fixed rate). But by the mid-2000s nonprime lending had taken off, and nontraditional products had proliferated.

Segmentation of the Mortgage Market

During the 1970s, 1980s, and most of the 1990s, the mortgage market was essentially segmented into three parts. Two were parts of the "conventional" market, defined as the market for loans that did not have explicit federal guarantees against the loss of principal. The largest segment of the mortgage market was the "conforming" side of the conventional market. This was the market for loans purchased by or placed into mortgage-backed securities (MBSs) guaranteed by Fannie Mae and Freddie Mac. These two shareholder-owned corporations were chartered by Congress. Because of their unique charters and small lines of credit from the Department of Treasury, these government-sponsored enterprises (GSEs) were

Figure 1-1. *GSE Share of Originations and Issuance of Mortgage-Backed Securities, 1990–2008*

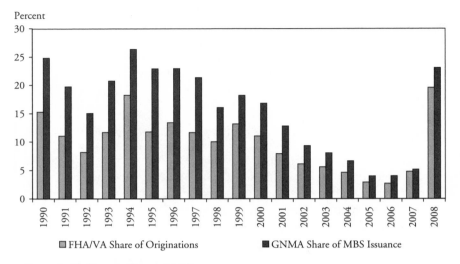

Percent

FHA/VA Share of Originations   ■ GNMA Share of MBS Issuance

Source: Inside Mortgage Finance (2009).

perceived by investors as having the implicit backing of the federal government. The two factors that made loans "conforming" is that they followed the exacting underwriting standards demanded by these two corporations and fell underneath loan size limits established by the federal government and benchmarked to a federal index. The other segment of the conventional market was the "jumbo" side. This was the market for loans above the conforming limits established for Fannie Mae and Freddie Mac or not acceptable because they deviated from the underwriting requirements of these two secondary mortgage market giants. While some small portion of these jumbo loans had more lenient standards or product features than Fannie Mae and Freddie Mac would accept, the overwhelming majority of loans simply were above the loan limits. Thus the conventional market for nearly the entire period also was the prime market. The third segment of the market was made up of loans or mortgage-backed securities explicitly guaranteed by the federal government. Loans insured by the government had more lenient down payment and debt-to-income requirements than conventional loans and were subject to relatively low mortgage limits established by Congress. The two major agencies insuring mortgages with the full faith and credit of the federal government were the Federal Housing Administration (FHA) and the Veterans Benefits Administration. Ginnie Mae was the agency that guaranteed the timely payment of principal and interest of securities backed by loans insured by the FHA. Figure 1-1 shows these shares over time.

Growth of the Secondary Mortgage Market

A hallmark of the evolution of the housing finance system since the 1970s has been the growth and development of the secondary market for mortgages, mostly in the form of securities they guaranteed. The secondary market developed rapidly over the course of the 1980s and continued to grow in the 1990s and 2000s. Initially, the movement away from holding whole loans in portfolios was precipitated by macroeconomic events in the 1980s and a series of laws that deregulated mortgage lending and supported the secondary market in general and Fannie Mae and Freddie Mac in particular. These included the Depository Institutions Deregulation and Monetary Control Act, the Alternative Transactions Mortgages Parity Act, and the Secondary Mortgage Market Enhancement Act. The macroeconomic events that facilitated the secondary market included the deep recession of the early 1980s and the wild gyrations in interest rates that hurt banks and thrifts stuck holding thirty-year fixed-rate mortgages when interest rates first rose sharply (because the interest rates they had to offer to attract depositors were above the interest rates on the loans they held in portfolio) and then when rates plummeted (because borrowers prepaid their mortgages and returned principal at a time when mortgage rates were much lower).[4]

These events led more and more lenders to seek ways to get the implicit backing of the federal government by selling loans to Fannie Mae and Freddie Mac or to get explicit backing by using FHA insurance and Ginnie Mae MBS guarantees. In addition, these events generated interest in finding ways to convert illiquid assets into more tradable and liquid homogeneous securities with implicit or explicit government backing. Financial engineering in the secondary market gave another reason: the capacity to buy different classes of multiple-class securities backed by a single pool, with each class having different priorities from principal and interest payments—and hence having different exposures to prepayment risks. This process was known as "structured" finance because classes were structured to appeal to a variety of different appetites for prepayment risk. Lastly, as banks and thrifts lost market share to pension funds and insurance companies and as appetite for dollar-denominated mortgage assets around the world increased, the demand for securities backed implicitly or explicitly by the federal government also grew. Investors who did not make the mortgage loans or specialize in mortgage lending could look past the credit risk that taking on such debt might pose when acquiring mortgage assets. Thus participants in the market were persuaded that credit risk was fully neutralized by the FHA and Ginnie Mae, Fannie Mae, or Freddie Mac guarantees (with private mortgage insurance playing a supporting role).

4. Curry and Shibut (2000).

Figure 1-2. *Broker Share of Originations, 1995–2005*

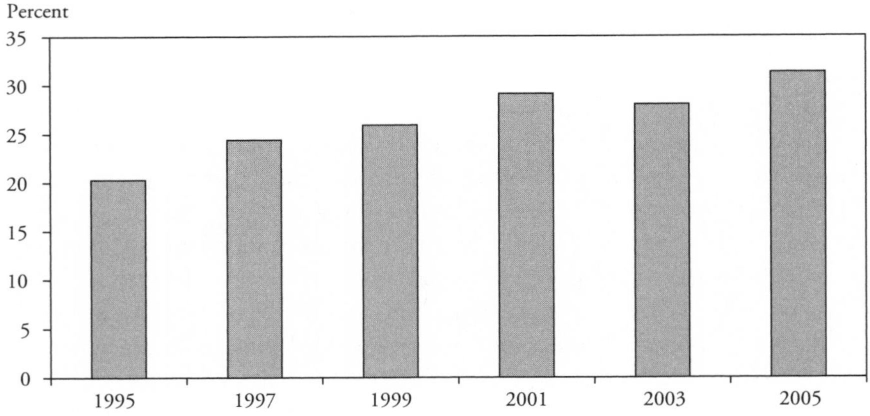

Percent

Source: Inside Mortgage Finance (2009).

Industry Consolidation and the Originate-to-Distribute Model

Two other important developments in the 1980s and 1990s are also worth noting. One—the increasing reliance on an "originate-to-distribute" model—is directly related to growth in the secondary market. The other was consolidation within the industry.

As the secondary market developed, more and more mortgages were originated by brokers, mortgage bankers, and banks and thrifts that collected a fee for originating loans (and sometimes for retaining servicing rights and the fees associated with them) but then conveyed loans to issuers of "agency" mortgage-backed securities (as MBSs guaranteed by Fannie Mae, Freddie Mac, and Ginnie Mae were called). During the 1990s, brokers steadily increased their share of the originations from 18.8 percent in 1994 to 27.9 percent in 2000 and to a peak of 31.3 percent in 2005 (see figure 1-2). The issuers of securities backed by loans conveyed by these brokers then assumed the credit risk on the loans. Furthermore, servicing rights became actively traded so that the originating lender often did not end up servicing the loans it originated. This system was efficient in that it allowed some firms to specialize in retail originations, others in pooling and wholesaling loans, and others in issuing securities and managing and pricing credit risk. The increasing use of mortgage brokers also allowed lenders to rely on variable rather than fixed costs to source loans, which had great advantages in the volatile and cyclical mortgage business. However, it also created a system in which credit risk was concentrated in a small number of entities and in which loan originators had more incentive to produce high unit volumes to earn up-front fees than to concern themselves with the long-term performance of the loans originated.

Figure 1-3. *Market Consolidation among Mortgage Originators, 1996–2008*[a]

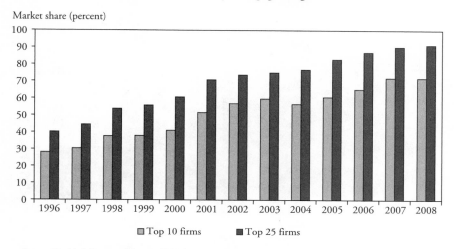

Market share (percent)

□ Top 10 firms   ■ Top 25 firms

Source: Inside Mortgage Finance (2009).
a. Market share is measured by dollar volume of loans.

Consolidation in mortgage origination and servicing was fueled by the increasing commoditization of mortgages that secondary markets and advances in information technology allowed as well as by consolidation in the banking industry (which was, in turn, fueled by deregulation, such as the lifting of interstate banking restrictions). In 1996 the largest twenty-five lending institutions accounted for 40 percent of the $785 billion in home purchase and refinance originations. By 2008 their share had grown to more than 90 percent (see figure 1-3). Mortgage servicing also was consolidating (see figure 1-4). Like the originate-to-distribute model, consolidation had strengths and weaknesses. On the one hand, economies of scale were achieved that brought down the costs of originating and servicing. On the other, a small customer base for Fannie Mae and Freddie Mac grew to have increasing market power in negotiating with these corporations. A handful could produce large exposures to counterparty risks (the risk that counterparties will work against the interests of another or that the failure of one will cause significant harm to another).

Emergence and Rapid Growth of Nonprime Lending

Beginning in the 1990s, the segmentation of the market into conventional conforming, jumbo, and government-insured mortgages that had been in place since the 1970s began to break down, and the nonprime market emerged. Finance companies that funded their operations with corporate bond issues began to lend to borrowers with previous credit problems who could not meet the conforming market standards. The subprime industry was born largely in an effort to serve

Figure 1-4. *Market Consolidation among Mortgage Servicing Firms, 1996–2007*[a]

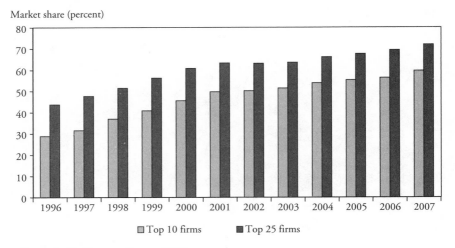

Market share (percent)

☐ Top 10 firms   ■ Top 25 firms

Source: Inside Mortgage Finance (2009).
a. Market share is measured by dollar volume of loans.

these borrowers.[5] The early pioneers reasoned that they could lend to these borrowers if the borrowers had gotten behind on their credit payments because of
temporary shocks to incomes or expenses that had largely passed *and* if the borrowers had substantial equity in their homes. The second condition offered
lenders protection if the bet that these borrowers could repay their loans and
rebuild their credit histories proved bad. Much of this lending was for second
mortgages. These lenders charged higher interest rates on the loans to cover higher
expected losses and found that borrowers were willing to pay them.

As a market emerged in which loans were priced based on risk, complaints
began to arise that some lenders were preying on unsuspecting borrowers. Consumer advocates labeled a slew of practices as "predatory," and they lobbied at the
federal, state, and local levels to protect consumers from these practices.[6] Concerns
also began to emerge that consumers could be discriminated against in the interest rate charged for the loan or the fees or conditions imposed rather than through
loan rejection.

Around the same time, the prime market began to use statistical credit and
mortgage scores to do a better job of discerning good from bad risks.[7] Mortgage
scores were based on modeling the performance of mortgage products that had

5. Gorton (2008).
6. Goldstein (1999).
7. Straka (2000).

been around for long periods of time and were based on performance under a range of interest rate environments and market conditions. These models were embedded in automated underwriting systems that increasingly supplanted manual underwriting. The advantage was that the automated systems were both better at modeling risk and less subjective, relying on colorblind models instead of on individual underwriters armed with detailed and large manuals that they could use to exercise discretion to approve variances from stricter underwriting and documentation standards. The large banks and Fannie Mae and Freddie Mac that developed these automated systems and scoring models found that the systems both drove down costs and allowed more borrowers to qualify for loans without adding to expected risk because the models allowed tighter underwriting on one standard to compensate for more lenient underwriting on another.[8]

Armed with mortgage-scoring models and some limited experience with nonprime mortgage lending, nonprime lending expanded rapidly after 2000 and most especially around 2004. At first, most of the subprime loans originated were held in portfolio. Increasingly, though, these loans were sold and placed into securities issued by investment banks or by large specialist subprime lenders. At the peak of the subprime lending boom in 2005 about eight in ten—and by 2007 fully nine in ten—subprime loans were placed into securities, according to Inside Mortgage Finance. With the exception of $13 billion wrapped by Fannie Mae, these securities had neither an implicit government guarantee against loss of principal from Fannie Mae or Freddie Mac nor an explicit guarantee from the FHA and Ginnie Mae. These securities were therefore called private-label securities and were traded in what was called the asset-backed securities (ABSs) market. This market was separate and distinct from the "agency" market where securities had implicit or explicit federal guarantees against the loss of principal (also called credit risk). From 1985 to 1995, the private-label MBS market grew from just $3.9 billion a year to fully $69 billion in constant 2008 dollars and continued to grow rapidly after 1995. While total MBS issuance increased more than 70 percent in real terms from $449 billion in 1995 to $769 billion in 2000, nonagency MBS issuance increased more, from a real annual level of $69 billion in 1995 to $170 billion in 2000. This lifted its share of MBS issuance from 15 percent in 1995 to 22 percent in 2000.[9]

Private-label securities dealt with credit risk by issuing multiple classes of securities from a single pool of mortgages with some classes "senior" and others "junior" in claim to principal in the event of loan defaults within the pool. Various other methods were also used to insulate investors from loss of principal, including third-party guarantees from bond insurers, overcollateralization of the pools, and excess spread income deposited into reserve accounts to absorb first

8. Gates, Perry, and Zorn (2002).
9. Inside Mortgage Finance (2009).

losses. Rating agencies rated large portions of the classes AAA or "money good," implying that the risk of loss of principal was extremely low. Classes of securities that were rated less than AAA were often recombined into collateralized debt obligations (CDOs) that then managed to receive AAA ratings for large portions of the issued classes. Indeed, Coval, Jurek, and Stafford argue that the essence of structured finance is to "repackage risks and create 'safe' assets from otherwise risky collateral" by creating tranches that are "viewed by investors to be virtually risk-free and certified as such by rating agencies."[10]

Not only were CDOs created, but CDO-squared securities were constituted from recombined CDOs, and "synthetic" CDOs were created in which credit-default swaps (CDSs) referencing the underlying CDOs and MBSs were bundled and issued as a way to hedge against and trade in the risk of these underlying assets and the issuers of securities. In this way, securities and credit-default swaps were created that were multiples of the underlying face amounts of subprime mortgages.

Subprime lending had a particular geography.[11] Lending by subprime lending specialists was much more concentrated in low-income, minority neighborhoods than in higher-income neighborhoods (see figure 1-5). From 1993 to 2001, the share of loans originated by subprime mortgage specialists, as identified by the Department of Housing and Urban Development (HUD) based on the specialization of lenders, increased in these neighborhoods from 2.4 to 13.4 percent of all home purchase originations and from 6.8 to 27.5 percent of all refinances. The share of loans originated by subprime lending specialists in predominantly white, low-income neighborhoods jumped as well, climbing from 1.0 to 11.5 percent of purchase originations and from 2.8 to 16.7 percent of refinances.[12] Without careful controls, it is difficult to judge whether this pattern entailed intentional discrimination. Indeed, one might expect this pattern since minorities have lower credit scores on average than whites. Nevertheless, using credit scores to distinguish those who would get a prime loan from those who would get a higher-priced subprime loan had a large disparate impact on minorities.

Also in the early 2000s, a range of boutique mortgage products that had been around for some time but had seen very limited use under tight underwriting standards started to be offered to more borrowers under more lenient standards. These "nontraditional" products became substantial fractions of the "prime" conventional and subprime mortgage markets by 2004. As home prices soared to record heights, the period also coincided with a dramatic increase in the vol-

10. Coval, Jurek, and Stafford (2008, p. 3).
11. Several studies have looked at the geographic dispersion of subprime originations prior to 2004, when these loans grew from a niche product to a popular means of reaching potential home-buyers with below-prime credit. See, for example, Scheessele (2002); Calem, Gillen, and Wachter (2004); Avery, Canner, and Cook (2005).
12. Joint Center for Housing Studies (2001).

Figure 1-5. *Subprime Loans, by Income Level and Race or Ethnicity of the Neighborhood, 1993–2001*[a]

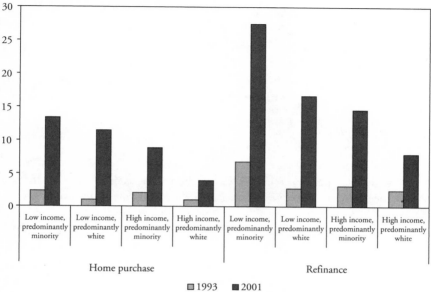

Subprime lender share of mortgage originations

Home purchase   Refinance

□ 1993   ■ 2001

Source: JCHS tabulations of enhanced HMDA database.

a. Includes only loans made in metropolitan areas. Predominantly white neighborhoods were less than 10 percent minority in 1990, while predominantly minority neighborhoods were 50 percent or more minority in 1990. Low-income neighborhoods had median income 80 percent of metro area median or lower in 1990, and high-income neighborhoods had median income 120 percent of metro area median or higher in 1990. Subprime loans are defined as all loans originated by lenders that were identified by HUD as subprime lending specialists.

ume of mortgage lending for home purchase, refinance, and home equity borrowing. Thus large volumes of nonprime loans were originated, often with nontraditional features, including 2/28 adjustable-rate subprime mortgages and interest-only and payment-option loans. Interest-only and payment-option loans were far more common in the prime and Alt-A loans than in the subprime market.

During the early and mid-2000s, Fannie Mae and Freddie Mac also became much more actively engaged in purchasing and guaranteeing Alt-A loans. These loans were issued mostly to borrowers who had good or better credit scores but who deviated in some other way from standard underwriting—most often because of limited documentation or verification of their income and assets. They also began to purchase private-label securities backed by subprime loans. However, they purchased only tranches that were rated AAA.

Causes of the Nonprime Lending Boom and Bust

While it is difficult to know for certain what caused the boom in nonprime lending and the particular character of the ugly bust that followed, four broad factors
likely played an essential role:

—Global liquidity, which led to low interest rates, expectations of rapidly rising home prices, and greater leverage

—The origination of mortgage loans with unprecedented risks through the
relaxation of mortgage underwriting standards and the layering of risk, especially
in the private-label securities market and in the portfolios of some large banks and
thrifts

—The magnification, multiplication, and mispricing of this risk through
financial engineering in the capital markets

—Regulatory and market failures.

These four factors did not work in isolation from each other. Low interest
rates (especially when combined with initially historically tight housing markets) sparked a house price bubble and motivated homebuyers to take on more
mortgage debt. The house price bubble, in turn, fueled strong demand for
homes and gave mortgage lenders comfort that the inflating value of the collateral backing loans was sufficient to overcome lax underwriting, while the lax
underwriting and nontraditional products fueled demand that helped to drive
prices higher. Low mortgage interest rates and strong home equity growth also
spurred record levels of cash-out refinances and other forms of home equity borrowing that added to household leverage. In addition, low interest rates caused
investors to use low-cost, often short-term, debt to lever up returns on low-
yielding underlying mortgage and other long-term interest-bearing assets. This
left investors vulnerable to liquidity risk if the value of their long-term mortgage
assets fell. Financial engineering in the capital markets resulted in large amounts
of nonprime securities receiving AAA ratings, which increased the demand for
risky nonprime loans and kept credit flowing to them. And the failure to price
and rate risk adequately, align incentives, and monitor counterparty risk effectively also contributed. Finally, the failure of regulation to prevent excessive
leverage, curb the origination of risky mortgages with aggressive underwriting,
or demand transparency in the capital markets also contributed to the boom and
the subsequent financial crisis.

It could be argued that the erosion of nonprime loan performance reverberated
through the global financial system because of the magnification of risk through
the issuance of credit-default swaps and synthetic collateralized debt obligations
referencing these CDSs, the lack of transparency in the CDS market, the difficulty in assessing the performance of loans underpinning CDOs and their inclusion in so many CDO issues, the amount of leverage that financial institutions
used to warehouse or purchase nonprime securities, and the lack of adequate

reserves against risk in the underlying subprime securities and the credit-default swaps referencing them.

Liquidity, Leverage, and Bubbles

A driving force behind the boom in nonprime lending was the excess liquidity created in the 1990s. While the United States enjoyed its longest economic boom in postwar history, several large nations—including China, India, and Brazil—scaled the steep part of the industrialization growth curve (see figure 1-6). Perhaps in tandem with expansionary monetary policy, beginning in the United States and then spreading to other nations, the liquidity glut led to low interest rates, which in turn stimulated both consumer spending and consumer borrowing.[13] As a result, a remarkable amount of cash began to look for opportunities to earn high returns. Pulling off such a feat required not only a search for ever more places to invest cash, but also leverage to boost returns.

In addition, the same low interest rates allowed American homebuyers to chase house prices higher and higher without adding to their monthly mortgage payments. Easy credit prolonged and extended the boom, which might otherwise have run out of steam due to affordability constraints. Moreover, the appreciating prices protected borrowers and lenders from losses. Low interest rates and strong income growth helped to lift home prices not just in the United States but also in many other developed nations, with the result that prices soared ahead of incomes in a remarkable number of countries (see figure 1-7). In fact, home prices did not increase nearly as much in the United States as they did in several other markets.[14] None of these nations was spared from a subsequent drop in home prices, but most did not suffer such a dramatic erosion in mortgage loan performance.

What was different in the United States was the impact of the decline on loan performance because lending standards were relaxed further in the United States

13. Caballero, Farhi, and Gourinchas (2008a, 2008b); IMF (2009). There is an active debate on how large the role of low interest rates was in sparking the crisis. Many have argued that low mortgage interest rates played a critical role in triggering the house price bubble (see, for example, Himmelberg, Mayer, and Sinai 2005), while others have argued that, although these rates did play a role, they were not central (see, for example, Glaeser, Gottlieb, and Gyourko 2010). An additional debate has sprung up over whether a glut of global liquidity or monetary policy caused the decline in long-term mortgage interest rates, with Taylor (2009) most famously arguing that it was monetary policy and Greenspan (2010) most famously arguing that it was not.

14. Still, low interest rates and changes in certain underwriting standards are not sufficient to explain the run-up in home price appreciation (Glaeser, Gottlieb, and Gyourko 2010). Apparently a bubble formed in part because people have backward-looking expectations about home prices. What might otherwise be a temporary rapid run-up in home prices produced by initially tight markets continued even after ample supply was added because people bought in anticipation of continuously and rapidly rising home prices, drawing more homebuyers and speculators into the market willing to pay more but driving an unsustainable number of new and existing home sales.

Figure 1-6. *Global S-Curve for Population in Select Countries, 2005*[a]

Per capita GDP (2005 US$)

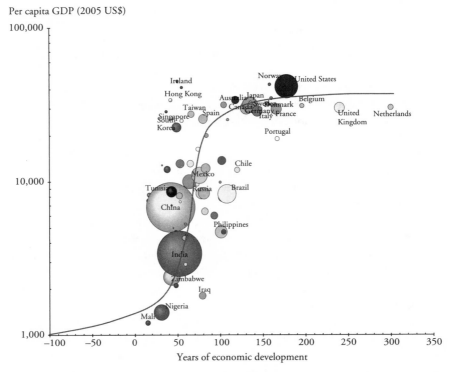

Years of economic development

Source: Jurrien Timmer, Director of Investment Research at Fidelity Investments.
a. Bubble size depicts each country's population as of 2005.

than in other countries (with the possible exception of the United Kingdom, which also experienced a boom in subprime lending). The U.S. experience can be contrasted with that of a country like Denmark, which also saw home prices rise sharply but which maintained an 80 percent maximum loan-to-value ratio and full income documentation requirements. Canada also maintained tighter standards. Its share of nonperforming loans managed to remain less than a fifth of that in the United States.[15]

The tendency for people to spend more when asset values are appreciating led to heavy home equity borrowing and rapidly growing consumer spending, feeding the economic and housing market boom.[16] According to Freddie Mac, real cash-out refinancing and consolidation of second loans through refinancing

15. Lea (2010).
16. Belsky and Prakken (2004).

Figure 1-7. *House Price Appreciation in Select Countries, 1997–2009*[a]

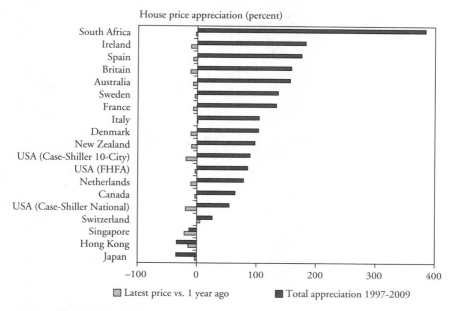

House price appreciation (percent)

Latest price vs. 1 year ago   Total appreciation 1997-2009

Source: *The Economist* (2009).
a. Data are as of the first quarter of 2009 or the latest available.

increased from $75 billion in 2000 to $263 billion in 2003, peaking at $370 billion in 2006. All this borrowing also shrank equity cushions, despite escalating home prices. The aggregate ratio of home equity to value reached a record low of 55 percent in 2006, even before house prices collapsed (see figure 1-8).

Lax Underwriting Standards and the Layering of Risk

Rapidly rising home prices in 2000–05 masked the risks posed by nonprime loans and lax underwriting standards. After all, borrowers who got into trouble repaying their mortgages early in the boom could either refinance their loans or readily sell their homes at a profit and repay their debt. On the investment side, demand for nonprime mortgages was strong, not only because the residential mortgage market was so big and offered an outlet for excess liquidity, but also because the mortgages carried higher yields than prime mortgages and the securities backed by them carried higher yields than many corporate bonds of the same rating. As a result, the number of investment companies focused solely on mortgage debt expanded.

As previously discussed, the lion's share of nonprime loans at the peak was sold into the secondary market and subsequently bundled into securities, with most "structured" so that a significant share of the issued classes received high credit

Figure 1-8. *Home Equity, Debt, and Ratio of Home Equity to Value, 1970–2008*

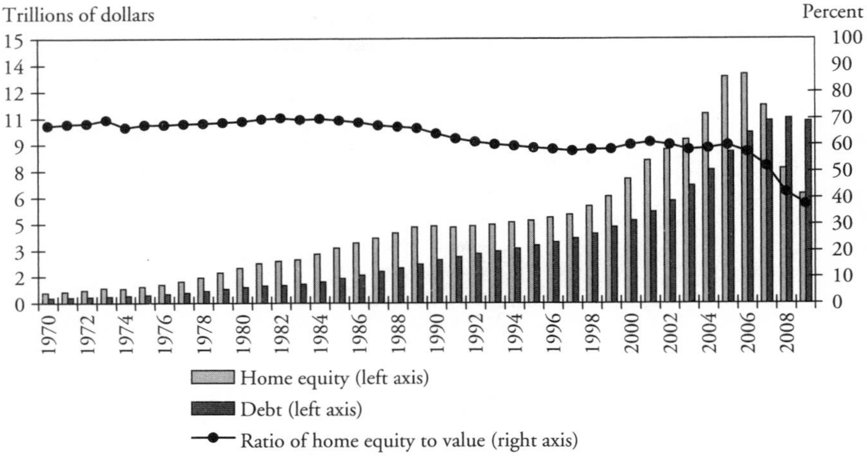

Source: Federal Reserve Board (various years).

ratings. To satisfy strong investor and borrower demand, investment banks were willing to source loans with increasingly lax underwriting, with deeper and deeper teaser rates that would reset much higher (unless interest rates fell sharply) within a year or two, and with other risky features that lowered initial monthly payments for borrowers. This led to what we call the "origination" of risk—that is, the origination of highly risky products that had heavy payment reset risks and that were underwritten in ways that often failed to require proof of income or to set high caps on debt-to-income ratios. Private conduits (investment banks and other originators selling directly into private securitizations) issued nearly all of the securities backed by subprime loans, although both Fannie Mae and Freddie Mac ended up purchasing significant amounts of the highly rated tranches of those securities. As of September 30, 2009, they reported owning $86 billion of subprime private-label securities. Private conduits also issued most of the Alt-A MBSs, although Fannie Mae and Freddie Mac stepped up their issuance of securities backed by Alt-A loans in 2000–07. As of September 30, 2009, they reported guarantees outstanding on Alt-A loans in their credit books of $415 billion of business. Some portfolio lenders also loaded up on nonprime debt.

In fact, nonprime mortgages grew explosively in the first half of the 2000s, measured both by dollar volume and as a share of refinance and home purchase loans (see figure 1-9). Subprime mortgage loans moved from being a niche product to being widely distributed to borrowers of all income levels beginning in 2000. Although a disproportionate share of subprime mortgages were originated to lower-income and minority households, the majority of all such loans were

Figure 1-9. *Nonprime Lending as a Share of First-Lien Mortgage Originations, 1995–2008*

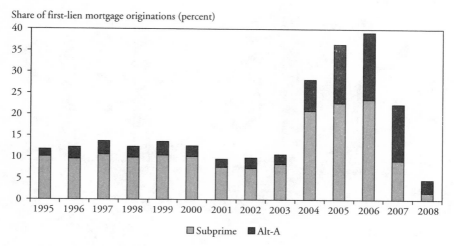

Share of first-lien mortgage originations (percent)

Source: Inside Mortgage Finance (2009).

taken out by middle-income white households. Even at the peak in 2005, Home Mortgage Disclosure Act (HMDA) data show that only about a quarter of all higher-priced home purchase loans were made in low-income communities, only a third in majority-minority communities, and only a fifth in low-income majority-minority communities.

Equally important, the product mix in the subprime market shifted from mostly fixed-rate to mostly adjustable-rate loans. In 2003 fully 66 percent of subprime loans were traditional fixed-rate loans. That share fell to 31 percent in 2005 and to 26 percent in 2006 (see figure 1-10). The most common loan became the 2/28 adjustable, making up fully 44 percent of subprime originations in 2005. In addition, the share requiring a balloon payment jumped from 5 percent in 2003 to 10 percent in 2005 and to 18 percent in 2006. The shift away from fixed-rate loans was even more dramatic among Alt-A mortgages. As a result, a much larger share of subprime and Alt-A borrowers than prime ones faced the risk that their payments would reset higher after the initial period. On top of this, lenders offered teaser rates so that borrowers' rates would rise when the discount expired even if interest rates did not increase between the origination and payment reset dates.

Meanwhile, issues of nontraditional loan products also skyrocketed. Interest-only and payment-option loans went from just a few percent of all loans in the first few years of the decade to a peak of about 19 percent in 2005.[17] These so-

17. This figure is based on LoanPerformance data from First American CoreLogic.

Figure 1-10. *Adjustable Mortgages as a Share of Mortgage Originations, 2003–07*[a]

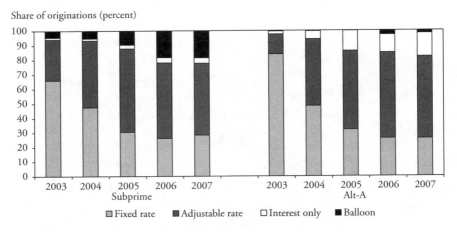

Share of originations (percent)

Subprime   Alt-A

☐ Fixed rate   ■ Adjustable rate   ☐ Interest only   ■ Balloon

Source: First American CoreLogic, LoanPerformance data.
a. Adjustable rate mortgages include hybrid loans with initial fixed rates.

called "affordability" or "nontraditional" products allowed borrowers to leverage their incomes. Interest-only loans typically offered a five-year period in which the borrower paid only interest and the principal balance was carried. At the end of this set period, the borrower would have to repay the principal over the compressed time period remaining on the loan, which meant sharply higher monthly payments. The payment-option mortgage was much like a credit card, giving borrowers the flexibility to make a minimum payment that could be even lower than the interest due. When a payment was less than the full amortizing amount, the rest was rolled into the mortgage balance, resulting in negative amortization. Eventually borrowers would have to increase their monthly payments to pay down this growing principal.

Remarkably, lenders often layered additional risks on top of these considerable payment reset risks. First, lenders began to require less and less documentation of income and assets. While low- and no-documentation loans were also available in the prime and subprime markets, they were most prevalent in the Alt-A market, where the share of full-documentation loans dipped to 15 percent (see figure 1-11). Second, the average combined loan-to-value (CLTV) for securitized loans increased during the post-2000 housing boom. Compared to loans originated in 1995–99, the share of Alt-A and subprime loans originated with more than 90 percent CLTV rose from 2000 to 2004, while the two categories also made up a higher share of all securitized loans. The result was that the share of all loans in private-label securities originated with 90 percent CLTV or higher climbed from 6 percent in the late 1990s to more than 10 percent for the first half of the 2000s (see figure 1-12).

Figure 1-11. *Share of Mortgage Originations with Full Documentation*[a]

Share of originations with full documentation (percent)

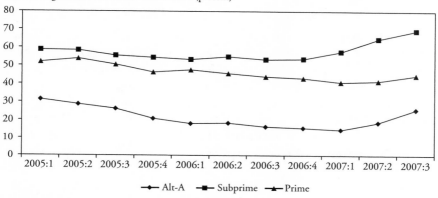

Source: First American CoreLogic, LoanPerformance data.
a. Origination share is based on loan volume.

Figure 1-12. *Share of Loans in Private-Label Securities with CLTV of 90 Percent or Higher, 1990–2007*

Percent

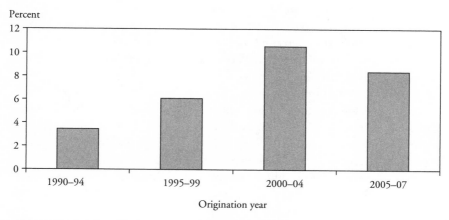

Origination year

Source: First American CoreLogic, LoanPerformance data.

Although relaxed underwriting standards (including credit score cutoffs, debt-to-income ratios, combined loan-to-value ratios, and income and asset documentation)—as well as widespread adoption of mortgage products with payment reset risks—may not have been the principal contributors to the run-up in home prices, they did cause mortgage loan performance to be much worse in the United States than elsewhere when house prices finally fell.

Multiplication and Mispricing of Risk on the Capital Markets

The risks being taken in the primary mortgage market were multiplied on the secondary market by financial engineering and by investors overleveraging and holding insufficient reserves against losses. Mortgage-backed security issuers created increasingly more complicated securities, and these securities were then referenced by CDSs and synthetic CDOs over and above the underlying mortgage loan amounts. Investors often purchased MBSs and CDOs with heavy amounts of short-term debt, while sellers of unfunded synthetic CDOs paid only a premium to buyers in return for protection against losses on the underlying referenced securities.

Investors snapped up these securities in large measure because of the high credit ratings most of the tranches received. A Fitch Ratings study from 2007 estimated that 60 percent of all global structured products (not just those backed by subprime mortgages) were AAA rated compared to less than 1 percent of all corporate issues.[18] It was the ability to manufacture such large shares of AAA-rated products from loans with underlying risks that caused these securities to grow so rapidly. These high ratings simultaneously gave investors confidence that the securities would perform well and attracted investors who wanted to bet against these high ratings and to hedge the risk that rating agencies were wrong. More generally, the growth of the nonprime and nontraditional mortgage market was fueled by the perception that the mechanisms in place to manage and mitigate subprime mortgage risk were effective. Indeed, the system appeared to have myriad ways to manage these risks well. In the first instance, the risks being taken and priced were being modeled and simulated by several separate firms, including portfolio lenders, those guaranteeing securities like the GSEs and the FHA, and, perhaps in some cases, third-party investors. Second, in the case of structured nonprime securities, rating agencies applied their own models to both mortgage-backed securities and collateralized debt obligations and judged these loans to be safe enough to assign AAA ratings to a large share of the tranches in an issue. Like others sizing up risk, rating agencies stress-tested the loans in nonprime mortgage-backed securities using assumptions drawn from past periods of stress in housing markets.

---

18. Ashcraft and Schuermann (2008) present a Bear Sterns chart suggesting that the typical structure of a subprime mortgage-backed security had 79.3 percent AAA-rated debt and that the structure of a typical Alt-A mortgage-backed security had 92.9 percent AAA-rated debt.

In hindsight, and with greater disclosure, it is now clear that these tests were insufficient and that fitting models of new products and practices to valid historical precedents was difficult because of the lack of history with the products and practices.[19] At the time, this was far less clear. Third, it was not just the ratings but also the structure of investments that prompted confidence in agency ratings. The issues were overly collateralized, excess spread was siphoned into reserves, and investment-grade tranches were senior in priority. Equity pieces were often held at least in part by the underwriters of the securities and in any event enjoyed strong demand, suggesting to senior note holders that yields in the equity pieces were rich enough to justify the risk. Fourth, the diversification of risk into other assets provided by CDOs also appeared to offer another level of protection against systemic risk. Fifth, those who wanted to hedge their risks had ample opportunities to do so. Monoline insurers offered protection on whole loans as well as tranches of nonprime securities. Purchasers of nonprime securities could buy protection through bilateral credit-default swaps with large writers of AAA protection or through CDS trades. All of these actions created the appearance that subprime risks were being managed well, hedged and diversified against, and distributed widely to those most able to bear or manage them.

But rating private-label securities involved making assumptions about default probabilities or expected losses that turned out to be overly optimistic. As an example, in 2007, even before the larger meltdown, the Bank for International Settlements reported that Moody's downgraded 31 percent of all the tranches it had rated. In June 2009 Standard and Poor's reported that only about one-tenth of its AAA-rated ABS collateralized debt obligations remained AAA, while nearly six-tenths had fallen to less than B. Rating CDOs involved making assumptions not just about the default probabilities or expected losses of the individual asset types in a pool, but also about the joint probability of defaults of tranches drawn from different security issues. As a result, CDO ratings were even more sensitive to small variations in the estimated joint probabilities of default. As early as 2004, a working paper released by the Bank for International Settlements noted, "It has been argued that the high numbers of downgrades of high-yield CDO tranches over recent years are at least partially the result of the under-modeling of both default and recovery rates and, hence, a manifestation of model risk."[20] Coval, Jurek, and Stafford provide simple illustrations and simulations of how sensitive ratings are to joint default-probability assumptions.[21] Indeed, the assumptions used discounted the risk of a nominal decline in house prices occurring nationally and, in the case of CDOs, relied on historical prices

19. Rossi (2010); Deng, Gabriel, and Sanders (2009).
20. Fender and Kiff (2004, p. 9).
21. Coval, Jurek, and Stafford (2008).

of credit-default swaps over a period in the 1990s to early 2000s when house prices were appreciating.[22]

But with high ratings and other appearances of safety, the market for these CDOs soared. The Securities Industry and Financial Market Association reported that total global CDO issuance stood at approximately $157.5 billion in 2004, more than tripling to $520.6 billion just two years later. But as quickly as CDO issuances rose, they fell at the first signs of trouble. Quarterly issuance peaked at $178.6 billion in the second quarter of 2007 and plummeted 87 percent to $23.6 billion a year later. CDOs denominated in U.S. currency made up the lion's share, averaging 76 percent of global issuance from 2005 to 2007.

CDS writers issued swaps that referenced these complex securities, and CDSs were used to create synthetic CDOs, literally adding to the amount of capital at risk in the event that nonprime mortgages performed worse than expected. Credit-default swaps are bilateral agreements between two counterparties to trade risk with reference to a third-party entity or security. The buyer pays a fee to the seller in return for a contingent claim on the seller should the reference security fail to make a payment or default. The seller either takes delivery of the defaulted bonds at par or pays the buyer the difference between the par value and the recovery value. CDSs bear a resemblance to insurance policies, but in most cases there is no requirement to hold any asset or prove adequate reserves against the total exposure to losses.

Estimates of the size of the CDS market vary, but even lower-range estimates place it at more than $40 trillion at the end of 2007. The emergence of this mammoth market multiplied risks in at least four ways. First, it introduced an additional layer of counterparty risk because settlements of CDSs require those writing protection to be able to make good on protection, yet they are not required to reserve against losses in the same way as an insurance company or a deposit-taking financial institution. Second, it introduced more systematic risk because a few enormous issuers dominated the market and the default of a single issuer could have serious ramifications. Third, the CDS market is not transparent, lacking both a central clearinghouse and a price discovery mechanism. This made it unclear who bore which risks in the system and who stood to lose if subprime performance was worse than anticipated. Indeed, not until the government stepped in to avert the failure of Bear Stearns and AIG and in the aftermath of the Lehman Brothers failure did the government become aware of just how many counterparties stood to lose from the failure of any one of these entities. Finally, the CDS market vastly

---

22. Salmon (2009). More sensitive still were CDO-squared securities, which draw from an underlying pool of CDO tranches that have been combined and repackaged. CDO-cubed securities take the process a step further and are structured from the tranches of CDO-squared securities. Coval and his colleagues show how even a CDO-squared security made up entirely of mezzanine tranches could yield large tranches that achieved AAA ratings.

expanded the exposure of investors to subprime credit because the supply of CDSs is not limited by the face amount of subprime debt but rather by the number of agreements that financial firms enter into that reference the face debt. Multiple contracts can and were written against the same issue. The Federal Reserve estimates that in 2005 exposure to collateralized debt obligations referencing BBB-rated subprime mortgage-backed securities was 60 percent greater than the BBB-rated subprime MBS issuance itself. In 2006 it was 93 percent greater.[23]

Making matters worse, investors also leveraged their long-term mortgage investments. Banks set up structured investment vehicles (SIVs) as off-balance-sheet entities to purchase MBSs and ABSs and lent them money to buy the assets. Hedge funds also purchased MBSs and ABSs with borrowed money. In many cases the loans extended were short term, leaving these funds and vehicles vulnerable to collateral calls and making it difficult for them to roll over their debts if poor performance eroded these long-lived assets. By the height of the subprime boom, off-balance-sheet SIVs had accumulated assets in the neighborhood of $400 billion.[24]

Investment banks also began to increase their leverage and were permitted to do so by a Securities and Exchange Commission (SEC) ruling in 2004 that dramatically changed the way the SEC measured banks' capital. The new rules allowed investment banks to use their own risk assessment systems to set their ratio of debt to net capital. Previously, the net capital rule had required broker-dealers to limit their ratio of debt to net capital to 15 to 1. After the ruling, several investment banks exceeded that ratio, with Merrill Lynch setting a high ratio of 40 to 1.[25]

In sum, the push to extend more and more credit emanating from the capital markets—as well as what was done to the credit when it was bundled and sold as securities on these markets—helped to magnify risks and increase the exposure of the financial system to deterioration in the performance of mortgage loans. For decades, the securitization process had worked successfully to place long-term, fixed-rate, prepayable mortgage loans with a variety of institutional investors, pooling and repackaging the loans into securities with a broad range of maturities, coupons, and credit risk protection. A large, liquid secondary market

23. Pozsar (2008).

24. SIVs were designed to operate as ongoing entities, providing sponsoring banks with healthy returns without increasing their capital reserve requirements. As part of the growing shadow banking system, the SIVs operated much like banks, using funds raised by issuing short-term commercial paper to invest in long-term assets, including MBSs. The asset-backed commercial paper market took the place of depositors in a traditional bank, with the SIVs borrowing at short maturity to invest at long maturity. The typical gearing for an SIV's capital structure was as much as 15 to 1, although some closed-end SIVs focusing on residential mortgage securities had much higher leverage (Felsenheimer and Gisdakis 2008).

25. Satow (2008).

provided increasing access to mortgage credit on more favorable terms than would otherwise have been possible. But the secondary market became dysfunctional when it permitted mass originations of highly risky loans that, through financial engineering, were repackaged as mostly AAA-rated securities.

Regulatory and Market Failures

Properly viewed, the problem in nonprime lending stemmed from the financial institutions that established the underwriting standards, the agencies that rated the securities backed by them, the firms that wrote credit-default swaps against them, and the regulators that were entrusted with policing the system. It was they—not mortgage brokers, mortgage bankers, or borrowers—that determined the products that could be offered, the underwriting standards that would be tolerated, the requirements for capital reserves against losses, and the incentive structure for mortgage brokers, mortgage bankers, and broker-dealers that rewarded volume more than long-term loan performance. In hindsight, these were significant regulatory and market failures.

Some of the biggest problems stemmed from lax regulation and the deregulation of credit and the capital markets, including the more limited and uneven regulation and supervision of financial institutions that do not take deposits. This resulted in a patchwork of federal and state regulators and regulations. Indeed, it is clear that the nonprime lending boom was strongly driven by the demand for private-label, asset-backed securities (securities not backed by Fannie Mae, Freddie Mac, or Ginnie Mae) and the mortgage brokers and bankers, securities broker-dealers, securities issuers, and rating agencies feeding that demand.

WEAK COUNTERPARTY RISK MANAGEMENT, REGULATION, AND MISALIGNED PRINCIPAL-AGENT INCENTIVES. The nonprime mortgage lending system relied on an originate-to-distribute model as well as on financial engineering of the capital markets, both of which increased the number of counterparties in the housing finance system. Although investors relied on rating agencies to appraise the creditworthiness of counterparties large enough to get rated, plenty of unrated entities like brokers and small finance companies also fed loans to the system, and some of the financial institutions with strong credit ratings even saw major downgrades when the credit markets froze. In addition, lack of transparency in the CDS markets and among hedge and private equity funds and SIVs made it difficult to know the extent to which counterparties were exposed to nonprime risk. All of this added to the importance and cost of counterparty risk assessment.

Yet the mechanisms in place to manage counterparty risk were also lacking. Fannie Mae and Freddie Mac had for decades relied successfully on approved seller standards and audits as well as representations and warranties to guard against counterparty risk. But these protections broke down at the height of the nonprime lending boom in ways that did not become apparent until after the fact. Safeguards in the private-label market were even weaker and likely even less successful. In addition, loan originators were often brokers or small mortgage banks that had little or no capital at risk. Even those that did have substantial amounts of capital at risk often did not have adequate capital reserves to cover losses. Furthermore, investment banks, Fannie Mae, and Freddie Mac were allowed high leverage ratios, the leverage ratios of SIVs and finance companies were not federally regulated, and CDS issuers were allowed to write insurance-like protection with an implicit premium on the swap rate. While no reserves were required, these instruments were marked to market with a capital requirement. When the tide went out, many counterparties could not make good on their claims, causing a collapse in investor confidence and a liquidity crisis. The posting of collateral created liquidity problems. The reliance on a thin market caused disputes on collateral posting and the inability to limit losses by getting out of trades.

Furthermore, incentives in the originate-to-distribute model between financial intermediaries serving as agents for the ultimate loan investors were not necessarily aligned. Brokers were paid an up-front fee for originations, and broker-dealers were paid an up-front fee for pooling and structuring securities. In essence, the financial intermediaries were rewarded primarily through volume, while investors were rewarded through the long-term performance of the loans. The compensation of rating agencies may have also created conflicts of interest because issuers pay for the ratings, not the investors who rely on the ratings to make investment decisions.[26]

The compensation structure for mortgage brokers and loan officers also created opportunities to pass along their up-front fees to borrowers in the somewhat shrouded form of yield-spread premiums built into interest rates. This may have provided brokers and loan officers with an incentive to originate loans in the non-prime market where pricing was more opaque, although no studies have confirmed that this was the case. In fact, even in the FHA channel, with simpler mortgages and easier price discovery, yield-spread premiums were widely dispersed.[27] Also brokers do have offsetting incentives to treat customers fairly and transmit quality loans to aggregators. The mortgage lending business is highly competitive. Customer service and referrals matter to brokers and so act as a check on their rent-seeking behavior. In addition, many lenders monitor the relative performance of loans originated by brokers and loan officers and will cease doing business with those who have poor track records.

For their part, sellers and servicers are compensated in part through servicing income, which is tied to the long-term performance and longevity of loans. These originators have significant incentives to originate quality loans because the efficiency and returns of their servicing portfolios depend on it. The fact that servicing is highly concentrated and has thin margins puts strong pressure on sellers and

---

26. Fender and Kiff (2004).
27. Woodward (2008).

servicers to attend to quality. This was less so in the nonprime market where more spread was retained by sellers and servicers.

DEREGULATION, REGULATORY SHOPPING, AND STATE PREEMPTIONS. Deregulation from the 1980s has been faulted for ushering in higher-priced lending and anything-goes underwriting standards and mortgage product offerings. The 1980s were a tumultuous time in mortgage funding and in the regulations governing mortgage and credit markets.[28] The first major piece of legislation deregulating financial markets was the Depository Institutions Deregulation and Monetary Control Act of 1980. In a context of raging inflation, this act lifted interest rate ceilings (including fees) on first-lien home mortgages. It also extended coverage of a 1978 Supreme Court ruling to all deposit-taking institutions and thus allowed national banks to export their home state's interest rates to other states. This effectively ended state usury caps because a bank could relocate its headquarters to a state with a very high or no ceiling and export rates elsewhere.

The second major piece of deregulation legislation was the Alternative Mortgage Transactions Parity Act of 1982. This act preempted state laws restricting the terms on adjustable-rate mortgages, balloon payments, and negative amortization, paving the way for interest-only and payment-option loans that would later contribute to mounting risks in the mortgage markets.

Deregulation is widely viewed as having had a powerful role in the collapse of the thrift industry. At both the state and federal levels, deregulation allowed thrift institutions to offer new and riskier loan products, while ushering in more relaxed capital requirements and accounting procedures. This proved a volatile mix, especially when combined with souring economic conditions in the Southwest and Midwest, an unprecedented increase in the chartering of new thrifts, and a weakening of bank oversight.[29] Lax oversight in a market when so many thrifts were investing in an overheated real estate market led to the failure of more than 1,000 institutions, at a cost to taxpayers of about $124 billion.[30]

The existence of multiple banking regulators has been faulted for allowing further de facto deregulation as a result of the more far-reaching preemptions of state law claimed by banking regulators competing for deposit-taking institutions that can shop for a preferred regulator.[31] This process, it is asserted, allowed thrifts and nationally chartered banks and their affiliates to avoid state laws aimed at restricting permissible lending practices and thus allowed high-risk lending to thrive.

WEAK FEDERAL REGULATION AND SUPERVISION OF THE SHADOW BANKING SYSTEM, INCLUDING LAX OVERSIGHT OF THE CAPITAL MARKETS. Most criticisms of the nation's regulatory structure in relation to the nonprime crisis focus on the part of the system that is beyond the reach of banking regulators. This so-called "shadow bank-

---

28. McCoy and Renuart (2008).
29. Curry and Shibut (2000).
30. Curry and Shibut (2000).
31. McCoy and Renuart (2008).

ing system" or "unregulated fringe" includes state-chartered insurance and finance companies, investment banks, hedge funds, rating agencies, private equity firms, special investment vehicles, and the brokers who deliver a substantial portion of loans from the retail level.[32]

Giving credence to this argument is the fact that the shadow banking system originated most of the nonprime loans. In addition, these loans increasingly ended up in private-label securities. When home prices fell, these loans suffered the heaviest and earliest losses. Virtually all of the subprime securities and much of the Alt-A issues were private-label issues. With subprime and Alt-A reaching securitization rates over 90 percent in 2007, the private-label market played a pivotal role.

It is clear that rating agencies, investment banks, hedge funds, private equity funds, state-chartered insurance companies, and state-chartered finance companies were not as closely supervised as deposit-taking institutions, nor were they generally subject to as tight or as uniform regulation. Opacity in these markets was permitted, and rating agency practices and models were not subjected to the scrutiny of federal regulators. Finance companies were regulated and supervised unevenly by state regulators, and mortgage brokers were subject to an uneven patchwork of state laws and licensing.

There were several specific problems with regulation and oversight of the shadow banking system and the capital markets. These include the adequacy of capital requirements for investment banks, CDS issuers, and the GSEs; measures to ensure transparency; oversight of rating agencies; oversight and regulation of CDS markets and capital standards for writers of CDS protection; assignment of liability for defects in loan originations; underwriting standards; and oversight of compensation.

The credit-rating agencies played a central role in determining the feasibility of nonprime lending in general, and of certain terms in particular, through their ratings of structured nonprime securities. Yet this crucial function was essentially unregulated until the Credit Rating Agency Reform Act of 2006, which gave the SEC authority over the agencies. In addition, the lack of a central clearinghouse and minimal regulation of the CDS market have been criticized for allowing both opacity and systemic risk to build in the capital markets. Furthermore, assignees' lack of liability for the practices of nonprime loan originators (many of which were small and thinly capitalized) has been faulted for letting large, well-capitalized financial institutions off the hook for policing their origination channels.

INSUFFICIENT CONSUMER PROTECTIONS. Credit regulations did not adequately protect consumers, especially when the nation's credit allocation system shifted from offering nearly uniform pricing only to borrowers who met prime standards

---

32. The term "unregulated" fringe is a misnomer. It would be more accurate to call the financial institutions in the shadow banking system less regulated or less closely supervised or the state-regulated fringe.

to offering credit at a risk-adjusted price to borrowers with subprime credit scores who were taking out loans with nonconforming underwriting standards and features. By the early 1990s—even before subprime lending took off—reports of abusive and predatory practices were on the rise. This led to passage of the Home Ownership and Equity Protection Act (HOEPA) of 1994. While HOEPA was intended to deal with potentially unsafe, unfair, or usurious rates and fees, it applied only to closed-end mortgages for refinance, had very high annual percentage rate (APR) triggers, and imposed only some restrictions on lending.[33]

Consumer disclosures have been faulted for being insufficient and confusing. For example, except for high-cost refinance loans as defined under HOEPA, the Truth in Lending Act (TILA) did not require lenders to disclose binding prices until closing. In addition, subprime lenders were permitted to advertise their best rates without disclosing to consumers that they might not qualify for them. Furthermore, variable-rate disclosures were viewed as weak and as calling insufficient attention to the risks associated with a floating interest rate.

In general, disclosures designed back in the 1960s did not anticipate the complex risks (including a range of payment reset risks) that consumers would take on. Therefore, they did not effectively disclose and underscore these risks. Even the APR, which is at the heart of both the prime and subprime disclosure regimes, is not easily grasped.[34] New changes to the Real Estate Settlements and Procedures Act (RESPA)[35] and the Truth in Lending Act[36] in place by 2010 have gone a long way toward improving disclosures and good-faith estimates.

Weaker responses to subprime lending practices came earlier in the form of an interagency guidance on subprime lending issued in 1999 and extended guidance in 2001. The guidance was mostly advisory in nature, although the 2001 exten-

33. Lenders were prohibited from offering such high-cost loans with a balloon payment due within five years or with negative amortization, from imposing a prepayment penalty for longer than five years, or from refinancing the loan within a year unless assignees that pooled and securitized loans were subject to liability. Further, lenders were required to disclose a final APR, the amount of monthly payments, any balloon payments due, principal borrowed, and fees for credit insurance and debt cancellation three days before closing.

34. Durkin (2008).

35. Changes to RESPA took effect in January 2010 and included a thorough revamping of the disclosure forms for good-faith estimates and HUD-1 settlement charges that made it easier to compare loans. The new good-faith estimates more clearly describe potential changes to interest rates, loan balances, and payments and lump all lender charges into a single origination charge. RESPA reforms also include restrictions on how much settlement charges can change between issuance of the good-faith estimate and closing. Lender-related fees must be identical from application to closing, and there is a 10 percent tolerance for estimates in other areas.

36. Changes to the TILA (which governs disclosure of the costs and terms of mortgage credit) took effect in July 2009 and applied to all noninvestor mortgages. Under the changes, lenders are required to provide good-faith estimates to borrowers within three days of loan application, with a seven-day waiting period between the good-faith estimate and closing. No fees can be collected from a borrower before a disclosure is issued except for the cost of obtaining a credit report. If the APR changes by more than 0.125 percent, the lender must provide a corrected disclosure and wait an additional three days before closing the loan.

sion stated that the portion of an institution's allowance for loan losses allocated to the subprime portfolio had to be sufficient to absorb estimated credit losses. The guidance only applied to federally regulated deposit-taking institutions. Despite this guidance, some banks and thrifts continued to put subprime loans on their books. And to the extent the guidance discouraged banks and thrifts from originating subprime loans, it did not do so in the ABS market, where the volume of mortgage lending exploded during the first half of the 2000s. Guidance on home equity lending, also aimed at deposit-taking institutions only, was issued in 2005 and 2006. Guidance on nontraditional loan products did not come until the fall of 2006.

It was not until HOEPA changes went into effect on October 1, 2009, that meaningful and enforceable steps were taken.[37] Although late in coming and not strong enough by some lights and too strong by others, the HOEPA changes were substantial. Additional changes in the form of stronger TILA disclosures took effect in July 2009, and revised RESPA good-faith estimates took effect in January 2010. Thus, while there eventually was a meaningful response, it did not take effect until some two years or more after the market had largely shut down nonprime lending anyway.

INSUFFICIENT MONITORING AND REGULATION OF SYSTEM RISK. Regulators did not take enough account of systemic risk. No single regulator was charged with attempting to measure and detect when investments and practices in the financial markets were adding to systemic risk. Off-balance-sheet SIVs allowed banks to take on more leverage, and piggy-back seconds allowed homebuyers to do so as well. Meanwhile, after 2004, investment banks were allowed to set their own leverage ratios. Massive volumes of CDSs were issued that were not regulated by banks or insurance commissioners. Securities with performance systematically related to the performance of the broader market were given AAA ratings. Fannie Mae and Freddie Mac had high leverage ratios. Making matters even worse, the systemic risk being created by concentrating risk in the hands of a few "too-big-to-fail" financial institutions was difficult to detect because the market for CDSs was opaque. With SIVs and other funds depending on constant access to the commercial paper markets to finance long-term assets, duration risk was allowed to flourish and went unregulated. This maturity mismatching caused

37. HOEPA reforms included a new definition of "higher-priced lending." First-lien mortgages are now considered higher priced if they are 1.5 percentage points or more above an "average prime offer rate" index based on Freddie Mac's mortgage survey. Subordinate mortgages are higher priced if they are 3.5 percentage points or more above this index. For these higher-priced loans, lenders are prohibited from making a loan without regard to the borrower's ability to repay the loan from income and assets other than the home's value, based on the highest scheduled payment in the first seven years. Lenders must verify income and assets and establish escrows for taxes and insurance, and prepayment penalties are severely restricted. The reforms also introduced new rules for all mortgages, which included prohibiting misrepresentation of home value, prohibiting pyramiding late fees, changing advertising rules, and expanding early-disclosure requirements.

many financial institutions to fail when they could no longer access the short-term debt markets. This, in turn, forced them to sell assets into an illiquid market, further depressing prices.

THE CRA RED HERRING AND LIMITED ROLE OF GSE GOALS. Some have blamed the problems with nonprime lending performance on regulations that encouraged banks and thrifts to lend to low- and moderate-income borrowers and areas rather than on lax regulation of a shadow banking sector that was under no obligation to lend to underserved markets. But the problem was not, as some have argued, the Community Reinvestment Act (CRA), which places affirmative obligations on banks and thrifts to lend in low- and moderate-income communities. CRA played a minor role at best. There is ample evidence from carefully controlled studies of loans made by CRA lenders in their assessment areas that the loans performed comparatively well.[38] Moreover, only 4.5 percent of all higher-cost loans (a proxy often used for nonprime lending) at the 2005 peak were made in areas where lenders were assessed for CRA performance.

Others have blamed affordable housing goals imposed on Fannie Mae and Freddie Mac by Congress beginning in 1992 and administered by HUD for causing nonprime lending to become such a large share of total originations. Indeed, both agencies were under pressure to purchase nonprime loans and the securities they backed, especially after regulators ratcheted up their goals for affordable lending and underserved areas in 2004 and established subgoals that forced them to meet targets through purchases of single-family rather than multifamily loans. Yet the GSEs had a much larger exposure to Alt-A loans than to subprime loans, even though Alt-A loans were not very goal rich. They also incurred heavy losses on interest-only and payment-option loans, yet these loans were goal thin. Equally plausible explanations for their behavior are that, as shareholder-owned companies, they were under pressure to regain market share they were losing to private-label issuers of Alt-A and subprime securities, to serve their large customers better, and to go after the higher yields offered in the nonprime market. Weighing the evidence and arguments, Jaffee concludes that market pressures probably played the larger role.[39]

Whatever the reasons, nearly all industry-identified subprime loans were non-conforming, and Fannie Mae and Freddie Mac participated in subprime markets almost entirely by purchasing AAA-rated tranches of private-label securities.[40]

38. Laderman and Reid (2008).

39. Jaffee (2010).

40. In September 31, 2009, Fannie Mae reported that 0.3 percent of its credit book of business was industry-identified subprime, but that loans with credit scores under 620 accounted for 4 percent of its book. Loans with such low credit scores would typically be considered subprime. Freddie Mac has not disclosed that it had any subprime loans, but it has reported that 4 percent of loans in its credit book had credit scores under 620. However, only Fannie Mae wrapped a guarantee around known subprime securities, but only about $12.8 billion worth.

While this added to the demand for subprime loans, the demand for exposure to these loans exceeded the total supply of them, so it is hard to conclude that the market would not have flourished without them. Indeed, synthetic CDOs and CDSs were issued so that investors could buy and sell protection against loss of the face amount of the subprime securities these derivatives referenced, so great were the demand and the appetite for subprime risk. It is also the case that private-label Alt-A securities outstripped the issuance of Fannie Mae and Freddie Mac Alt-A mortgage-backed securities and GSE purchases of private-label Alt-A originations combined. Indeed, Pinto estimates that in the peak years for Alt-A originations, 2005 and 2006, the GSE share of the Alt-A market was 25 and 36 percent, respectively.[41] Furthermore, looking just at private-label Alt-A securitizations, the GSE share was an even lower 11 percent in 2005 and 12 percent in 2006.

Understanding and sizing the GSE contribution to the expansion of risk in the financial system, however, are difficult. Subprime and Alt-A loans are typically based on industry self-identifications. As a result, both Pinto and Jaffee have attempted to estimate GSE exposure to high-risk loans other than those self-identified as subprime and Alt-A.[42] Using information that Fannie Mae and Freddie Mac themselves disclosed on the credit profiles of their guarantee business and portfolios, Jaffee creates an "other" high-risk category that includes all loans and securities that were not identified as Alt-A or as subprime *but* that had credit scores under 660, had loan-to-value ratios higher than 90 percent, or were interest-only or payment-option loans. Together with self-identified subprime and Alt-A, this book of business generated the lion's share of losses at the GSEs. At $1.0 trillion on the guaranty books as of September 30, 2009, "other high-risk loans" is a large category—larger than the less than $0.5 billion of self-identified subprime and Alt-A loans on their guaranty books. Jaffe estimates that about 30 percent of the guaranty books and 10 percent of the investment portfolios of the GSEs on September 30, 2009, were "other high-risk," subprime, and Alt-A loans combined. However, he does not attempt to estimate the GSE share of the total mortgage debt outstanding that was high risk as of that date. In contrast, Pinto considers any loan with a credit score of less than 660 on the books of the GSEs to be subprime and adds these directly to the number of self-reported subprime loans, creating his own set of subprime loans. Unlike Jaffee, he does try to estimate the GSE share of the total subprime market (including all loans with credit scores under 660). By this definition, he concludes that the GSEs were responsible for 34 percent of the subprime loans outstanding in 2008.

---

41. Pinto (2010) concludes that Alt-A originations reported by Inside Mortgage Finance do not include GSE-purchased Alt-A whole loans and therefore adds reported GSE-purchased Alt-A loans to the total Alt-A originations reported by the International Monetary Fund to obtain the GSE share.
    42. Pinto (2008, 2010); Jaffee (2010).

Although the exact numbers and market shares are tough to settle on and depend on definition, the foray of the GSEs into higher-priced, subprime, Alt-A, other high-risk, and nontraditional loans has been responsible for a disproportionate amount of the asset impairments and credit losses taken by the GSEs on their guarantees and portfolios. But it is important to recognize that the pressure on the GSEs would not have been as great as it was if the financial institutions and rating agencies involved in the private-label market had been more tightly regulated and supervised or if more regulatory constraints had been imposed on the nonprime products and practices of all financial institutions.

Summing Up

Nonprime lending and capital market problems largely arose as a result of widespread regulatory lapses: rating agencies and finance companies were barely subject to federal review and regulation, CDS markets were allowed to flourish with a striking lack of transparency, federal laws preempted state laws that might have curbed the riskiest lending practices, and efforts by states that opted out of the preemptions were stymied by federal banking regulators claiming preemptions anyway.

Moreover, regulators set the capital standards that proved inadequate throughout the financial system. They pressed Fannie Mae and Freddie Mac to boost home purchase loans at the height of the nonprime market. If there is fault to be found with capital requirements and the goals of Fannie Mae and Freddie Mac, it is not with the effort to regulate capital standards or to impose goals for low- and moderate-income lending, but rather with the actual standards that were promulgated. By the time the rule changes made by the Federal Reserve to inhibit risk layering took effect in October 2009, the damage from issuing such risky nonprime and nontraditional loans had already been done.

Creating Safer and Healthier Mortgage Markets

With so many people facing credit problems and foreclosures in the wake of the Great Recession, reestablishing a functional nonprime housing finance system is increasingly important to the future of homeownership and asset building. The causes of the boom and bust in nonprime lending point to several important steps that government and the private sector should take to restore mortgage markets to health. Many of the steps that will move the nation decisively in this direction have already been taken in new rules under existing regulations and newly passed laws. These include new TILA, HMDA, RESPA, and HOEPA rules, the Dodd-Frank Wall Street Reform and Consumer Protection Act (the financial reform act), and the Secure and Fair Enforcement for Mortgage Licensing Act (SAFE act). Although the details of many of the steps have yet to be hammered out, they will be pounded out in the process of promulgating new regulations and setting up the Consumer Financial Protection Bureau. Still others have not yet begun, including reforming the federal role in regulating secondary mortgage markets and supporting mortgage markets with guarantees and insurance at the loan and MBS level.

From the ashes of a broken mortgage finance system, a stronger one must rise. This section offers steps that could be taken to move forward in a way that provides credit to borrowers who might otherwise be excluded and makes room for specialized mortgage products and future innovation, while also protecting consumers and containing systemic risk.

Put Prudent Nonprime Lending with Traditional Products to a Fair Test

The evolution of nonprime lending in the mid-2000s was unfortunate not only because it inflicted so much damage, but also because it provided an unfair test of lending to borrowers with past credit problems. The wholesale relaxation of lending standards, when combined with marketing of riskier nontraditional products near the peak of an overheated housing market, was a recipe for heavy defaults and severe losses. Had the financial system itself contained the risk better—through effective self-policing or stronger regulation—the performance of nonprime loans (and prime loans for that matter) might well have been much better.

At least one test of nonprime loan performance—set up by Self Help, the Ford Foundation, and Fannie Mae under carefully controlled conditions—suggests that nonprime lending can be sustainable even under difficult market conditions. In 2000 Self Help began purchasing loans under the Community Advantage Program (CAP) that were originated by CRA lenders but did not conform to Fannie Mae's underwriting standards. Although tame by the standards for nonprime lending and products offered in the mid-2000s (most CAP loans were thirty-year fixed-rate mortgages with no prepayment penalties and complete income documentation), at the time the experiment was designed the underwriting standards used were considered so risky that Fannie Mae agreed to participate only in a second-loss position, with a large first-loss reserve funded by a grant from the Ford Foundation.

Ding, Quercia, Ratcliffe, and Wei compare the performance of subprime mortgages originated outside CAP to CAP loans.[43] They find that subprime loans carried a significantly higher risk of default and prepayment than CAP loans, even for comparable borrowers. For subprime loans with specific characteristics, such as adjustable rates or prepayment penalties, the relative risk of default on CAP loans (which prohibited these practices) was even higher. The channel of origination also appeared to make a difference, with default risk three to five times higher for borrowers who had obtained their mortgages through brokers, all else equal. The study also shows that, in combination, risky loan features magnified risk.

43. Ding and others (2008).

Figure 1-13. *Share of Fixed and Adjustable Subprime Mortgages That Are Delinquent or in Foreclosure, 2006–09* [a]

Share of loans 90+ days delinquent or in foreclosure

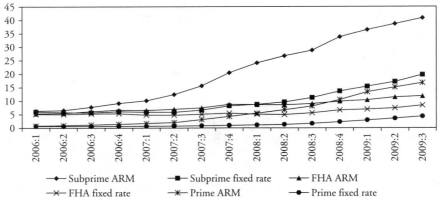

—◆— Subprime ARM   —■— Subprime fixed rate   —▲— FHA ARM
—✕— FHA fixed rate   —✳— Prime ARM   —●— Prime fixed rate

Source: Mortgage Bankers Association, National Delinquency Survey.
a. Serious delinquencies include loans ninety or more days delinquent or in foreclosure. Delinquent loan shares are not seasonally adjusted.

Borrowers were four to five times more likely to default on subprime loans that combined broker origination, adjustable rates, and prepayment penalties than on CAP loans. These findings demonstrate that borrower characteristics were not solely responsible for the higher risk of subprime loans and that features of the loans and their origination channels contributed significantly to risk.

Ding and others conclude that, when done correctly, lending to low-income and risky borrowers can be viable. And there is other evidence that the type of loan matters. Indeed, the difference between serious delinquency rates on fixed-versus adjustable-rate subprime loans indicates that the type of product matters a great deal (see figure 1-13). For example, serious delinquency rates in the third quarter of 2009 stood at a remarkable 40.8 percent for subprime adjustable-rate mortgages, but at a much lower 19.7 percent for fixed-rate subprime loans. In part, this difference reflects the fact that more adjustable-rate than fixed-rate mortgages were originated in 2004–06, when home prices peaked. But even after controlling for the vintage of loans, fixed-rate subprime mortgages performed far better (see figure 1-14).

It is now time to put prudent nonprime lending to a broad and fair test. The ingredients of such a test should include more careful licensing of brokers, a return to more traditional lending products, verification of incomes, efforts to ensure that borrowers have the capacity to handle mortgage payments at a fully indexed rate, and the requirement of escrows. This would restore commonsense underwriting. Important strides in this direction have already been made through the regulation

Figure 1-14. *Share of 2005 and 2006 Mortgage Originations That Are Delinquent, by Number of Months after Origination and Type of Nonprime Loan*[a]

Delinquent share of 2005 mortgage originations (percent)

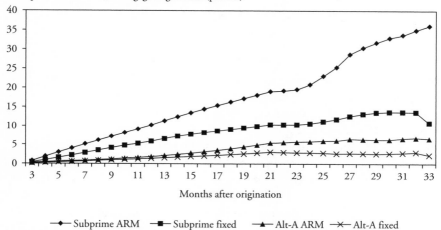

Months after origination

— Subprime ARM　— Subprime fixed　— Alt-A ARM　— Alt-A fixed

Delinquent share of 2006 mortgage originations (percent)

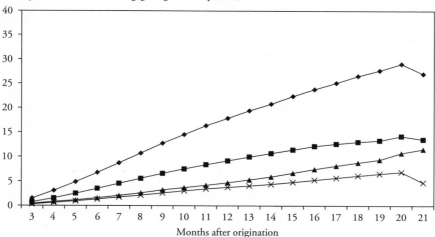

Months after origination

Source: First American CoreLogic, LoanPerformance data.
a. Delinquent loans are sixty or more days delinquent or in foreclosure.

of "higher-priced" loans as defined by new HOEPA regulations, newly mandated national licensing of brokers, and changes to good-faith estimates under the Truth in Lending Act. Provisions of the financial reform act go further by establishing minimum underwriting standards, enhanced disclosures on adjustable-rate and interest-only loans, a prohibition on prepayment penalties for all but certain fixed-rate qualified loans, and a prohibition on payments to the originator (broker) for all types of loans that are based on terms such as type of loan or interest rate (although the act does allow the ability to pay a broker points based on loan size).

Recognize That Properly Underwritten, Nontraditional Loans Have Their Place

When prudently underwritten—and when systemic risk was not ballooning—many nontraditional loan products performed well. It would therefore be wrong to conclude from the poor overall performance of nontraditional prime loans that the products themselves should be prohibited. Indeed, there are good reasons to offer nontraditional products, such as payment-option loans that allow for flexibility in deciding on monthly payments, hybrid adjustable-rate mortgages that allow people to amortize loans over thirty years but lock in lower rates for a shorter period matching their expected stay, or products that bank on future income gains. For example, a 5/25 loan affords borrowers who intend to move within five years a lower interest rate, with the only risk being that the rate will reset if the borrower remains in the home longer than expected. This ought to be viewed as a useful and workable loan option rather than one to be avoided.

The housing market crisis exposed nonprime lending to exceptional stresses that even prime loans were unable to withstand. The steep decline in home prices experienced in many areas, when combined with high unemployment, took a toll on the performance of prime mortgages as well. Indeed, serious delinquency rates on prime loans reached 6.3 percent in the third quarter of 2009 and were still rising. By comparison, during the previous three recessions (none of which featured as steep a drop in home prices), serious delinquency rates for all loans peaked at less than 2 percent.

Build Models That Can Serve as a Foundation for Sustainable Nonprime Lending

The failure to model nonprime default probabilities and loss severities properly could be interpreted as a sign that modeling cannot be used to assess nonprime and nontraditional product risk. But the history of these models in the prime mortgage market suggests otherwise. As noted, the orderly process of expanding the pool of eligible borrowers in the prime conforming market was extended by the GSEs into the nonprime market gradually at first. Fannie Mae created the expanded approval program in 2000 to provide credit to borrowers with underwriting variances that constituted higher expected risks. Expanded approval was a risk-based pricing system, but its use was limited to select lenders, volumes were kept low, loan products were typically fixed, and at least initially a hard 620 credit score cutoff was used.

But the private conduits relaxed underwriting dramatically, relying heavily on simulations based on borrower credit scores and loan-to-value ratios that assumed overly optimistic home price appreciation or drew conclusions from past performance of similar products that were more strictly underwritten.[44] These models relied far less on past precedent than the models in the prime market where there was much more relevant historical data to examine.

Moving forward, it should be possible to build a sustainable nonprime lending system that is based on careful modeling of and experimentation with different underwriting standards and products. The goal must be to manage nonprime risk better by undertaking sounder underwriting and by requiring greater reserves to buffer losses.

Engage in a Serious Public Debate about Acceptable Levels of Risk

Even before subprime foreclosures skyrocketed, there was a question of what level of expected default was reasonable for lenders to accept. Until the second half of 2007, subprime defaults were under 10 percent. As a result, about nine in ten subprime borrowers who would otherwise have been denied credit were able either to refinance their mortgages or to buy homes and benefit from the potential to earn a leveraged return on an investment in housing, pay down principal, and enjoy the pride of ownership.

A serious public debate over what level of expected risk is reasonable for individuals to assume, from a safety and soundness perspective, has never been initiated. An argument can be made in favor of lending under standards that produce higher expected default rates than in the prime market as long as three conditions are met. First, estimates of expected defaults should be considered reliable and based on actual performance history before pilot programs are expanded. Second, yields should be high enough to cover and reserve against expected losses, although this is much easier said than done because there is no consensus on how to get the expected loss calculations right. Third, borrowers must understand the risks they are taking on. Under these circumstances, borrowers can make informed choices and lenders can cover themselves for the added risk of lending to borrowers who have failed to repay previous debts on schedule.

Of course, the debate over what constitutes an acceptable level of risk would not be simple and would take place against a backdrop of lost faith in the models used to form expectations of default and loss. However, lenders will almost certainly continue to rely on modeling past data and simulating performance in making underwriting decisions. These models will come under closer scrutiny—whether or not regulations demand it—because investors will be less likely to go along with

44. Rossi (2010); Lang and Jagtiani (2010).

modeling assumptions and approaches used in the past. In addition, information will now be available on how different types of loans performed under a truly disastrous set of circumstances. As time passes, credit-scoring models will also be improved by modeling the ability of those who defaulted on their mortgages to repay other debts, providing an even stronger basis for underwriting decisions.

Take Steps to Limit Systemic Risk

Scanning the wreckage caused by the financial crisis in September 2008, as well as six other episodes since the 1980s,[45] Larry Summers, head of the National Economic Council for the first two years of the Obama administration, concludes, "Regulation will have to shift from its traditional focus on regulating individual institutions to focus on the stability of the entire system."[46] While it is likely that policymakers will move in this direction, it is instructive to note that during the height of the housing bubble and nonprime lending boom, many serious and thoughtful observers failed to appreciate the depth and magnitude of the systemic risk being taken, and regulators failed to heed the warnings of those who did. This underscores how difficult it is to agree that a bubble is forming and take steps to stop it, especially ones that restrict credit practices and products.

Limiting systemic risk is politically unpopular because it can constrain economic growth and inhibit financial innovation. Measures that could be taken include imposing stiffer capital requirements on more financial institutions so that they can lend less from a given asset base; subjecting financial institutions that are not federally chartered to more rigorous federal examinations for compliance with safety and soundness regulations and consumer protection rules; creating an agency to prohibit credit products viewed as unsafe for consumers (and by extension the financial system); or, as Pollock has suggested, raising capital requirements when asset prices deviate from long-term trends.[47]

Although unpopular, one or more of these actions may be preferable to leaving the current set of regulations unchanged, and recent reforms have already begun to change them. The downside of not making these reforms is obvious: the world would remain exposed to periodic financial crises stemming from permissible practices in the financial system that may cost taxpayers a great deal of money and have disastrous consequences for the economy. In the end, some combination of imposing stiffer capital reserve requirements, paying into federal insurance funds, and limiting the risks to lenders by enforcing basic underwriting standards—especially on riskier loan products or higher-priced loans to risky

45. These other crises are the 1987 stock market crash, the savings and loan crisis of the middle to late 1980s, the commercial real estate crash of the late 1980s and early 1990s, the peso crisis in Mexico in 1994–95, the Asian financial crisis of 1998, and the collapse of Long Term Capital Management in 1998.

46. Summers (2008).

47. Pollock (2009).

borrowers—are important. It remains to be seen whether HOEPA's higher-priced lending requirements and provisions of the financial reform act for minimum mortgage-lending standards go far enough in constraining risky mortgage lending and if the broader oversight and stronger capital and risk-retaining requirements on banks and nonbank financial institutions within the financial reform act will be enough to contain systemic risk. But containing systemic risk through proper management of risk is a critical adjunct to stronger capital reserve requirements that limit the supply of credit.

In short, containing and managing risk through underwriting, not just through pricing, must be restored to nonprime markets while still allowing a market serving borrowers with subprime credit records to thrive. In addition, if lenders continue to have wide latitude to offer products and apply underwriting standards of their choosing, there should be some way for regulators to step in if there is a sense that the collective action of lenders is contributing dangerously to systemic risk.

Improve Consumer Protections and Disclosures

The admonishment "buyer beware" as a predicate of consumer protection works best when buyers can easily comparison-shop, prices are transparent (and borrowers do not incur costs for price discovery), the product features being compared are nearly identical, buyers and sellers have equal information and power in the negotiation, the risks of purchasing a product are clear, and buyers have a clear and well-informed perspective on the product that is best for them.[48] All of these conditions were lacking in the nonprime mortgage market.

As discussed, steps to protect consumers have already been taken in the form of HOEPA reforms that curb underwriting excesses around capacity to pay for the newly created category of "higher-priced loans" and to better inform consumers through TILA and RESPA disclosures that make interest rate, interest fee, and settlement cost estimates more binding for all loans secured by homes. Additional steps aimed at underwriting are in the financial reform act, such as mandatory verification of income and minimum underwriting standards to ensure a borrower's ability to pay (including the use of a fully indexed interest rate on hybrid adjustable-rate mortgages to ensure the ability of a borrower to absorb reset shock should it occur).

An important step that the government could also take is to help nonprime borrowers to comparison-shop by demanding greater pricing transparency. Government could explore the feasibility of requiring lenders to post prices for comparable loan products on a public website. The disclosure could take the form of grids showing the interest rates that borrowers with particular credit scores would be charged if they took out a particular product with a particular set of terms. Alternatively, when an automated scoring model is used, the borrowers could be

---

48. Laibson and Zeckhauser (1998).

granted access to the wholesale loan interest rate (net of broker commissions) and also be told the cost of running their information through another automated system to get another price quote when working with brokers who work with multiple lenders.

As it stands now, buyers and sellers do not have equal information or bargaining power. Sellers of mortgages have much more information than borrowers on the rates and terms being offered on nonprime mortgages. Brokers are faxed—or otherwise have access to—rate sheets along a number of dimensions from multiple lenders and are under no obligation to share that complete information with borrowers. Correspondent and retail branch lenders know the minimum interest rate that wholesale aggregators are looking for, but they are not required to make those prices known to the borrower.

By prohibiting yield-spread premiums on all residential mortgages, amending the Truth in Lending Act to require lenders to disclose the aggregate fees paid to brokers related to each loan, and imposing the additional prohibition against any other person paying compensation to the loan originator for a transaction if the consumer pays the loan originator's compensation directly, provisions of the financial reform act will also enable borrowers more easily to see all the compensation they cede to their lenders and the amount of interest they will be paying on their loan.

Beyond the challenges posed by the specific features of the nonprime market are the cognitive biases of consumers in making mortgage decisions, which leave borrowers vulnerable to taking on risks and failing to pick the lowest-cost loan. These biases include discounting future risks and assuming that their own level of risk of an adverse event is lower than average. There are also cognitive biases that result from innumeracy, which is widespread, and the use of rules of thumb to solve complex problems with future uncertainties, such as focusing on the monthly payment rather than the annual percentage rate in sizing up the true cost of the loan.

While all of these biases apply in a more extreme way in the nonprime market, they exist to some degree in the prime market as well. The challenges in relying entirely on educated consumers to protect themselves in mortgage transactions are apparent. The RESPA and TILA reforms in effect in 2010 go a long way toward achieving greater clarity about payment reset risks on products that contain them and in giving firmer fee and rate quotes to borrowers, but their influence on consumer behavior has yet to be tested. The financial reform act calls for other amendments to the TILA, requiring lenders to give borrowers six-months' notice prior to the reset of any hybrid mortgage, along with an explanation of the change, a good-faith estimate of the new amount, and a list of alternatives the borrower may pursue before the reset.

The sense that disclosures are not enough has added to the pressure on lawmakers to strengthen consumer protections further. In considering new regulations, lawmakers are faced with the challenge of protecting consumers without inhibiting financial innovations that might serve borrowers well or without prohibiting mortgage products and underwriting standards that lenders want to offer and that consumers can use to finance consumption or investment. For example, the Consumer Financial Protection Bureau will have to walk a fine line between protecting consumers and not stifling innovation.

Improve Affirmative Obligations and Duties to Serve Low-Income Markets

With pockets of concentrated foreclosures dotting low- and moderate-income communities, especially where minorities make up half or more of the population, there is a significant risk of a return to a time when it was especially difficult to get mortgage loans in these communities. A strong economic argument can be made that absent collective action, lenders will pull back from low-income lending in ways that will have disparate impacts on minorities, on low-income neighborhoods in general, and on low-income minority neighborhoods in particular.[49]

As argued, it is easy to confuse the reasons for the poor performance of loans to these borrowers and in these communities and to blame the victim. But these low-income, especially minority, communities were "reverse redlined," with unfettered lending practices permitting borrowers to take excessive risks they sometimes did not understand, including some degree of predatory lending and the use of products and underwriting standards that allowed buyers in low-income communities to drive prices to unsustainable levels. There is a risk that lenders will deny credit in the future on the basis of the abysmal performance generated by the reckless practices that thrived at the top of an overheated housing market. Just as when CRA and HMDA were initially passed, it may take collective action that only regulation can bring about to keep lenders looking for ways to reach out to low-income communities and working together to restart lending under a more sustainable model in these places.

There is ample reason to want to review and reconsider how CRA is implemented and how widely it should apply.[50] This review is already well under way—with many opposing views—but it is important that the review lead to concrete steps to improve how CRA grades are assessed and potentially expand its reach.[51] As it stands now, only loans made by banks and thrifts in areas where they have branch offices count, reducing the law's relevance since only a fraction of all mortgage loans fit this bill. Its critics have pointed out that at least in some cases large banks responded to regulatory pressures by extending below-market-interest-rate loans to borrowers who already had a higher-than-typical risk profile. While some cross-subsidization has long been a part of the broad prime market—so that

49. Litan and others (2000).
50. Willis (2010).
51. Chakrabarti and others (2009).

the same price has been charged on loans to borrowers who constitute different risks—this sort of treatment has struck some observers as evidence of an act implemented in an overreaching way or interpreted unwisely by the regulated. Although the extent to which such market-distorting behavior was practiced is unclear, most observers believe that it was done mostly by a handful of lenders in large metropolitan areas that were competing for outstanding ratings.

Like CRA, the notion of the duty for secondary-market firms to serve certain markets where the risk of being underserved either remains or could reemerge is sensible. It should not be abandoned, even if it is viewed as having contributed to the unwise embrace of Alt-A lending by the GSEs in the mid-2000s, without first diagnosing if how the goals were set is what created the problem. Fannie Mae and Freddie Mac from 1999 onward complained about the increase in the goals and even more vocally about their inflexibility. They argued that the goals should be modified for years in which the volume of refinance is especially heavy or the share of adjustable-rate mortgages is especially high, and in 2004 the industry challenged HUD's calculations and estimates of the market. Then in 2005 they complained that forcing them to meet specific single-family home purchase subgoals was ill advised and limited their ability to meet goals in a more prudent and safe fashion.

Improve Transparency in the Capital Markets

As Federal Reserve Chair Ben Bernanke has pointed out, "Because mortgage-backed securities are complex amalgamations of underlying mortgages that may themselves be complex to price, transparency about the underlying assets and the mortgage-backed security itself is essential."[52] Yet transparency in the asset-backed securities market was lacking because only a limited amount of detailed information on the underlying assets was passed along when the assets were placed into securities. In addition, investors had an even more difficult time following the characteristics of underlying loans and predicting how their performance would affect payouts when tranches were recombined to manufacture even more tranches in collateralized debt obligations. When CDO tranches were recombined again to form CDO-squared securities, transparency suffered even more.

Credit-default swaps and synthetic CDOs (CDOs made up of CDSs referencing the underlying loans and mortgage-backed securities) did not trade on public markets and did not have a central clearinghouse or repository of record. Indeed, the Commodity Futures Modernization Act of 2000 ensured that the derivatives market would remain largely unregulated. A dispute between the SEC and the Commodity Futures Trading Commission over which had jurisdiction over derivatives like CDSs had inhibited the market for them in the United States while the market was developing rapidly in Europe. As a result, regulators, let

52. Bernanke (2008).

alone investors, could not gauge total exposure to nonprime credit risk, which entities held it, and who the counterparties to CDS were.

This lack of transparency proved a major failing, turning a useful method for managing and hedging risk into a means for propagating it. In the aftermath of the financial crisis, efforts have been made to have credit-default swaps and other derivatives traded on public exchanges or clearinghouses, backed by capital reserves, such as is written into the financial reform act through the requirement that several classes of derivatives be traded on an exchange and routed through derivatives-clearing organizations registered with the Commodity Futures Trading Commission. The opacity of capital markets may also lead investors to demand, or regulators to require, greater disclosure of pertinent information on the loans backing mortgage securities. The lesson here is that these efforts are important and worthwhile. As part of the financial reform act, the SEC is required to adopt rules requiring the issuers of ABSs to disclose information regarding the underlying assets within each tranche or class, including disclosures of loan-level data. These are all important steps in addressing transparency.

Improve Measurement, Monitoring, and Management of Counterparty Risk

The lack of transparency in the capital markets and the reliance on rating agencies to judge the creditworthiness and business practices of counterparties resulted in counterparty risk that was undetected and poorly managed. In addressing this problem, there is a tendency to prescribe retention of more credit risk by the mortgage originators to better align counterparty interests, while also creating cushions against losses. While this makes sense, there are limits to how far down the supply chain such demands can reasonably reach, and it is likely that putting more capital at risk is not sufficient in and of itself to manage counterparty risk properly.

Imposing stiff capital requirements on brokers and small mortgage companies on all products is impractical, and doing so could drive them out of business. Yet the originate-to-distribute model has relied—and will likely continue to rely—on mortgage brokers. The reason the broker network has been so durable is that it allows larger lenders to avoid the fixed costs of operating a large retail mortgage origination system. Consumers can also benefit from working with brokers who are able to offer products, pricing, and underwriting from a wide array of lenders. Given their scale and business model, brokers are often not in a position to retain much credit risk. Thus the carve-out for "qualified loans" in the financial reform act is essential to supporting a competitive market for loan origination that allows smaller community banks and mortgage brokers to continue to originate loans. While "qualified loans" are, as of the release of this book, yet to be defined, the intention is to waive risk retention for well-established traditional loan products like thirty-year fixed-rate mortgages that are prudently underwritten.

While larger mortgage banks, finance companies, banks, thrifts, and investment banks are in a better position to retain more of the risk—and there are good reasons to want them to do so—this does not guarantee that fewer risks will be taken, especially if origination and brokerage fees remain up-front and substantial. In fact, many banks did have capital at risk, which is why their losses related to nonprime mortgages were so large, such as Bear Stearns and Lehman Brothers.

In addition to requiring counterparties to put capital at risk, there are other ways that counterparties can and should monitor, manage, and contain risk. Instead of relying on the ratings of rating agencies, entities that aggregate loans—or insure or guarantee loans or the securities they back—can impose their own strict requirements for sellers and servicers. Fannie Mae, Freddie Mac, and others have long operated with such rules. In addition, these aggregators can constantly monitor the performance of sellers and brokers to detect those with loans that perform significantly worse than their peers. Regulations could require all aggregators to impose certain requirements on sellers and servicers and to have systems in place for monitoring counterparty risk. These systems would look for statistical outliers in the performance of their sellers and servicers and prescribe methods for investigating whether they warrant breaking off business with the outliers. The financial reform act calls for new regulations on ratings procedures and further disclosures of credit-rating methodologies by the credit-rating agencies, with emphasis on qualitative detail on the data used and assumptions made as well as some quantitative reporting of the impact of various changes in market conditions.

A recent step in the direction of both greater counterparty strength and ability to monitor performance is the requirement that mortgage brokers meet national licensing standards and be listed in a national registry. Licensing standards help to ensure the professionalism of brokers, and registration allows the performance of brokers to be monitored more closely. Employees of regulated financial institutions must be federally registered but do not need state licenses, diminishing the reach of the law.

The extent to which counterparty rules as strong as those in the conforming market were in place in the private-label channels is less clear. The incentives to police distribution channels were weaker because the broker-dealers who structured the securities were not guarantors and were insulated from assignee liability. One way to ensure that broker-dealers police their distribution channels, therefore, would be to hold assignees liable for certain conditions under which loans were originated, although efforts to impose assignee liability in the 1990s strongly suggest that conditions would have to be limited, clear, and compelling and that liability would have to be capped so that securities backed by loans in private conduits could be rated. Even so, such a move could have a chilling effect on market participants.

Lastly, counterparty risks can be reduced by aligning the incentives of agents to avoid principal-agent problems. This could be done by tying some portion of mortgage broker and MBS broker-dealer compensation to the long-run performance of loans, such as the requirement in the financial reform act that issuers retain a minimum of 5 percent of all securitized assets unless the security is backed entirely by qualified mortgages as defined by the act. Rather than front-loading all the incentives, some portion could come out of the payment streams from the mortgages the brokers originate or the securities they issue. This is how servicers are compensated. But it would be difficult to achieve this without a transition period because up-front fees are more immediate. It would also likely take regulation because brokers prefer up-front fees. Thus any firm offering them would likely gain market share from those paying a portion from recurring monthly payments tied to loan performance and prepayment characteristics.

Improve Regulation and Supervision of the Shadow Banking System

The lack of oversight by federal authorities meant that many important practices occurred out of the sight and reach of federal regulators (except for practices already prohibited by federal credit laws like TILA, RESPA, HOEPA, and the Equal Credit Opportunity Act). Finance companies, mortgage brokers, rating agencies, CDS issuers and markets, investment banks, and investment funds would benefit from more federal oversight and regulation.

While many of those that might be subjected to such regulation and oversight are resisting it, at least one major trade association representing firms in the so-called shadow banking system has acknowledged the value of subjecting the firms it represents to federal oversight. The Mortgage Bankers Association has called for establishing a federal regulator to develop uniform national mortgage standards and regulate independent mortgage banks and brokers.[53]

It appears likely that at least some players in the shadow banking system will come under closer federal scrutiny and regulation. As noted, the federal government has already taken that step with mortgage brokers through licensing and registration, but it is likely that efforts will also be made to improve federal oversight and regulation of the rating agencies, issuers of credit-default swaps, and investment banks acting as broker-dealers. The Consumer Financial Protection Bureau goes a long way toward doing this by granting a single bureau within the Federal Reserve the authority to examine and enforce regulations for all mortgage-related businesses, including all lenders, servicers, mortgage brokers, and bank and non-bank financial companies.

53. The Mortgage Bankers Association's proposal calls for legislation that incorporates and extends borrower protections in HOEPA, including taking into account a borrower's ability to pay using fully indexed rates and fully amortized payments. It also improves appraisal and servicing rules. The proposal establishes a duty of care for loan originators requiring them to present a choice of appropriate loan products to borrowers, fully disclose their costs, and disclose all forms of compensation received by the broker or loan officer in connection with the loan. Under the proposal, borrowers would have to agree in writing to the terms of a nontraditional loan product before closing.

Retool the Federal Role in Guaranteeing Mortgage Debt

For decades, the markets perceived that Fannie Mae and Freddie Mac had the implicit backing of the federal government because they were chartered by Congress, enjoyed special privileges, and had modest but symbolic lines of credit with the Treasury. When the federal government stepped in and placed Fannie Mae and Freddie Mac into conservatorship, this perception was borne out for its debtors and the purchasers of its MBSs (if not for equity holders). It is important to point out, however, that other large financial institutions, notably AIG and several of the nation's largest banks, received significant federal backing for their obligations as well and, in some cases, on terms less onerous than those imposed on the GSEs. Thus the expectation has been raised that the federal government will step in to prop up any institution deemed too large to fail and to honor their debts. Be that as it may, the experience with Fannie Mae and Freddie Mac must cause a rethinking of how government should support mortgage liquidity and the stability of the financial system through insurance and guarantees of mortgages and mortgage-backed securities.

In rethinking this role, several important lessons outlined in this chapter should be kept in mind. First and foremost, absent FHA and the federal government stepping in to honor the debt and guarantee commitments of Fannie Mae and Freddie Mac, the mortgage market would have utterly collapsed. The prospect of such a collapse is terrifying. Had it occurred, for some period of time no one could have bought or sold a home without paying cash or accepting onerous terms, no one could have refinanced to take advantage of lower rates, and no one could have borrowed against home equity. Homes would have been as devalued and untradable as subprime securities were in the fall of 2008. Thus it is clear that federal insurances and guarantees are vital to the stability of the mortgage finance system, the broader financial system, and the national economy. It would be ill advised for the federal government not to have mechanisms in place to provide these insurances and guarantees and be able to activate them immediately on a massive scale should conditions demand it. Indeed, the ability of the federal government to go in over a weekend and seize control of the two companies was vital to keeping the financial system from collapsing and credit flowing from the thousands of private firms that originate and service loans. In addition, Fannie Mae and Freddie Mac ran large-scale federal loan modification programs and allowed the Federal Reserve to operate an agency MBS purchase program that lowered mortgage interest rates and kept credit flowing.

Second, even if the federal government provides only an implicit guarantee (and it is doubtful whether such an implicit guarantee makes sense moving forward or whether only explicit guarantees should be offered), it has a compelling interest in charging fees for these guarantees, as it does with the FHA, to protect against losses. It must also sort out ways to make sure that the proper counterparty risk management measures are in place, including adequate reserve requirements against losses and other risk-sharing arrangements that limit moral hazard and principal-agent problems.

Third, the need for federal guarantees goes beyond the need to insure whole loans and extends to guarantees of mortgage-backed securities, especially of securities structured to allow interest rate risk to be parsed and better managed. As discussed in this report, the secondary market—which is driven by large players that can enforce standardization—has enormous benefits, including liquidity that lowers mortgage interest rates, the capacity to tap into deeper pools of capital, which also lowers costs, and the ability to match asset and liability duration by issuing securities with a range of maturities, coupons, and privileges to cash flows from otherwise long-term, illiquid mortgage assets. Absent structured securities aimed at managing interest rate and related prepayment and asset-liability matching risks, it would be difficult to source so much capital for thirty-year fixed-rate products. Even pension funds and insurance companies focus their purchases on real estate mortgage investment conduit tranches with short-term maturities. Absent federal guarantees, those structured securities may not be issued at all times, and pension funds and insurance companies will have to revert to the tricks of structuring credit risk that backfired so badly in the private-label ABS and CDO market for subprime mortgage securities.

Fourth, if the lowest common denominator lenders are allowed to thrive anywhere in mortgage credit markets because regulatory oversight is weak, any shareholder-owned company like Fannie Mae and Freddie Mac that offers an implicit (or explicit) mortgage guarantee will come under pressure to move toward that lowest denominator to retain market share and possibly boost short-term earnings if yields are attractive. Thus the federal government has a compelling interest in managing counterparty risk not only through capital requirements and risk-sharing arrangements but also through care in the loan products and underwriting standards it will allow these enterprises to insure or purchase (perhaps above and beyond regulations already in place to limit products and standards for all mortgage loans, as is starting to occur as a result of the financial reform act, new TILA rules, and the new HOEPA rules governing higher-priced lending).

Lastly, the FHA has been criticized over the years for being too rule bound by law to act decisively to manage the risks in its own portfolio or to innovate in ways that might better serve the consuming public. It has also been faulted for being too sensitive to political pressure to police its private partners as effectively as a private company can. And it has long been viewed by experts as having antiquated information technology systems, salary structures that make it difficult to attract the necessary talent, and other problems that stem from being a government agency subject to annual appropriations. While many strides have been made to improve and reform the FHA, few would say that these reforms have solved many of the agency's structural challenges. Moving forward, old reform proposals should be dusted off and revisited in light of recent events and the FHA's evolution.[54] Ginnie Mae, which guarantees timely payment of principal and interest on securities backed by FHA-insured loans, provides a model that is now being considered as a way for the federal government to provide wraparound securities issued by firms that would become chartered entities for the purposes of issuing MBSs explicitly backed by the federal government.

Beyond the loans and MBSs it guarantees, the federal government also has a role to play in regulating originators, issuers, rating agencies, mortgage loan products, mortgage derivative products, consumer disclosures, and public disclosures of lending information, like HMDA, to protect consumers and investors and promote fair lending. It has long exercised this role and is in the process of rethinking and reforming it.

Improve Loan-Level Disclosures

The lack of disclosure and lack of uniformity in disclosure have made it extremely difficult to reach common conclusions about the basic facts of the boom and bust in nonprime lending.[55] Subprime and Alt-A loans were self-defined by lenders. There was no statutory definition: even credit score cutoffs varied widely in defining subprime. While proprietary databases often contained sufficient information to parse data based on features of the underlying loan product, underwriting standards, and credit scores of borrowers, these data were not widely available to the public at a detailed level.[56] This has inhibited meaningful analysis. To gauge the nature and extent of nonprime lending, it would be helpful to get away from umbrella terms such as Alt-A, prime, and subprime and to substitute much more specific categories that are reported in common ways. For example, it would be useful to cross-classify loans into common categories of combined loan-to-value ratios, debt-to-income ratios, credit scores, degree of documentation of income, whether loans require escrowing of taxes and insurances, if the applicants intend to occupy the home as a primary residence or not, and type of product (such as interest-only loans with reset dates of less than five years or five years or more; payment-option loans; fixed-rate loans of less than fifteen years or more than fifteen years; and adjustable rates with reset dates of less than one

54. Vandell (1995); Wartell (2002).

55. See Edward Pinto's detailed testimony on the subject to the Committee on Oversight and Government Reform of the House of Representatives, December 9, 2008.

56. Wall Street analysts often released reports that drew on such detailed information, and some of the vendors were quite forthcoming in recent years to researchers and policymakers on a case-by-case basis. But these vendors are businesses, and there are both limits to the amount of time they can spend formatting tables for outside parties to inform public debates and inefficiencies in doing so in ways that are thought out in advance as the most fundamental to policy formulation. Coming up with required national disclosures as described in the text would bring efficiency and consistency to the process and could be developed based on a process facilitated by regulators.

year, two to four years, and five years or more). Common CLTV categories might be 80 percent or less, 80–90 percent, 91–95 percent, 96–97 percent, greater than 98 percent, and so forth. Private vendors could be required to provide information on the number as well as the performance of loans cross-classified in this way after a certain threshold number of loans within a cell has been reached. This could be required at the national level and only for particular categories and threshold numbers of loans so that vendors would still be able to sell more detailed geographic and loan-level data.

Many loan-level disclosure reform proposals are circulating that would demand much greater disclosure than this, especially on loans in private-label securities. These may gain traction. The approach described here is aimed specifically at gauging the national patterns of the kinds of loans that are being originated and under what sorts of underwriting standards, how much risk is being layered, and how these loans are performing. These other reforms, such as those included in the financial reform act, are aimed mostly at improving the ability of investors to know what is in the ABSs and CDOs they invest in and to track the performance of these securities. Others are pushing to do the same for privately placed securities or to improve disclosures around broker markups and loan modifications.[57] Others seek to link loan information to borrower characteristics by forming a common identifier between HMDA data and loan-level data reported to and aggregated by third-party data vendors.[58] Additional HMDA disclosures required by the financial reform act include a universal identifier for each loan and information on the age of the borrower or applicant, credit score, total points and fees payable at origination, the difference between the loan APR and a benchmark rate for all loans, the months of a prepayment penalty, the value of collateral property, the proposed terms of the loan in months, terms that would allow the payments to be not fully amortizing, the channel through which the application was made, a unique identifier for the loan originator, a parcel identifier for the property, and other information that the bureau may see fit to acquire.

Revisit Servicing Arrangements in Securitizations

The jury is still out on whether the differing interests of tranche holders and the pooling and servicing agreements that govern servicing arrangements for loans held in trust by special-purpose entities inhibited servicers in their response to massive subprime loan defaults. As a result, the legal agreements governing trusts and the conduct of servicers are worthy of closer attention, and efforts to strengthen them are worth making.

57. For an excellent review of these proposals as well as the issues they pose, see the chapter by Howell Jackson in this volume.
58. See the chapters by Howell Jackson and by Allen Fishbein and Ren Essene in this volume.

Where Next?

The severe global recession sparked by the meltdown in credit markets poses important questions for business leaders and policymakers about the best ways to reform the U.S. capital markets and housing finance system. The answers are difficult because they involve the perennial trade-off between, on the one hand, limiting access to credit by imposing harsher capital standards, restrictions, and prohibitions on products and underwriting practices and, on the other hand, ensuring that credit is as available as possible, consistent with sound underwriting, for businesses and households seeking to borrow for consumption and investment purposes.

Even those who have criticized many nonprime lending practices express a strong interest in seeing the market succeed because, by definition, it opens up access for borrowers and allows the use of loan products and terms not available in the prime market. Whatever solutions are worked out, it is more important than ever to strike a fruitful balance in this perennial trade-off. The hope is that market corrections and regulatory reforms in the nonprime market will allow a broad range of households to have access to mortgage credit, but in ways that are more sustainable, involve fewer risks, and do not become fodder for excessive financial risk taking in the capital markets.

By 2010 regulatory reform proposals were proliferating, and on July 21, 2010, the Dodd-Frank Wall Street Reform and Consumer Protection Act was passed into law. The other proposals yet to be acted upon have a wide range of sponsors, including trade organizations, investment banks, think tanks, academics, lawmakers, and the administration. It is uncertain how these proposals will be received and which will ultimately succeed. But what emerges will govern the safety and soundness of the financial system, access to and cost of mortgage credit, and the fairness and clarity of mortgage lending for years to come.

References

Ashcraft, Adam B., and Til Schuermann. 2008. "Understanding the Securitization of Subprime Mortgage Credit." *Foundations and Trends in Finance* 2, no. 3: 191–309.

Avery, Robert B., Glenn B. Canner, and Robert E. Cook. 2005. "New Information Reported under HMDA and Its Application in Fair Lending Enforcement." *Federal Reserve Bulletin* 91 (Summer): 344–94.

Belsky, Eric S., and Joel Prakken. 2004. "Housing Wealth Effects: Housing's Impact on Wealth Accumulation, Wealth Distribution, and Consumer Spending." Harvard University, Joint Center for Housing Studies.

Bernanke, Ben. 2008. "The Future of Mortgage Finance in the United States." Presentation at the University of California Berkeley and University of California Los Angeles symposium, "The Mortgage Meltdown, the Economy, and Public Policy," Berkeley, Calif.

Caballero, Ricardo J., Emmanuel Farhi, and Pierre-Olivier Gourinchas. 2008a. "An Equilibrium Model of 'Global Imbalances' and Low Interest Rates." *American Economic Review* 98, no. 1: 358–93.

————. 2008b. "Financial Crash, Commodity Prices, and Global Imbalances." In *BPEA*, no. 2: 1–68.

Calem, Paul S., Kevin Gillen, and Susan Wachter. 2004. "The Neighborhood Distribution of Subprime Lending." *Journal of Real Estate Finance and Economics* 29, no. 4: 393–410.

Chakrabarti, Prabal, David Erikson, Ren S. Essene, Ian Galloway, and John Olson, eds. 2009. *Revisiting the CRA: Perspectives on the Future of the Community Reinvestment Act.* Federal Reserve Bank of Boston and Federal Reserve Bank of San Francisco.

Coval, Joshua D., Jakub Jurek, and Erik Stafford. 2008. "The Economics of Structured Finance." Harvard Business School.

Curry, Timothy, and Lynn Shibut. 2000. "The Cost of the Savings and Loan Crisis: Truth and Consequences." *FDIC Banking Review* 13, no. 2: 26–35.

Deng, Yongheng, Stuart A. Gabriel, and Anthony B. Sanders. 2009. "CDO Market Implosion and the Pricing of Subprime Mortgage-Backed Securities." National University of Singapore; University of California, Los Angeles; Arizona State University.

Ding, Lei, Roberto G. Quercia, Janneke Ratcliffe, and Wei Li. 2008. "Risky Borrowers or Risky Mortgages: Disaggregating Effects Using Propensity Score Models." University of North Carolina, College of Arts and Sciences, Center for Responsible Lending.

Durkin, Thomas A. 2008. "Should Consumer Disclosures Be Updated?" In *Understanding Consumer Credit.* Harvard University, Joint Center for Housing Studies.

Economist, The. 2009. "Global House Prices." *The Economist,* June 4, 2009.

Federal Reserve Board. Various years. "Flow of Funds, Balance Sheet of Households and Non-profit Organizations." Washington.

Felsenheimer, Jochen, and Philip Gisdakis. 2008. *Credit Crises: From Tainted Loans to a Global Economic Meltdown.* Weinheim: Wiley-VCH.

Fender, Ingo, and John Kiff. 2004. "CDO Rating Methodology: Some Thoughts on Model Risk and Its Implications." Basel: Bank for International Settlements.

Gates, Susan Wharton, Vanessa Gail Perry, and Peter M. Zorn. 2002. "Automated Under-writing in Mortgage Lending: Good News for the Underserved?" *Housing Policy Debate* 13, no. 2: 369–91.

Glaeser, Edward L., Joshua Gottlieb, and Joseph Gyourko. 2010. "Did Credit Market Policies Cause the Housing Bubble?" Policy Brief. Harvard University, John F. Kennedy School of Government.

Goldstein, Deborah. 1999. "Understanding Predatory Lending: Moving towards a Common Definition and Workable Solutions." Harvard University, Joint Center for Housing Studies.

Gorton, Gary. 2008. "The Subprime Panic." ICF Working Paper 08-25. Yale University, International Center for Finance.

Greenspan, Alan. 2010. "The Crisis." *BPEA* (Spring).

Himmelberg, Charles, Christopher Mayer, and Todd Sinai. 2005. "Assessing High House Prices: Bubbles, Fundamentals, and Misperceptions." *Journal of Economic Perspectives* 19, no. 4: 67–92.

IMF (International Monetary Fund). 2009. "Lessons of the Global Crisis for Macroeconomic Policy." Washington: IMF, Research Department.

Inside Mortgage Finance. 2009. *The 2009 Mortgage Market Statistical Annual.* Bethesda, Md.

Jaffee, Dwight M. 2010. "The Role of the GSEs and Housing Policy in the Financial Crisis." Paper prepared for presentation to the Financial Crisis Inquiry Commission, Washington, February 27. www.fcic.gov/hearings/pdfs/2010-0227-Jaffee.pdf.

Joint Center for Housing Studies. 2001. *The State of the Nation's Housing.* Harvard University.

Laderman, Elizabeth, and Carolina Reid. 2008. "Lending in Low- and Moderate-Income Neighborhoods in California: The Performance of CRA Lending during the Subprime Melt-down." Federal Reserve Bank of San Francisco.

Laibson, David, and Richard Zeckhauser. 1998. "Amos Tversky and the Ascent of Behavioral Economics." *Journal of Risk and Uncertainty* 16, no. 1: 7–47.

Lang, William W., and Julapa Jagtiani. 2010. "The Mortgage and Financial Crises: The Role of Credit Risk Management and Corporate Governance." University of Pennsylvania, Wharton Financial Institution Center.

Lea, Michael. 2010. "Alternative Forms of Mortgage Finance: What Can We Learn from Other Countries?" In *Moving Forward in Addressing Credit Market Challenges: A National Symposium.* Harvard Business School Press.

Litan, Robert E., Nicolas P. Retsinas, Eric S. Belsky, and Susan White Haag. 2000. "The Community Reinvestment Act after Financial Modernization: A Baseline Report." Washington: Department of Treasury.

McCoy, Patricia A., and Elizabeth Renuart. 2008. "The Legal Infrastructure of Subprime and Nontraditional Home Mortgages." In *Borrowing to Live: Consumer and Mortgage Credit Revisited,* edited by Nicolas P. Retsinas and Eric S. Belsky, pp. 110–37. Harvard University, Joint Center for Housing Studies; Brookings Institution Press.

Pinto, Edward J. 2008. "The Role of Fannie Mae and Freddie Mac in the Financial Crisis." Testimony before the Committee on Oversight and Government Reform, U.S. House of Representatives, December 9.

———. 2009. "Establishing the Role of the Community Reinvestment Act in the Financial Crisis." Washington: Cato Institute (November 18).

———. 2010. "Memorandum: High LTV, Subprime, and Alt-A Originations over the Period 1992–2007 and Fannie, Freddie, FHA, and VA's Role." www.aei.org/docLib/Pinto-High-LTV-Subprime-Alt-A.pdf.

Pollock, Alex J. 2009. "Ten Ways to Do Better in the Next Financial Cycle." *The American,* July 28.

Pozsar, Zoltan. 2008. "The Rise and Fall of the Shadow Banking System." *Regional Financial Review,* 44, no. 1: 13–15.

Rossi, Clifford V. 2010. "Anatomy of Risk Management Practices in the Mortgage Industry: Lessons for the Future." Washington: Research Institute for Housing America.

Salmon, Felix. 2009. "Recipe for Disaster: The Formula That Killed Wall Street." *Wired Magazine,* February 23.

Satow, Julie. 2008. "Ex-SEC Official Blames Agency for Blow-up of Broker-Dealers." *New York Sun,* September 18.

Scheessele, Randall M. 2002. "Black and White Disparities in Subprime Mortgage Refinance Lending." Washington: Department of Housing and Urban Development.

Straka, John W. 2000. "A Shift in the Mortgage Landscape: The 1990s Move to Automated Credit Evaluations." *Journal of Housing Research* 11, no. 2: 207–32.

Summers, Lawrence. 2008. "The Future of Market Capitalism." Keynote address given at the Centennial Global Business Summit.

Taylor, John B. 2009. *Getting off Track: How Government Actions and Interventions Caused, Prolonged, and Worsened the Financial Crisis.* Palo Alto, Calif.: Hoover Institution Press.

Vandell, Kerry D. 1995. "FHA Restructuring Proposals: Alternatives and Implications." *Housing Policy Debate* 6, no. 2: 291–393.

Wartell, Sara Rosen. 2002. "Single-Family Risk Sharing: An Evaluation of Its Potential as a Tool for FHA." Unpublished report. Millennial Housing Commission.

Willis, Mark. 2010. "Give Credit Where Credit Is Due: An Approach to Revamping CRA." Harvard University, Joint Center for Housing Studies.

Woodward, Susan. 2008. "A Study of Closing Costs for FHA Mortgages." Washington: U.S. Department of Housing and Urban Development.

2

How Should We Serve the Short-Term Credit Needs of Low-Income Consumers?

RACHEL SCHNEIDER AND MELISSA KOIDE

A lmost one-third of the 30 million U.S. households who are unbanked or underbanked borrow to pay for small-dollar, short-term needs. They obtain loans through payday lenders, rent-to-own centers, pawnshops, refund anticipation lenders, or any of a variety of other nonmortgage–related sources, including friends and family.[1] These individuals either conduct their financial lives entirely outside of traditional banks and credit unions (unbanked) or maintain a checking or savings account while also using alternative providers (underbanked). Lower-income and certain minority groups are disproportionately represented among unbanked and underbanked households.[2]

Almost 40 percent of those borrowing do so to pay bills or to cover basic living expenses. Other major reasons to borrow include making up for lost income, paying for home repairs or a major purchase such as an appliance, or helping friends and family.

1. According to the Federal Deposit Insurance Corporation, 27 percent of the 9 million unbanked and 40 percent of the 21 million underbanked households in the United States borrow from alternative financial services providers, yielding a total of 10.8 million borrowers among the 30 million unbanked and underbanked households. The FDIC also points out that its estimate of 30 million such households may be low because there are an additional 5 million banked households about whom insufficient data were gathered to determine if they are underbanked. See FDIC (2009).

2. Almost 54 percent of black households, 45 percent of American Indian or Alaskan households, and 43 percent of Hispanic households are either unbanked or underbanked, compared with 26 percent of the total population. Nearly 20 percent of lower-income households—those with incomes lower than $30,000 a year—are unbanked compared with 8 percent of the total population (FDIC 2009).

These statistics are open to various interpretations. They suggest that some unbanked and underbanked borrowers have too little income to cover their expenses and thus require better income supports or budgeting guidance. The numbers also reveal a substantial need for more households to accumulate savings so that they can weather disruptions in earning power or fund major purchases without taking on debt.

For several reasons, however, income supports, budgeting guidance, and additional savings do not entirely fill the need that credit satisfies.

First, well-structured credit can support a household's ability to save. It can do so directly by incorporating a savings feature into a debt product or indirectly by providing a means to fund short-term spending without dipping into longer-term savings.

Second, building a credit history is a critical financial asset in its own right. Because credit scores are used by mortgage lenders, employers, insurers, landlords, and others, a positive credit history is crucial to long-term financial prosperity. Developing a sound credit history requires taking on and then paying down debt.

Third, credit can facilitate an investment or purchase that provides the foundation for other wealth-building activities. In many cases, taking on credit can lead to financial prosperity more quickly than saving for the same investment or purchase. Home mortgages are the traditional example of this use of credit. But this logic can be applied equally well to short-term debt that pays to fix a car that allows someone to get to a better-paying job, pays medical bills that allow a person to obtain essential health care, or goes to purchase a washer-dryer that frees time for child care or education instead of visits to the laundromat.

To meet these goals, small-dollar, short-term credit must be high quality. It must be marketed transparently and priced fairly. It must be affordable and structured to support repayment, without creating a cycle of repeat borrowing or "rolling over" of the loan. Repayment must be reported to the credit bureaus. Ideally, it may be accompanied by other features, such as savings accounts or budgeting advice that can prepare the borrower for greater financial prosperity over time. However, the additional complexity created by such features must be balanced against the convenience, speed, and privacy that consumers demand and the additional costs created for the lender.

Unfortunately, there is a shortage of high-quality, small-dollar, short-term credit in the marketplace today. This gap in supply exists despite the fact that the last decade or more saw a dramatic and traumatic excess of availability and overuse of credit. The gap in the supply of well-structured credit is evidenced by the fact that underbanked consumers use a great volume of payday and other expensive loans.[3] Furthermore, this gap is likely exacerbated by the current recession and the

3. The growth and use of payday lenders are well documented. See Herrman and Tescher (2008) for a bibliography of some of this research.

tightening of credit. Certainly some consumers who previously relied on credit card debt or overdraft protection now have to identify other means of obtaining credit, even as their need for credit may be growing because of job loss or other financial stress. This is an especially pressing issue for the millions of consumers who have seen their credit scores drop over the past two years and who lack not only a loan product to meet their credit needs, but also a means to reenter the system and begin to rebuild their credit scores.

While excess credit is hardly desirable, it is important to increase access to appropriate forms and amounts of credit for all households who need it and can benefit from it.

In a previous paper, the Center for Financial Services Innovation (CFSI) described the broad landscape of small-dollar loan providers.[4] This paper builds on that discussion by examining the demand for short-term credit and the credit products that hold potential to meet that demand. It seeks to explore the challenges these products face in order to identify business strategies and public policies that can support the development of an efficient marketplace for high-quality, small-dollar, short-term credit.

Unbanked and Underbanked Consumer Demand for Credit

According to the *National Survey of Unbanked and Underbanked Households*, released by the Federal Deposit Insurance Corporation (FDIC) in December 2009, at least 25 percent of U.S. households are unbanked or underbanked.[5] This includes 9 million unbanked households, in which no adult has a checking or savings account, and 21 million underbanked households, in which at least one adult has a bank account but the household also relies on alternative financial services.[6] To conduct this survey, the FDIC partnered with the Bureau of the Census to contact approximately 47,000 individuals in person. The survey included several questions about the use of credit products provided by payday lenders, pawnshops, rent-to-own stores, and refund anticipation loan providers. It is the largest survey on this topic, providing invaluable and authoritative data about the behavior of unbanked and underbanked households.

The FDIC found that the percentage of households who are unbanked declines sharply with increasing income, education, or age. Nearly 20 percent of U.S. households earning below $30,000 a year are unbanked compared with the national estimate of 8 percent. The likelihood of being underbanked also declines

4. Herrman and Tescher (2008).
5. FDIC (2009).
6. Specifically, the FDIC defines alternative financial services as nonbank money orders, nonbank check-cashing services, payday loans, rent-to-own agreements, pawnshops, and refund anticipation loans.

with income, education, and age, but less markedly. For example, households with incomes between $30,000 and $50,000 are almost as likely as those with incomes under $30,000 to be underbanked.

Race and ethnicity also affect banking status: 22 percent of black households, 15 percent of American Indian or Alaskan households, and 19 percent of Hispanic households are unbanked compared with 4 percent of Asian and 3 percent of white households. Similarly, minority groups are more likely to be underbanked: 32 percent of black households, 29 percent of American Indian or Alaskan households, and 24 percent of Hispanic households compared with 7 percent of Asian and 15 percent of white households.

A significant portion of unbanked and underbanked consumers borrow. According to the FDIC, 27 percent of unbanked households have used a payday loan, entered into a rent-to-own agreement, or borrowed from a pawnshop within the prior year or have taken out a refund anticipation loan within the past five years. Among underbanked households, 40 percent have done so.

The FDIC's findings validate the size and importance of the underbanked marketplace and generally confirm CFSI's findings in its 2008 *Underbanked Consumer Study.*[7] In that study, CFSI interviewed approximately 2,800 unbanked and underbanked individuals by phone and mail. The survey included a series of questions about credit use, defining credit more broadly than in the FDIC survey to include not only alternative financial services providers such as payday lenders, but also friends and family, credit cards, auto loans, student loans, and other types of credit. The CFSI study also included questions about the amounts borrowed and the respondent's attitudes and preferences about borrowing.

Taken together, these two studies paint a vivid picture of who is borrowing and why, how, and where they are doing so.

Who Borrows?

The CFSI's study found important behavioral and attitudinal differences between unbanked and underbanked individuals who have borrowed within the previous twelve months and those who have not.[8]

First, those who have borrowed are more likely to be underbanked or previously banked as opposed to never banked: 61 percent have a current checking account, 27 percent have had a checking account in the past, and only 12 percent have never had a checking account. This is consistent with the FDIC's finding that borrowing from alternative financial services providers is higher among those

---

7. CFSI (2008) found a similar number of underbanked households in the United States (21 million) as the FDIC study, but a much larger number of unbanked households (19 million compared to the FDIC's 9 million). Some of this variation probably results from methodological differences.

8. The FDIC has not yet released results with which to analyze how borrowers behave differently than nonborrowers.

with bank accounts—related in part to the fact that a bank account is necessary to access many types of credit, including payday loans.

Second, they are not comfortable with banks and bank products. For both borrowers and nonborrowers, the number-one reason reported for having no bank account is that the respondent thinks he or she has too little money to make using a bank account worthwhile.[9] However, among unbanked households who have borrowed within the last year, trust issues are also apparent: 21 percent reported that they do not trust banks or credit unions or they had a bad experience with banks in the past, compared with 15 percent of the total unbanked and underbanked population. In addition, 18 percent said they do not know how to manage a bank or credit union account, compared with 10 percent of the total unbanked and underbanked population.

Third, those who have borrowed are more likely than nonborrowers to use the Internet: 51 percent of borrowers said they had used the Internet within the prior week, compared with 35 percent of nonborrowers and 40 percent of all unbanked and underbanked respondents.

Fourth, they are more willing to ask questions about financial matters. More borrowers than nonborrowers said that they are willing to ask household members (44 and 35 percent, respectively) or banks and credit unions (37 and 27 percent, respectively) about money.

Among those who have borrowed within the last twelve months, there seem to be two distinct behavioral patterns within the CFSI study respondents. One group said that they generally borrow larger amounts once a year, with 83 percent borrowing more than $1,000. Their top reason is to purchase a car or truck.

The other group of frequent borrowers said that they generally borrow smaller amounts—between $100 and $1,000—two to four times a year. This group relies on a wide array of debt products, including personal loans (51 percent), lines of credit (39 percent), and cash advances on credit cards (37 percent). More than a third of this group (36 percent) said that they borrow from family and friends. They reportedly borrow to pay for utilities (32 percent), home repairs (31 percent), basic living expenses (22 percent), repayment of other debt (21 percent), or medical bills (17 percent).

There are meaningful differences in the borrowing behaviors of different demographic groups, with whites borrowing larger amounts than African Americans and Latinos (see figure 2-1) and older people borrowing larger amounts than younger people. These findings correlate with the fact that underbanked individuals are more likely to borrow larger amounts than unbanked individuals (see figure 2-2) and are also more likely to be white and older. Similarly, these findings are likely connected to income, with higher-income individuals borrowing larger

---

9. This finding was common to both the FDIC and CFSI studies.

Figure 2-1. *Among Borrowers, Amount Borrowed, by Ethnicity*

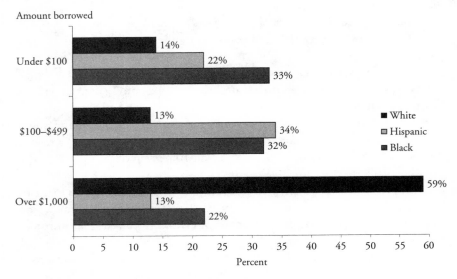

Source: Center for Financial Services Innovation (CFSI 2008).

Figure 2-2. *Among Borrowers, Amount Borrowed, by Banked Status*

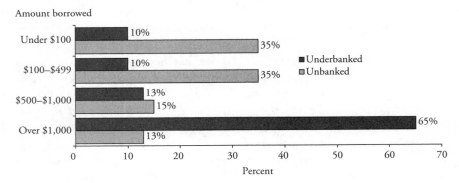

Source: Center for Financial Services Innovation (CFSI 2008).

amounts. That said, 38 percent of all unbanked and underbanked individuals with incomes between $20,000 and $30,000 reported borrowing more than $1,000 the last time they borrowed.[10]

These findings suggest that market segmentation is crucial to designing loan products that meet consumer needs. Cultural differences are key, but so is variation in borrowing patterns across many other criteria. One group of borrowers

10. CFSI (2008).

needs to borrow small amounts, perhaps regularly. Another segment would benefit from larger installment loans with longer repayment periods. Still other segments need solutions that recognize the meaningful financial ties that borrowers have with their families and broader communities.

Why Do They Borrow?

Both the FDIC and CFSI studies cite the need to pay bills and cover basic living expenses as the biggest reason that unbanked and underbanked households borrow (38 percent). Other major reasons include making up for lost income (15 percent) or paying for home repairs or an appliance (7 percent).[11]

Among specific demographic groups, additional reasons to borrow are particularly important.[12] For example, according to the CFSI study, 18 percent of Latino unbanked and underbanked households and 17 percent of African American unbanked and underbanked households reported that they have borrowed to help friends and family compared with only 7 percent of white unbanked and underbanked households. Similarly, 16 percent of Latinos and 15 percent of African Americans said they have borrowed to pay back money owed compared with 8 percent of whites.

It should come as no surprise that medical expenses cause more older individuals to borrow, with 16 percent of those between the ages of sixty-five and seventy-five and 26 percent of those older than seventy-five reporting medical bills as a reason they have borrowed. This compares with 7 percent of the total unbanked and underbanked population. Younger people are more likely to borrow for education, with 15 percent of those between the ages of eighteen and twenty-four citing education as a reason to have borrowed compared with 8 percent of the population overall.

How Do They Borrow?

Unbanked and underbanked individuals borrow in a variety of ways. According to data from the CFSI study, they use personal loans, lines of credit, home equity loans, auto title loans, credit cards, and payday loans (see figure 2-3). When asked to name the first place they would turn for a loan of less than $1,000, however, unbanked and underbanked respondents ranked banks and credit unions (36 percent) and family members (34 percent) almost equally, followed by friends (9 percent).

Latinos appear to borrow from friends and family even more often: 42 percent of Latinos said they would go first to a family member to borrow less than $1,000, and only 23 percent would go first to a bank or credit union. For white borrowers,

11. FDIC (2009). Note that 23 percent of respondents answered "other." CFSI also found that automobile purchases are a major reason to borrow (17 percent).
12. CFSI (2008). These findings do not control for income.

Figure 2-3. *Among Borrowers, Types of Loans Used, by Banked Status*[a]

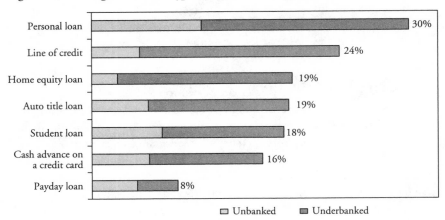

Source: Center for Financial Services Innovation (CFSI 2008).
a. Numbers total to more than 100 percent, reflecting that some borrowers have accessed more than one type of loan.

these numbers are reversed, with 42 percent preferring banks or credit unions and 30 percent saying they would go first to a family member. Black borrowers evidence no real preference for banks or credit unions, with 33 percent going first to a bank or credit union for less than $1,000 and 31 percent going to a family member.[13]

The lesson from this is that lenders to the underbanked must determine how best to leverage social networks. The strength of personal networks for Latino and African American borrowers in particular cannot be ignored. An opportunity exists either to lend directly to groups of borrowers, as Grameen America is doing, or otherwise to engage social networks in encouraging repayment.

In addition, providers of credit products to unbanked and underbanked households should not discount the reach of the Internet. It is clearly a viable way to market to potential borrowers and to communicate with current borrowers, as evidenced by the growth of online lenders such as Prosper, Elastic, and Swish in the United States as well as Wonga in the United Kingdom. Online and mobile models could be critical for both new and traditional providers of credit.

Early evidence indicates that customers value credit innovations from new or nontraditional sources, such as retailers, as well as from banks and credit unions: 45 percent of unbanked and underbanked consumers who have borrowed in the last twelve months identified banks and credit unions as places where they would

13. CFSI (2008). These findings do not control for income.

prefer to conduct financial transactions, while 38 percent would prefer retailers. These findings are consistent with the preferences of unbanked and underbanked households overall, regardless of borrowing behavior.

Older individuals appear to be more inclined to access banks and credit unions to meet their credit needs. Among unbanked and underbanked individuals between the ages of eighteen and twenty-four, 17 percent said they would go first to a bank or credit union, while 61 percent would go first to family. Among those between fifty-five and sixty-four, these numbers are reversed, with 45 percent going first to a bank and 20 percent first to family.[14]

Similarly, those with higher incomes are more likely to report a preference for banks and credit unions for their borrowing needs. Among individuals with household incomes between $40,000 and $50,000, 48 percent said that they would borrow first from a bank or credit union, while 26 percent would prefer to borrow first from family. For individuals with household incomes under $20,000, these figures are 27 and 39 percent, respectively.[15]

No group of respondents said that their first choice would be a payday lender. In the CFSI study, only 2 percent of unbanked and underbanked individuals said that they would go first to a payday lender to borrow less than $1,000, although 8 percent of this group said that they have used payday lenders. The FDIC survey uncovered even higher use of payday lenders, with 7 percent of unbanked and 16 percent of underbanked individuals estimated to have obtained a loan from a payday lender within the last year.

Although the data are insufficient to explain the full range of reasons why borrowers use payday loans, convenience and ease of application clearly are major factors (see box 2-1). The FDIC found that 26 percent of payday loan borrowers use payday lenders because of their convenience—evidence that borrowers want their credit needs to be met quickly and without application processes they perceive as onerous or intrusive.

The difficulty of qualifying for a bank loan is both a real and a perceived issue for underbanked consumers. Among payday loan borrowers, 43 percent said that they use alternative credit because it is easier to qualify for a payday loan than for a bank loan.[16] This could refer to the application process, as banks generally take longer to make lending decisions than payday lenders, but it also likely pertains to underwriting standards.

The disconnect between borrowers' stated preference for how to borrow and their actual borrowing behavior indicates a significant opportunity for alternative lenders who can provide a product that meets the same consumer needs as payday lenders but is better structured. Faster underwriting and greater transparency

14. CFSI (2008).
15. CFSI (2008).
16. FDIC (2009).

Box 2-1. *Reasons for Using a Payday Lender*

Easier to qualify for a payday than for a bank loan (43 percent)
Payday loan location more convenient than a bank (26 percent)
Do not qualify for a bank loan (16 percent)
Payday loan service feels more comfortable than a bank (2 percent)
Other (11 percent)

Source: FDIC (2009).

in underwriting are part of the solution. In addition, lending models that do not require any underwriting may also have a role to play in this market.

Opportunities to Meet Demand in New Ways

Several key findings emerge from this analysis of the available data about borrowing behavior and preferences among unbanked and underbanked consumers. Perhaps the most important finding is that it is critical to segment the market: there is a significant diversity of borrowing needs in terms of loan purpose, size, duration, and repayment structure. As a result, successful lending models must customize the product being offered for different consumer needs. The models described below each attempt to accomplish this in different ways.

Emerging Models to Supply Small-Dollar, Short-Term Credit

Despite consumers' need for access to a variety of small-dollar, short-term loan products, there is insufficient availability of products that are profitable for the provider, yet affordable and responsibly structured.[17] The inadequate supply of high-quality, small-dollar credit options appears to stem from a variety of inter-related factors, including capital constraints on lenders, perceived or real regulatory challenges for banks and credit unions, negative stigma attached to small-dollar credit providers, and underwriting methods that inadequately assess risk. These factors have contributed to an inefficient marketplace and reduced competition, resulting in limited product options and suboptimal prices for consumers.

In the discussion that follows, we examine products that hold potential for increasing the supply of high-quality, small-dollar, short-term credit and explore the challenges that they face in an effort to identify business strategies and public

17. For a description of the history of small-dollar credit in the United States and the market dynamics that have led to this phenomenon, see Herrman and Tescher (2008).

policies that can support this expansion. See table 2-1 for a summary of the advantages and challenges of each business model.

Lenders must achieve sufficient profitability, whether on a product or a customer-relationship basis, to become sustainable businesses over time. Of course, different types of institutions aim for different levels of return. Some of the lending models profiled here are motivated by social or regulatory returns as well as by financial returns. But in all cases, effectively covering costs and generating some profit is a requirement for long-term sustainability.

It is challenging for several reasons to achieve a break-even point with small-dollar loan products that are affordable to consumers. One of the most significant is that many of the costs to offer a loan are the same whether the loan is large or small. These include processing and verifying the application, paying for staff and overhead expenses, underwriting, issuing the funds, processing payments, and pursuing collections. When these costs are applied against smaller loans with shorter terms, they result in higher annual percentage rates (APRs) or higher fees per dollar loaned.

In addition, it is necessary to invest in technology to handle applications, underwriting, servicing, collections, and customer support. While an opportunity exists to create seamless, low-cost platforms for various channels of delivery—and some platforms to do so are emerging—for now lenders must invest in developing their own customized technological solutions. Furthermore, while in some cases it makes economic sense to develop a platform that can be used in place of high-touch personal interaction, in others the success of the business model relies in part on face-to-face engagement with the borrower. That personal interaction requires staff engagement as well as a costly physical presence.

Scale and volume of lending are necessary for profitability. However, capital to fund operations and lending, particularly in this highly credit-constrained environment, is both scarce and expensive. The high cost of funds and constraints on the supply of capital are significant barriers to growth and sustainability, particularly for nonbank lenders.

A final, major factor limiting profitability deserves particular attention: losses stemming from high default rates. Each of the lending models profiled below has taken a different approach to managing this issue. Installment lenders establish a physical presence in the community. Some banks work with nonprofit partners to identify and counsel customers. Workplace and account advance models employ very little underwriting and instead rely on automatic payment mechanisms. The major differences in the cost drivers of various lenders stem largely from these choices.

Depository Participation in Small-Dollar Lending

Historically, banks and credit unions, along with installment lenders, have provided the bulk of small-dollar consumer credit. The prominence of banks and

Table 2-1. *Types of Loans Discussed and Relative Expenses*

Indicator	Salary advance	Depositories	Installment lending	Workplace lending
Provider examples	Wells Fargo, US Bank, Fifth Third, MetaBank	El Banco, FDIC small-dollar pilot depositories, credit unions	Highly fragmented industry	Virginia State Employee Loan Program, United Way of Chittenden County
Loan amount (approximate)	Up to $500	Tranches of $1,000 or less or $1,000 or more	Up to $5,000 or more	Varies: up to $500
Stated APR	120–150 percent	16–36 percent	Varies	36 percent or less (requires financial institution participation)
Repayment term	Up to a month (repaid with succeeding direct deposit)	Biweekly, monthly, multiple years	Up to three years	Up to one year
Underwriting criteria	Account with direct deposit	Varies (may include credit check, budget analysis, proof of income)	Varies (may include credit check, budget analysis, proof of income)	Must be an employee in "good standing"

Relative expenses

Up-front costs[a]	Low (highly automated process with very limited underwriting)	Varies (may include standard underwriting along with in-person assessment and use of nontraditional data)	High (in-person underwriting process with little automation)	Medium (limited underwriting cost, but requires synchronized processing procedures)
Servicing and customer support	Low-medium (automated repayment)	Varies (depending on the customer targeted, servicing and support range from medium to high)	High (maintenance of physical outlets, in-person payments)	Medium (automated repayment, but loans serviced at traditional financial institutions)
Cost of funds	Dependent on funding source	Varies	High (typically sourced through syndicates; seen as "high risk")	Low (loans funded by partnering financial institution)
Credit losses	High	Medium	High (dependent on underwriting, but can reach the mid-teens)	Low (limited by payroll repayment; defaults typically occur only in cases of severance)
Primary cost driver	Infrastructure investment	Customer support	Up-front costs (in part because of physical outlet)	Costs to manage a partnership

Source: Authors.

a. Up-front costs include customer acquisition, application processing, and underwriting costs.

credit unions in the consumer loan market, however, fell with the widespread use of credit cards and the emergence of other types of small-dollar lenders. Nevertheless, some depositories—including both banks and credit unions—have continued to make small-dollar loans to consumers. The products typically include installment loans and secured credit products, and banks and credit unions are increasingly adding savings and financial education as part of the offering. The depositories making these loans tend to be community banks or credit unions that serve primarily minorities and lower-income consumers.

For example, El Banco de Nuestra Comunidad, a division of the Peoples Bank, a Georgia-based bank focused on serving the unbanked and underbanked Hispanic market, offers a variety of credit products designed for Hispanic customers with little or no credit history. El Banco underwrites loans to these borrowers using a wide range of nontraditional credit data, including check-cashing activity, money transfers, bill payments, prepaid card and bank account usage, rental history, employment verification, and length of residence in the United States.

El Banco's initial credit application requires face-to-face interaction, with significant time spent with customers, who often lack the application information and require education on the importance of maintaining a good credit history. Since El Banco started a lending program in 2006, it has lent more than $13 million in consumer and credit-builder installment loans, $55 million in residential mortgages, and $3.5 million in small business loans. Throughout this period, it has experienced relatively low losses and delinquencies with its loan products.

Thirty community banks are participating in a two-year small-dollar credit demonstration project initiated by the FDIC. The demonstration, which began in 2008, is designed to increase understanding of the dynamics of depositories offering small-dollar, short-term loans with APRs of 36 percent or less. The thirty participating banks are providing loans in two categories: less than $1,000 and between $1,000 and $2,500. Over the first year, banks originated 8,346 loans of less than $1,000, with a total balance of $5.5 million. The FDIC reports that, while delinquencies have been above average, defaults are in line with national trends in consumer loans.

Although data about costs and profitability of these loans are not available, information is available that sheds light on the banks' motivations and challenges. The FDIC has found that participating banks offer small-dollar loans for three reasons: to build new customer relationships and enhance existing ones, with the goal of achieving per-customer profitability over the long term, to build goodwill with the community and fulfill their responsibilities under the Community Reinvestment Act, and to issue a profitable product in the immediate term. Of the banks that have met the goal of generating profit from the loans in the immediate term, most if not all are located in lower-income areas, where consumer demand for the loans is strong.

Many of the participating banks offer or require financial education as part of their small-dollar program. One participating bank found a strong positive correlation between the size of loan requested and the borrower's interest in financial education.

One-third of participating banks require their small-dollar loan customers to open savings accounts linked to the loans, and nine encourage but do not require savings accounts. By the end of the demonstration project's fourth quarter, 300 linked savings accounts had been opened, with an aggregate balance of $78,000. There appears to be greater interest in and use of the savings accounts among borrowers who take out larger loans for longer periods, a useful insight for designing small-dollar loans that both meet consumers' needs and help to build longer-term financial stability.

Credit unions are also increasingly offering small-dollar loan products at some of the lowest prices in the market, in part because of guidelines established by the National Credit Union Administration, which set an 18 percent interest rate ceiling on loans made by credit unions. In some cases, additional benefits such as automatic savings and financial education are part of the loan package. The Pennsylvania Credit Union Association in partnership with the Pennsylvania Treasury, for example, established the Better Choice short-term installment loan, with terms of thirty, sixty, or ninety days and payment options of weekly, biweekly, or monthly. To facilitate savings, 10 percent above the requested loan amount is loaned and automatically deposited into a savings account for the borrower, and that money cannot be withdrawn until the loan is paid in full. The Better Choice loan is intended to break even, and losses on the loans have been relatively low, ranging between 5 and 6 percent. To induce credit unions throughout the state to offer the product, the Pennsylvania Treasury reimburses losses on the loans up to 50 percent.

Installment Loans

While not a new product, installment loans are receiving renewed attention as a potentially high-quality option for small-dollar, short-term credit. Installment lenders, which operate out of brick-and-mortar stores, are located predominantly in the southeastern United States, where state laws governing consumer loan products and terms are less restrictive. The installment lending industry is composed of many small, independent stores and a handful of large companies. The World Acceptance Corporation, a large installment lender with stores in the United States and Mexico, operates 900 offices throughout the Southeast. In 2009 it loaned $1.9 billion in 1.9 million transactions, yielding an average loan size of a little over $1,000, with an average term of eleven months.[18]

18. World Acceptance Corporation (2009).

Given the structure of installment loans, consumers typically borrow more money for longer terms than is the case with other small-dollar, short-term credit providers. Two types of installment loans are generally available: small unsecured loans of less than $1,000 with a term of one year and larger secured loans, ranging between $1,000 and $5,000, with terms of one to three years. Loans are offered at fixed rates—APRs can vary from 36 percent for larger, longer-term loans to as high as 450 percent for smaller, shorter-term loans[19]—and are repaid in equal periodic installments of principal and interest, with no balloon payment at the end.

Like traditional bank lenders, installment lenders operate out of physical stores, and they assess the borrower's creditworthiness before deciding whether to make a loan and at what price. Installment lenders usually examine the borrower's credit report and score, although that information is not the sole factor in the lending decision. Other considerations include the borrower's job tenure, employment history, monthly income and expenses, and ability and willingness to repay the loan.

In some cases, the installment lender develops its own credit assessment system, which can enhance its ability to qualify consumers with thin or no credit histories. Progreso Financiero, a relatively new and growing installment lender with twenty-three locations in California, uses a proprietary underwriting system modeled after small-dollar lenders in Latin America. The company, which provides lower-income Latinos with short-term installment loans, has made almost 40,000 loans with its underwriting tool.

Once the installment loan is made, repayment history is reported to the major credit bureaus and becomes part of the borrower's credit record. Thus installment loans, unlike many other small-dollar, short-term credit products, enable consumers to build or repair their credit scores.

Because consumers must deliberately decide to apply for an installment loan, some planning and intentionality are required of borrowers. The fact that installment loans are offered at a fixed rate and are paid back in equal payments may help to ensure that the loan remains an affordable part of a consumer's budget.

Installment loan companies typically locate stores in the communities in which they operate. Lenders report that this interaction helps them to assess the borrower's financial situation and keeps them abreast of any potential challenges the borrower may have in repaying the loan. Lenders consider their direct interaction with consumers and physical presence in the community as critical to controlling default rates.

Because of the high-touch aspects of this model, installment loans are costly to provide. The primary cost drivers of the installment lending model arise from the operation of physical stores and from underwriting expenses, including credit

---

19. Installment loans were explicitly excluded from the 2006 Talent Amendment, which effectively barred payday lenders from operating in close proximity to military bases by capping the rate that could be charged at 36 percent.

checks and bank fees. One industry representative estimates that achieving breakeven on a $200 loan requires charging borrowers an APR of about 250 percent. The break-even APR drops to approximately 145 percent if the volume of $250 loans reaches 1,000. Larger loans in the amount of $2,500 require APRs closer to 44 percent, and the break-even APR drops to a projected 35 percent if 1,000 loans at that amount are made.

Although the installment lending industry has been around for decades, the difficulty of finding adequate capital keeps many lenders from scaling up, which would enable higher profitability and lower prices. Raising necessary capital from banks and other lenders has long presented challenges, given the stigma attached to the small-dollar, short-term loan industry. That challenge has intensified amid the general credit constraints of today's economy.

Account Advance Loans

A handful of large banks offer "salary advance" or "account advance" products, whereby a checking account holder with direct deposit into his account can access short-term, small-dollar lines of credit. The account holder requests the advance and can do so in increments of as little as $20 and up to a maximum of $500. The fee charged for these products is generally $2 for every $20 borrowed. The advance is automatically repaid from the next direct deposit into the account, and the entire amount must be repaid within thirty-five days. Banks generally restrict access to the account advance products following consecutive use of the product for nine to twelve months. Banks often include materials in the marketing of advance products explaining that the products are costly and advising consumers to explore other sources of low-cost credit.

An analogous product is the Meta iAdvance loan, which is offered by Metabank, a federal savings institution with a division that specializes in payment products, including prepaid cards and credit cards. With the iAdvance loan, the advance is authorized and repaid based on direct deposit to a prepaid card rather than a checking account. The consumer applies online or by phone, and the loan is made and becomes available in a matter of minutes. The fee is $2.50 for every $20 advanced. Metabank limits access to the advance feature for borrowers who have used it at least once a month for more than twelve consecutive months. After that point, the consumer's credit limit is reduced repeatedly in $100 increments until it reaches zero. Following a one-month cooling-off period, Metabank then recalculates the individual's credit line.

Rather than being triggered by the simple act of overdrawing one's account, these products require the borrower to apply for the funds. While they have higher APRs than many other forms of bank credit, they carry substantially lower APRs than typical payday loans. They can also cost less than overdraft, especially for consumers who overdraw small amounts. According to Bankrate.com, the average fee charged for a courtesy overdraft is $29.

Account advance lines of credit do not require the kinds of application process or extensive underwriting that credit cards or typical bank installment loans require. Customers may apply for the account advance, or the bank may solicit a customer following an assessment of the customer's cash flow and tenure with the bank. From the bank's perspective, there is no application to review or verify, no underwriting expenses, no paperwork or processing costs. From the account holder's perspective, there is no application to complete, little concern about acceptance, and no waiting. Once the credit is available, it can be withdrawn from the automated teller machine.

Because this streamlined process lowers the bank's cost of offering credit, the bank can afford to offer credit in much smaller increments while still managing costs. In the case of iAdvance, Metabank's operating costs are lowered even further because it does not need to support a branch network or a physical presence. An initial technology investment is necessary to build the product platform, but most of the product delivery is then automated, leading to variable costs that are likely much lower than those of traditional or payday lenders.

In addition, some account advance lenders limit their default-related losses by offering initial loans in amounts as small as $20. Even though default rates on these first loans can be quite high, total losses can be manageable. As the lender sees positive repayment patterns emerge, the amount of credit available to a borrower can be increased.

Criticisms of the account advance products currently on the market are that the repayment period is short—generally one pay cycle—which is often too little time for the borrower to amass the funds to repay the loan, and that repeat usage of the product leads to high total costs. The fact that borrowers can access such small amounts may help to mitigate this problem for many, because they borrow only what is necessary.

Workplace Loans

The workplace may represent an important channel for reaching underbanked consumers with a wide variety of financial products and services because of its advantages in scale, facilitation, and timing. Financial services companies gain access to a large base of potential customers by catering to a company's workforce. The infrastructure of the workplace facilitates the distribution of financial services. Meanwhile, employees enjoy the convenience of making decisions about their saving and spending in the context of when and how they receive their earnings.[20]

Using the workplace to provide small-dollar loans can reduce the costs of the loans in two ways. First, the use of e-mail and other workplace communication systems can significantly cut marketing costs. And second, direct access to the payroll system can help to offset underwriting costs and facilitate repayment.

20. See Berke and Schneider (2009) for further discussion of this idea.

Two companies, eDuction and DFM, have designed small-dollar loan platforms that use the payroll system to authenticate the potential borrower for the loan, determine the appropriate amount and cost of the loan, and facilitate repayment through automatic payroll deduction, significantly reducing delinquencies and defaults.

Another workplace model involves credit unions partnering with local employers to provide small-dollar, short-term loans; in some cases, these partnerships have been brokered by community organizations. The United Way of Chittenden, Vermont, for example, facilitates partnerships between local credit unions and a number of small and mid-size employers. The credit products offered typically consist of installment loans that must be repaid before a subsequent loan can be taken out. The borrowing employee must be in good standing with the employer. Automatic payroll deduction is used to facilitate repayment, and loans are offered at an APR of 18 percent. At the end of the loan tenure, instead of closing out the automatic payroll process, employees are offered the option of continuing the wage deduction, with the money deposited into a savings account, something installment lenders could not do without a bank partner. Approximately half of participating employees have chosen to use the automatic savings option. Of the 184 loans that have been made in the program so far, ten borrowers have defaulted.

The State of Virginia is piloting a workplace loan program for state employees in conjunction with the Virginia Credit Union. Six months after it was launched, the program had lent almost $1.4 million. Loans are available from $100 to $5,000, in increments of $100. Employees have up to six months to repay the loan in full, and no more than two loans can be taken out in a calendar year. The APR, regardless of loan amount or term, is fixed at 24.99 percent. Direct deposit facilitates repayment from a Virginia Credit Union account. The employee must be a credit union member and must complete an online financial education module. Data are not available on the profitability of or losses on these loans.

The workplace small-dollar loan approach can offer a simple, automated enrollment and payment process to access the loan. The use of automatic payroll deduction should reduce the administrative costs and the likelihood of delinquencies and defaults. Lenders report that they value the opportunity to strengthen their relationships with employers. And the use of automation can facilitate additional features such as savings and personalized financial education information.

Models of Short-Term, Small-Dollar Credit: Challenges and Potential Solutions

Each of these models, in its own way, addresses part of the demand for credit among unbanked and underbanked consumers (see table 2-2). But there is still a significant gap between the demand for and supply of affordable short-term,

Table 2-2. *Innovations or Advantages and Challenges of Various Business Models*

Type of model	Innovation or advantage	Challenge
Small-dollar bank or credit union loan	Cross-subsidizes costs; generates a long-term customer relationship	Underwriting requires access to multiple data sources; customer engagement can be time-intensive; demand varies by geographic location; maintaining a branch network entails costs
Installment lending	Entails larger loans and longer terms as well as fixed rates and equal repayments; loan data are reported and accepted by major credit bureaus; application decision and direct interaction may facilitate responsible borrowing	Requires a high APR; securing capital for stability, growth, and expansion is difficult; brick-and-mortar model entails costs
Account advance product	Streamlines application, disbursement, and repayment options; eliminates underwriting, with manageable impact on default losses	Requires initial investment in technology, such as systems development to facilitate loan requests, disbursement, and repayment; the high-risk nature of the loans leads to a high cost of funds or high reserve requirement; a high acceptance rate leads to high default rates
Workplace lending	Reduces marketing and administrative costs; entails low to no defaults via automatic repayments through payroll debits; benefits employers as well as employees; provides an opportunity to add savings and education components	Obtaining capital for loans is difficult; repayment may be given priority over consumer necessities; underbanked individuals may not be employed by employers offering workplace loans; the costs to establish and maintain an effective partnership could be substantial

Source: Authors.

small-dollar credit. The models described face significant challenges to scale, which inhibit their ability to continue to improve their products for the benefit of consumers. While some of these challenges can be solved in the marketplace, some potential systemic or public policy solutions could help to resolve some of the common challenges to expanding and attaining scale, thus ensuring that under-banked individuals have access to credit products.

Three major challenges are discussed in this section: the lack of generally accepted criteria to define high-quality credit products, insufficient availability of capital to support lending and the growth of small-dollar lenders, and high operating costs inherent in the business model.[21]

Lack of Common Product Definition: Create Loan Standards

In addition to meeting the requirements for consumer acceptance and struggling for profitability, innovative lenders must develop credit products that are structured to help borrowers to achieve their short-term goals and improve their financial prosperity over the longer term. There is increasing agreement about what responsible lending like this might mean. Certainly, high-quality, small-dollar, short-term credit must be marketed transparently and priced fairly. It must be affordable and structured to support repayment—without creating a cycle of repeat borrowing or "rolling over" of the loan—and repayment must be reported to the credit bureaus. However, the specific definition of each of these criteria and their prioritization if they cannot all be achieved equally are still hotly contested.

Furthermore, some argue that high-quality loans should be accompanied by other features, such as savings accounts or budgeting advice, that are designed to enable borrowers to achieve greater financial prosperity over time. These features increase complexity for both the lender and the borrower and so must be balanced against cost concerns and the convenience, speed, and privacy that consumers demand.

The lack of consensus around defining responsible loans creates several real challenges for lenders. Because it increases the reputational risks of offering these types of products, it decreases the number of potential entrants into the marketplace. This makes price competition, which would be positive for borrowers, less likely. It also makes it more difficult for small-dollar lenders to access capital. Fewer lenders make capital available to small-dollar, short-term loan providers because they are concerned about reputational risk themselves.

Common metrics about the best ways to structure small-dollar, short-term loans could provide a foundation for many other possible solutions to the challenges facing new entrants into this market. They could aid in the creation of policies and regulations related to small-dollar, short-term lending, while providing the financial services industry with clarity and direction. Such metrics would have to take into account the need for diversity in the marketplace, allowing for revolving credit as well as installment loans of varying size and duration. They would ideally be designed as guideposts, in order to allow for new product developments and market changes.

---

21. Some of the solutions are being explored as part of a CFSI–Pew Charitable Trusts Working Group on Small-Dollar Lending.

These metrics could be encouraged via public policy, with policymakers defining the criteria—as opposed to explicit definitions—for safe loan products by establishing minimum qualifications for "good" small-dollar, short-term credit. Such criteria could be used for assessing loans under consumer protection rules and for determining eligibility for government incentives that encourage lenders to offer high-quality products. In designing its loan pilot, the FDIC has taken a step toward articulating such qualifications, but policymakers could do more to engage industry, advocates, and other stakeholders in formulating criteria for a greater diversity of loan products offered by both bank and alternative financial services providers.

At the same time, the industry could create such metrics for itself. Lenders are beginning to gather the knowledge and establish the infrastructure needed to determine some industry guidelines for high-quality products, which may benefit both consumers and providers in setting out clear terms and thresholds for what constitutes high-quality, small-dollar products and services.

Need for Capital: Form a Loan-Loss Reserve Fund and Clarify Bank Capital Requirements

Adequate access to capital is necessary for achieving scale and reaching sustainability, while offering products at affordable prices. The ability of nonbank lenders to raise the necessary capital from banks and other lenders has long presented challenges, given the stigma attached to the small-dollar loan industry and the relative risk associated with such loans. That challenge has intensified amid the general credit constraints of today's economy.

To the extent that available capital is scarce because of the potential risks of such loans, lenders could take advantage of several ways to ensure the availability of additional capital for innovative, responsible lenders. Options might include facilitating the development of a secondary market for small-dollar loans (which would likely require some common definitions of high-quality, small-dollar loans) or the formation of a loan fund enabling investors to pool their investment dollars and diversify their exposure to multiple types of loans. Alternatively, public policy could facilitate the formation of a loan-loss reserve fund.

The challenge facing depositories pertains to the regulatory oversight of capital reserves, and policymakers could provide greater clarity and consistency with regard to the capital requirements for depositories making small-dollar loans.

One public policy option for making capital more available to alternative small-dollar lenders could be to create a loan-loss reserve fund, which qualified firms could tap to offset a portion of the costs associated with making small-dollar loans to underserved consumers. The fund's primary purpose would be to enable small-dollar lenders to acquire more capital to expand their businesses and offer more affordable loans. Over time, participating lenders would achieve sufficient scale to operate independently of the loan-loss reserve fund. To help to ensure that participating firms will ultimately reach and maintain sustainability, only firms that are adequately capitalized would be eligible to use the fund. To encourage firms to make prudent loans, the fund would be structured to reward firms that keep losses low; those with lower losses would be eligible for higher reimbursement rates.

Such a program could improve the availability of small-dollar credit to underserved consumers in several ways. By offsetting a portion of the costs of providing credit, it could expand the number of loan providers in the marketplace and the amount of credit available to consumers. It could induce larger financial institutions to extend credit to small-dollar lenders. And if it were created by the federal government, it could bring valuable attention and legitimacy to the small-dollar credit needs of low-income and financially underserved consumers.

Such a program could also enable the federal government to target programs that build consumers' financial capability at a financially relevant point by requiring or encouraging lenders to provide financial information when the loan is made.

As a general regulatory rule, banks are required to maintain levels of capital that are commensurate with the risk associated with their loan portfolios. Increased regulatory scrutiny and higher capital requirements are required when total subprime loans are greater than 25 percent of an institution's Tier I capital. Very few banks, however, reach this threshold in short-term, small-dollar lending. Nevertheless, in this economic environment, regulators are paying significant attention to higher-risk loans in general, and banks are reporting that regulators are imposing greater scrutiny on these loans even when they are not at the threshold, which serves as a disincentive for offering such loans.

As a policy matter, both depositories and regulators who are concerned with promoting access and ensuring safety and soundness would benefit from an analysis of the risk of carrying a small portfolio of small-dollar loans. The insights from the analysis could offer greater clarity for industry and regulators on useful techniques for managing risk, ensuring compliance, and reporting effectively. While no one wants to see these types of products put the depository institution at risk, regulatory attention and clarity regarding whether and what requirements are needed to guard against risk for loans that are less than 25 percent of Tier I capital would aid banks seeking to provide small-dollar loans.

High Operating Costs: Encourage Partnerships and Technology Investments

High operating costs for small-dollar lenders must be lowered if lenders are to sustain their ability to offer small-dollar loans to borrowers. There are several routes to reducing costs, and smart market solutions and public policies can facilitate their growth and development. First, partnerships among lenders, nonprofits, and employers can shift the business model of the lender in crucial ways. Second, the development of streamlined delivery and processing platforms could improve the economics for a wide variety of small-dollar lenders.

By partnering with nonprofits, employers, or both, lenders can leverage the trust, infrastructure, and physical presence of those institutions. This can create substantial benefits for lenders and consumers alike. For lenders, advantages to this model include lower marketing costs, streamlined loan processing, and lower default rates. Benefits for borrowers include lower prices, faster application processes, and the ease of accessing credit in locations and environments that are convenient and comfortable for them.

The federal government could help to promote the benefits of such partnerships to employers and their employees by examining existing workplace loan programs and seeding new workplace loan demonstrations that would yield deeper insights into employees' demand for small-dollar loans. In addition, the government could develop policies that encourage employers to provide small-dollar loan options to employees and that induce lenders to partner with employers. Tax incentives to employers for providing small-dollar loan programs, for example, or targeted use of the loan-loss reserve fund described above could expand the availability of small-dollar loans through the workplace.

Minimizing the cost of lending requires significant technological infrastructure. By reducing the cost of application, underwriting, servicing, and customer support processes, technology solutions can help to make small-dollar lending viable at lower prices. Opportunity clearly exists to create seamless, low-cost platforms for various channels of delivery that would meet consumer needs and make products sustainable.

Without standard platforms, lenders must develop customized technological solutions. Lenders should explore ways to maximize the utility of this type of investment. Credit unions in particular have been effective at creating service bureaus or cooperatives through which they share back-office costs. These could provide relevant models for coordination. Given the strong consumer demand for small-dollar loan products and the changing dynamics of this part of the consumer credit industry, technology vendors should also be looking closely at this opportunity.

Conclusion

Although unbanked and underbanked consumers clearly need better access to small-dollar, short-term credit, meeting those needs is challenging, as the descriptions of the loan products attest. However, there is considerable opportunity to offer small-dollar, short-term credit products that meet consumers' needs, are structured responsibly, and offer the promise of profitability for the lender. An encouraging variety of business models is emerging, including credit products offered by traditional financial institutions and new entrants.

Lenders are balancing significant trade-offs in the design of these credit products. In designing their business models, some lenders choose to support fairly intensive interactions with their borrowers—whether created through physical locations or partnerships with community organizations—while others offer automated, more distant connections. Lenders either invest in manual underwriting that takes into account detailed information about the borrower and a wide range of alternative data sources or simply evaluate whether or not direct deposit cash flow is sufficient to support repayment. Lenders also offer a range of credit products, including revolving credit and installment loans of all sizes.

These choices result in substantially different cost structures. Additional information about the underlying economics of these businesses and the riskiness of the loans they offer is needed to understand more deeply the extent to which the variation in cost structures explains the wide variation in APRs evidenced in the marketplace. This deeper understanding of the economics of supply is critical to informing public debate about the appropriate use and structure of credit. Such baseline information will enable the development of appropriate public policy interventions to support the growth of an efficient small-dollar loan marketplace.

A related point is that more information is needed to understand the relative merits and impact on consumers of the loan products available today. This would help policymakers and others to invest their resources in advancing types of credit that are most beneficial for consumers.

Still more innovation is necessary to meet consumers' full need for credit. Nonetheless, because there is meaningful diversity among the credit needs of the almost 10 million unbanked and underbanked consumers who borrow, the diversity of the emerging business models is positive for consumers. Fostering access to a range of high-quality credit products offered through many different, attractive, convenient channels will help to narrow the current gap between demand and supply, enabling individual borrowers to access the type and amount of credit they need when they need it.

References

Berke, Sarah, and Rachel Schneider. 2009. "Employer-Based Collaboration: Lessons from Financially Fit Minnesota." Chicago: Center for Financial Services Innovation.

CFSI (Center for Financial Services Innovation). 2008. *Underbanked Consumer Study.* Chicago (June).

FDIC (Federal Deposit Insurance Corporation). 2009. *National Survey of Unbanked and Underbanked Households.* Washington (December).

Herrman, Michael, and Jennifer Tescher. 2008. "A Fundamental Need: Small-Dollar, Short-Term Credit." Chicago: Center for Financial Services Innovation.

World Acceptance Corporation. 2009. *Annual Report, 2009.* Greenville, S.C. www.world acceptance.com/annual_report.php.

3

A Changing Credit Environment and Its Impact on Low-Income and Minority Borrowers and Communities

MARSHA J. COURCHANE AND PETER M. ZORN

T he recent tumult experienced in residential mortgage markets in the United States has left many struggling to determine what caused the crisis, what can be done to prevent a future crisis, and what can be done to mitigate the consequences of the current crisis. These are big and important questions, and accurately resolving them requires a clear and precise understanding of what transpired over the past several years.

This chapter provides an empirical analysis of a key five-year period—2004 through 2008—that was characterized by changing credit standards and, potentially, varying use of risk-based pricing. We broadly explore these changes in the market's "management" of credit risk and the impact that these changes have had on low-income and minority borrowers and neighborhoods.

Some observers have speculated that the current crisis had its roots in the expansion of risk-based pricing to residential mortgage markets, and if not for that expansion we would not be in the predicament we are in today. Our view is that the roots of the crisis are far more complex and that risk-based pricing is just one aspect of market risk management. In the United States in recent years, default and credit risk has been broadly managed through the use of submarkets and

The views expressed in this chapter are those of the authors and do not necessarily reflect the views of Charles River Associates and its board of directors, Freddie Mac and its board of directors, or any of Freddie Mac's regulators. The authors thank Matt Osborn and Rajeev Darolia of Charles River Associates and Jonathan Liles, Melissa Narragon, and Vanessa Patterson of Freddie Mac for their very able assistance.

channels (prime versus Federal Housing Administration [FHA] versus subprime), with different credit standards and pricing guidelines adopted within each submarket. We explore this dynamic and attempt to assess its impact on overall market outcomes.

Our data include information on all mortgage originations for a sample of the top twenty lenders from 2004 through 2008. Our measure of default or credit risk for each loan is its cumulative default rate (CDR), estimated as the probability that a loan will ever go into default over its lifetime (that is, ever become real estate owned or ever go into a foreclosure alternative status). Our measure of each loan's price is its reported annual percentage rate (APR). We assess the extent of the adoption of risk-based pricing by looking at the relationship between the APR and the CDR—the more the APR increases with the CDR, the greater the adoption of risk-based pricing.

Using these metrics, we compare how changes over the years 2004 through 2008 differentially affected the access to and cost of credit for low-income and minority borrowers and neighborhoods. We also attempt to decompose the impacts of changing submarket shares and the differing credit standards (access to credit) and pricing of default risk within each submarket. We conclude with a discussion of the policy implications of our empirical findings. We note, among other things, that the period 2004 to 2006 experienced a real "democratization" of credit and that risk-based pricing, at least in our analysis, is far from the unmitigated evil it is sometimes portrayed to be.

Background and Relevant Literature

The expansion of credit during the last decade resulted from a confluence of changes. Public policy emphasized the benefits of a general rise in homeownership rates and focused on reducing the gaps in homeownership rates between minority and nonminority households and between higher- and lower-income populations. Mortgage market changes also reflected the impact of low credit spreads and an influx of capital in search of a high return. Without low credit spreads, which created the potential for greater profitability as a result of expanded lending, the policy goals of expanding homeownership may not have been adopted so readily. It was this coincidence of the alignment of tightened spreads and homeownership-focused public policy that encouraged and supported the movement into higher-risk lending.

The availability of credit expanded rapidly, with just a few voicing any contemporaneous concerns about that expansion. Critics included Collins, Belsky, and Case, who stated, "The emergence of risk assessment tools, particularly regarding an applicant's willingness to pay, in theory can help overcome inefficiencies due to imperfect information available to lenders. This has the potential to complete an otherwise truncated market, add to allocative efficiency, and potentially increase the positive externalities of homeownership. Each of these gains, however, is conditional on how the subprime industry matures and on prevailing consumer and lender practices. Mis-pricing, principal agent distortions, and asymmetric information are all potential threats."[1]

Change in residential mortgage markets was facilitated by key developments in four broad areas: regulation, technology, securitization, and innovative homeownership-qualifying products. Developments in these four areas changed the structure of mortgage markets, as evidenced by a shift toward risk-based pricing, increased reliance on nonagency securitization, and changes in the market share of different financial institutions (particularly the shares of federally regulated depositories and independent mortgage companies). Each of the four areas of development affected, in some way, the homeownership outcomes for low-income and minority borrowers.

On the regulatory front, both the Community Reinvestment Act and the Federal Housing Enterprises Financial Safety and Soundness Act of 1992—the so-called government-sponsored enterprise (GSE) act—focused on serving the needs of low- and moderate-income borrowers and providing liquidity for housing markets.[2] The Community Reinvestment Act directs the federal banking regulatory agencies to encourage the institutions they regulate to meet the credit needs of their entire communities, including low- and moderate-income areas, to the extent consistent with safe and sound banking practices. The 1992 GSE act established income-based and geographically targeted housing goals for the purchase of mortgages by each government-sponsored entity. The housing goals were intended to ensure that an appropriate share of GSE mortgage purchases was targeted to low- and moderate-income families and neighborhoods underserved by the mortgage market.

On the technology front, advances along several dimensions have affected access to mortgage credit by reducing the costs associated with applying for a mortgage and by affecting the structure of the mortgage market.[3] These technological developments have included improved access to consumer credit information; adoption of credit scoring, automated underwriting, and automated appraisal technologies; advances in financial modeling; and innovation in secondary market debt instruments. Adoption of credit scoring, automated underwriting, and automated appraisal technologies increased the accuracy of credit risk measurement, encouraging and enabling the increased use of risk-based pricing and the introduction of new mortgage products. These technological developments, along with advances in financial modeling and the design of new debt instruments, also reduced the costs of securitization and facilitated the growth of

1. See Collins, Belsky, and Case (2004, p. 1).
2. The GSEs include Fannie Mae and Freddie Mac.
3. See Gates, Perry, and Zorn (2002) and Lax and others (2004) for a discussion of the impacts of automated underwriting on the expansion of credit to underserved populations.

a secondary market outside of the GSEs. In turn, growth in non-GSE securitization increased the liquidity available to mortgage lenders for serving higher-risk or nontraditional borrowers.

Risk-based pricing has its roots in a seminal article by Stiglitz and Weiss.[4] They suggest that credit rationing is the result of imperfect information regarding the risks of loan applicants. Because borrowers know their credit risk, but lenders only know it with uncertainty, lenders must ration the availability of credit.

In a special volume of the *Journal of Real Estate Economics and Finance* on subprime lending, several authors look at early segmentation in the United States mortgage markets. Chinloy and MacDonald consider the advent of subprime lending as a "completion" of the mortgage market and state, "With a subprime market, there is a more complete credit supply schedule with the market pricing for poorer credit quality in the mortgage rate. By completing the capital market, subprime lenders reduce borrowing constraints. The result is a social welfare gain. Low-credit applicants otherwise denied funding are able to qualify by paying higher interest rates in exchange for offering more equity or lower loan-to-value ratios."[5] Cutts and Van Order similarly discuss the economics of the subprime sector, laying out models for option-based pricing of mortgages, with different options leading to different contracts and terms in subprime mortgages. They also consider asymmetric information between borrowers and lenders and between lenders and the secondary market.[6] Deng and Gabriel look at the differences in default and prepayment risks of borrowers with FHA loans and suggest that pooling and risk-based pricing with respect to FHA loans can substantially reduce housing finance costs and increase homeownership among underserved populations.[7]

In a paper presented at a conference sponsored by the Joint Center for Housing Studies at Harvard University, Collins, Belsky, and Case lay out the trade-offs between the gains or potential losses from risk-based pricing. They state, "The potential for efficiency gains from subprime lending and risk-based pricing are real. If risk can be more accurately measured, the benefits to low-income and low-credit-score households and to society as a whole are great. Consumer choice is enhanced, risk is more efficiently priced, capital is increasingly allocated to highest and best use, while numerous households that would have been denied credit, find access to the ownership market. A major source of asymmetric information and adverse selection may be reduced as we gather increasingly accurate and reliable predictors of default. Other households are given the incentive to generate positive neighborhood externalities. On the other hand, if the risks of subprime lending are underestimated, the result may be very costly and inefficient."[8]

4. See Stiglitz and Weiss (1981).
5. See Chinloy and MacDonald (2005, p. 153).
6. See Cutts and Van Order (2005).
7. See Deng and Gabriel (2006).
8. See Collins, Belsky, and Case (2004, p. 15).

The Management of Default Risk

There has been, as discussed, research pertaining to the application of risk-based pricing to credit markets. However, there has been little explicit recognition that the evaluation of credit risk and responses to those risks is multidimensional. In some research, risk-based pricing refers simply to pricing up for higher loan-to-value (LTV) loans.[9] In other research there is recognition that risk-based pricing incorporates pricing for risk characteristics in addition to LTV, including, for example, recognition that FICO scores, debt-to-income (DTI) ratios, and other factors may influence default risk.[10] In this chapter we explicitly recognize the multidimensional characteristics of risk as well as the various methodologies that lenders and markets employ to manage higher default risks.

In the United States in the past decade, mortgages were originated through three separate submarkets or channels: prime, which generally originates the lowest-risk loans; subprime, which generally originates the highest-risk loans; and FHA, which focuses on originating loans to first-time homeowners and low- and moderate-income borrowers and generally has risk tolerances between prime and subprime. Lenders tend to limit their efforts to one submarket, and, especially between prime and subprime, the characteristics of business, marketing, and borrower demand can vary quite substantially across submarkets. Within each submarket, lenders manage their risks—and, indirectly, the market share across submarkets—by setting credit standards for the loans they will originate and by differentially charging for the default risks of those loans they do originate (that is, through risk-based pricing). As a consequence, the market "manages" default risk through a combination of the share of originations across submarkets and pricing and credit standards within submarkets.

All three of these components changed, at times dramatically, between 2004 and 2008. Much of our empirical effort is directed toward identifying and assessing the separate impacts of these changes. Moreover, because low-income and minority neighborhoods and borrowers tend disproportionately to have higher-risk credit characteristics, they also are likely to be disproportionately affected by changing submarket shares, credit standards, and movement toward, or away from, risk-based pricing. Our other empirical effort is directed toward assessing and decomposing these impacts.

Data and Methodology

The data used in our analysis include information on all mortgage originations for a sample of the top twenty lenders from 2004 through 2008. In combination,

---

9. For example, Chinloy and MacDonald (2005).
10. For example, Collins, Belsky, and Case (2004).

these lenders originated prime, FHA, and subprime loans, and all of the lenders in our data originated loans in most states. As a consequence, we believe our data are representative of loans originated in each submarket over our period of study.

Our primary focus is on the overall market, which we define as the sum of the prime, FHA, and subprime origination submarkets. Lenders are defined as either prime or subprime on the basis of their self-assessment. The non-FHA loans originated by each lender are therefore all labeled either prime or subprime, consistent with the self-designation of the lender. Regardless of lender designation, all FHA loans are considered FHA.

Because our lender data are a convenience rather than a random sample from each submarket, we are concerned that simply adding together our data will give an inaccurate view of the total market. To address this concern, we use Home Mortgage Disclosure Act (HMDA)–derived origination shares of the three submarkets (prime, FHA, and subprime) to construct weights that we then use to aggregate our lender data into the "total market." We believe, therefore, that if the lenders in our sample are representative of their submarket, our HMDA-weighted aggregate total market analysis will also be representative of the overall market.

Our lender data are rich in information for each loan. In particular, they include commonly used underwriting variables (for example, FICO score, LTV, and DTI), loan terms and characteristics (for example, fixed versus adjustable rate, purpose of the loan, and type of documentation), APR, property location (state, county, and census tract), and key borrower demographics (race, ethnicity, and income). These data enable us to conduct detailed ex ante analysis, but the lack of information on performance (for example, delinquency or default rates) prevents us from conducting any ex post analysis.

Critical to our analysis is assessing separately the ex ante distributions of default risk and mortgage prices, as well as the relationship between default risk and price (interpreted as the extent of risk-based pricing). We use the APR as our measure of mortgage price because it is a single price that combines contract rates with the amortized value of points and fees paid at closing, is part of standard loan disclosures, and is directly available in our data. However, use of the APR is not without problems. Most critical among these is the assumption embedded in the APR calculation that loans will last until maturity, an assumption that is often not met and can therefore understate the annual "cost" of up-front points and fees. That said, APR is the best measure of all-in price that we have available, and so it is what we use.

We believe the cumulative default rate—the expected probability that a loan will ever go into default over its lifetime—is a reasonable measure of default risk, where default is defined as becoming "real estate owned" or going into foreclosure alternative status. The attraction of the CDR as a metric is that it simply summarizes the complex interactions of multiple risk factors. It is also intuitive to interpret and representative of the metric that underwriting processes are designed to manage.

Unfortunately, CDR is not directly included in our data. To address this lacuna, we use a proprietary model to estimate CDR from available variables. The variables used in our CDR prediction include the type of mortgage product (adjustable, balloon, fixed rate, or interest only), purpose of the loan (purchase or refinance), type of documentation (no, low, or full documentation), type of property (single-family or manufactured housing), type of occupancy (investment, owner occupied, or second home), number of units (one, two, three, or four), DTI, LTV, and FICO score.[11] The CDR model we use gives a time-invariant view of default risk, meaning that loans with identical observable characteristics originated in different years have identical cumulative default rates. In all likelihood, however, CDR models used at the time of origination were not time-invariant because expectations about the future paths of house prices and other determinants of default evolved over time, affecting views of default risk for otherwise identical mortgages. While these contemporaneous and changing views of default risk would be interesting to study, the appropriate CDR models for doing so are not available to us. Our time-invariant CDR approach is nonetheless useful, because holding constant for changing expectations helps to isolate and identify the role of other factors affecting the default trends from 2004 through 2008.

With the APR and CDR available for each loan, our first step is to consider how the distributions of these characteristics vary in the total market for the years 2004 through 2008. We use box and whiskers plots to present this information compactly. The "box" in the box and whiskers plot demarcates the interquartile range (the values that encompass the twenty-fifth through the seventy-fifth percentile of the distribution), and the "whiskers" extend "down" to the first fifth percentile of the distribution and "up" to the ninety-fifth percentile of the distribution. Side-by-side placement of the box and whiskers plots allows for easy assessment of the changing distributions over time.

Our next step is to assess the adoption of risk-based pricing. We do this by considering the relationship between the APR and the CDR. The assumption made is that the more that price (APR) increases with default risk (CDR), the greater is the "adoption" of risk-based pricing. First, we provide a scatter plot of loans in CDR-APR space.[12] We then illustrate the central tendency of the relationship between the APR and the CDR by plotting a LOESS smooth fit through the scat-

11. A significant number of loans in our data have missing debt-to-income ratios. We impute DTI for loans where it is missing to avoid dropping these observations from our analysis. Details of this imputation are available on request from the authors.

12. To make the scatter plots more easily interpretable, we group loans into "buckets" of 100 loans with similar CDR and APR values and plot each bucket based on the average CDR and APR for the 100 included loans.

ter plot.[13] The more upward sloping the LOESS fit, the greater the adoption of risk-based pricing. The "slopes" of the LOESS fit lines can therefore be compared across time to determine trends in the adoption of risk-based pricing.

We next turn to the question of whether and how these trends affect key policy-targeted subpopulations—borrowers in low-income tracts (defined as tracts with median incomes equal to 80 percent or less of area median income [AMI]), borrowers in minority tracts (defined as tracts where 30 percent or more of the population are not non-Hispanic whites), low-income borrowers (defined as borrowers with incomes less than or equal to 80 percent of AMI), and minority borrowers (defined as borrowers who are not non-Hispanic whites). We consider impacts across two separate dimensions: accessibility to credit and the prices paid by borrowers who obtain credit.

We assess accessibility to credit by comparing CDR distributions across time. The CDR distribution of loans originated in a given year depends on the risk distribution of actual and potential loan applicants and the underwriting standards adopted by lenders in the granting of credit. Our observed CDR distributions commingle both impacts, and we are sensitive to the reduced-form nature of our empirical analysis. Our belief, nonetheless, is that the CDR distributions of potential mortgage applicants have remained relatively constant over time and that the primary factor affecting any observed time trend in CDR distributions is changes in lenders' credit standards (both directly and through the impact on the mortgage characteristics or risks "chosen" by potential applicants).

Consistent with this belief, we argue that years when CDR distributions are lower (that is, years when fewer loans with high CDRs are originated) are years when lenders impose "tighter" credit standards and that years when CDR distributions are higher are years when lenders impose "looser" credit standards. Relying on this framework, we conduct the conceptual experiment of imposing the "tightest" credit standards, which occurred in 2008, on all other years. Specifically, we identify the borrowers in earlier years who would not have received loans under the tighter standards of 2008 and then compare the composition of these "excluded" borrowers in terms of the subpopulations of interest.[14] So, for example, if 22 percent of low-income borrowers in an earlier year are excluded under

13. A LOESS smooth provides a semiparametric fit of the relationship between the APR and the CDR.

14. We assume that the ninety-fifth percentile in the cumulative default rate represents the implicit or effective credit limit in the "tightest" year and apply this standard to all other years. We use the ninety-fifth percentile rather than the maximum because we judge that the top 5 percent of default risks are more likely to represent loans that "slipped through the cracks" rather than truly reflecting contemporaneous credit standards. To conduct our experiment we calculate the percentage of originated loans above this tightest-year ninety-fifth percentile CDR value, subtract 5 percent, and interpret the remaining value as the percentage of borrowers in "looser"-credit-standard years who would have been denied credit had the tighter-year credit standards been applied.

the tighter credit standards of 2008, while only 15 percent of non-low-income borrowers are excluded, we say that low-income borrowers are disproportionately affected by 7 percentage points (22 minus 15 percent).

We compare the prices paid by borrowers who received credit by looking at APR distributions. Specifically, for each year we compare the APR distributions of each key subpopulation and its complement. For example, we compare the APR distribution of low-income borrowers to non-low-income borrowers and compare minority borrowers to nonminority borrowers. We do this first by simply comparing the box and whiskers plots of APR distributions for each subpopulation. More quantitatively, we compute the Kolmogorov-Smirnov (KS) statistic for the distributions of each key subpopulation and its complement.[15] In our data the subpopulations of interest always have higher APR distributions than their complements, so we interpret the magnitude of the KS statistic as a measure of the disproportionate impact on subpopulations of interest—the larger the KS statistic, the more disproportionately do subpopulations of interest face higher APRs. We compare trends in KS statistics across time to assess trends in the disproportionate impact on policy-targeted subpopulations.

We first apply these various techniques and metrics to the total market and then apply them separately to each submarket (prime, FHA, and subprime). Finally, we attempt to attribute the observed effects and impacts to changing submarket shares (primarily the rise and then fall of subprime) and changing credit standards.

Empirical Analysis

Our first step is to assess the time trends in the cumulative default rates of originations for the total market, provided in the left-hand panel of figure 3-1. The box and whiskers plots show significant changes from 2004 through 2008. The overall trend indicates increasing CDRs from 2004 to 2006 (illustrated by increasing medians, seventy-fifth percentiles, and ninety-fifth percentiles) and then dramatically declining CDRs in 2007 and 2008. This trend is not surprising. The 2004 through 2006 time period was the height of the credit bubble, and 2007 and 2008 reflect the tightening credit standards imposed after the financial crisis. Other sources—for example, the survey of Office of the Comptroller of the Cur-

---

15. The KS statistic is commonly used for testing whether two distributions are identical. In intuitive terms, the KS statistic calculates the difference between the cumulative density function of two distributions at the point when this difference is at a maximum. Under the null hypothesis these distributions are identical. If the KS statistic is large enough, the null is rejected, implying that the distributions are significantly different. A common application of the KS statistic in mortgage finance is as a test of the effectiveness of underwriting (default) models. Models with KS statistics above 30 are often considered to do a "good" job of distinguishing between well and poorly performing loans.

Figure 3-1. *Trends in the Distribution of Default Risk and Pricing in the Total Market, by Origination Year, 2004–08*

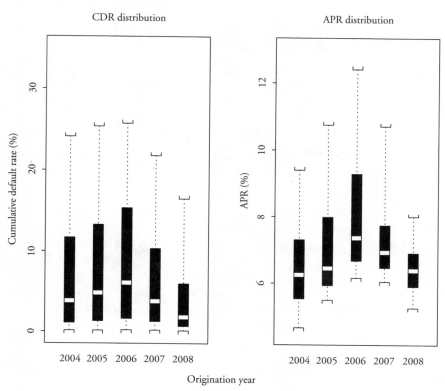

Source: Authors' calculations based on data from a sample of the top twenty lenders in 2004–08 and on HMDA data.

rency examiners—have documented the same loosening and then tightening of credit standards during this period.[16]

The uniqueness of these data is the quantification of this trend. For example, our data suggest that even in 2006, the period of most relaxed credit standards, 75 percent of originations had a 15 percent or lower expected probability of going into default. Moreover, roughly 95 percent of originations had CDRs less than 25 percent, meaning that about seven in ten borrowers were expected to pay back their loans. Obviously, these same data suggest that roughly three out of ten were expected to go into default, and this may be an unacceptable cost for increased access to mortgage credit. Moreover, as demonstrated in figure 3-6 below, the CDR distributions vary greatly across the submarkets. Nonetheless, these data show that

16. See www.occ.treas.gov/survey/2008UnderwritingSuvey.pdf.

Figure 3-2. *Trends in Risk-Based Pricing in the Total Market, by Origination Year, 2004–08*

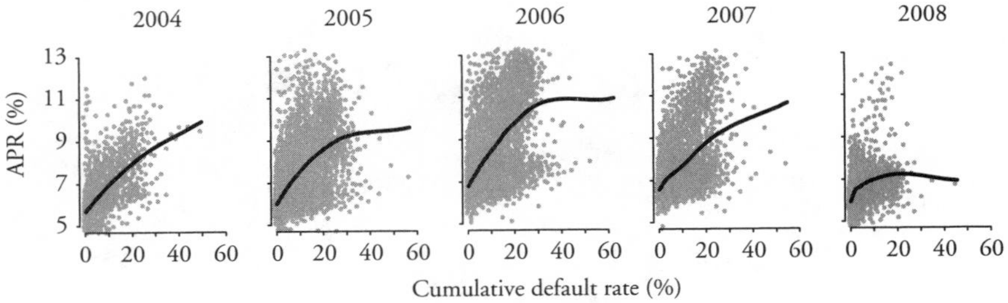

Source: Authors' calculations based on data from a sample of the top twenty lenders in 2004–08 and on HMDA data.

credit standards were not completely abandoned during this period, contrary to opinions expressed in the popular press and by critics of the mortgage industry.

The right-hand panel of figure 3-1 shows the accompanying time trends in APR distributions. Here we see a pattern similar to the time trend in CDR distributions: APRs increased from 2004 through 2006 and then declined in 2007 and 2008. Another trend worth noting is the expansion of the high-side tail of APRs through 2006 and even 2007 and the dramatic contraction in 2008. The relatively tight APR distribution in 2008 reflects the virtual absence of subprime originations. But, as shown in figure 3-7 below, the high-side APR tail in 2006 was apparent in both the subprime and prime submarkets. Wider APR distributions are a broad trend in a market with loose credit standards and risk-based pricing.

Figure 3-2 addresses the issue of risk-based pricing more directly. Here scatter plots of loan originations in the CDR-APR space (the gray dots) are used to assess the tendency of the APR to increase with the CDR, and we highlight this relationship by fitting a LOESS smooth fit (the dark line drawn on top of the scatter plot). Greater "adoption" of risk-based pricing is defined as an increasingly steep LOESS fit, and the plotted fits are provided separately by year, 2004 through 2008.

The scatter plots echo the trends in the box plot distributions of figure 3-1. Specifically, credit expands and then contracts (as shown by the increasing number of dots farther to the right on the CDR axis in 2004 through 2006 and then by the decline in the number of dots in 2007 and 2008) and the accompanying increase and then decrease of APRs (shown by the increasing number of dots farther up the APR axis in 2004 through 2006 and then by the declining number in 2007 and 2008). The LOESS plots show the relationship between the APR and the CDR. We focus on the "slope" of these plots in the 0–20 percent CDR range, because this is where the bulk of originations are located.

The plots show a clear and persistently strong relationship, illustrating that the market as a whole strongly embraced risk-based pricing during this time period. Nonetheless, there is an apparent trend to this adoption. Specifically, the slope of the LOESS fit in the relevant range increases between 2004 and 2006 and then declines in 2007 and 2008. This suggests that, at least in terms of an overall tendency, the total market most strongly embraced risk-based pricing in 2006, precisely when credit standards were the most lenient.

Next considered is the question of how these overall market trends affected low-income and minority neighborhoods and borrowers. First measured is the impact of changing access to credit, followed by a comparison of the percentage of each policy-targeted subpopulation (and its complement) that would have been denied credit in 2004 through 2007 under the tight credit standards of 2008.

The first column of figure 3-3 shows, for each policy-targeted subpopulation and its complement, the percentage of borrowers who would have been excluded under 2008 underwriting standards, that is, the percentage of each subpopulation that "benefited" from the expanded access to credit of earlier years. The second column of figure 3-3 provides a measure of the extent to which the target subpopulations disproportionately received this benefit. This measure is calculated as the difference between the impacts on the targeted subpopulation and its complement, which are plotted in the first column.

The first row of figure 3-3 focuses on borrowers in low-income tracts. Borrowers in low-income tracts benefited substantially from relaxed credit standards. At the peak in 2006, roughly 25 percent of all borrowers from lower-income tracts obtained mortgages because credit standards were significantly looser than in 2008. Borrowers not in low-income tracts benefited as well, however, and the right-hand column shows the extent that borrowers in low-income tracts benefited disproportionately. Borrowers from policy-targeted subpopulations uniformly benefited disproportionately from the increased access to credit relative to 2008, so all of the bars in the second column are positive.

Two overall trends are worthy of note. First, borrowers from low-income and minority tracts, as well as minority borrowers, obtained an increased benefit as credit standards loosened from 2004 through 2006 and then obtained a smaller benefit in 2007 as credit standards tightened. This reflects the tendency of policy-targeted subpopulations to have disproportionately higher risk characteristics and so, as a consequence, to benefit disproportionately from relaxed credit standards.

Second, the trends for low-income borrowers are in stark contrast to those for the other policy-targeted subpopulations. This may reflect a fundamental issue with our data rather than a "real" market trend. Specifically, the incomes available in our data are those reported for mortgage underwriting. For fully documented loans, the lender as part of the underwriting process verifies this income. For low- and no-documentation loans, however, income is less frequently or even infrequently verified, and the reported income is simply whatever the borrower

Figure 3-3. *Impacts of Changes in the Distribution of Default Risk on Targeted Subpopulations in the Total Market, by Origination Year, 2004–07*

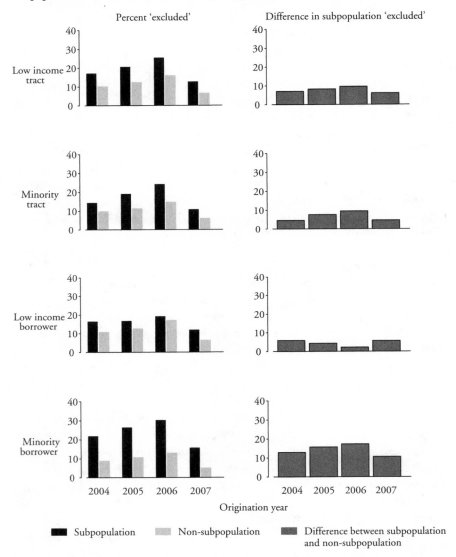

Source: Authors' calculations based on data from a sample of the top twenty lenders in 2004–08 and on HMDA data.

provides at application. Although we have no direct evidence from our data, we believe that this process results in an overstatement of incomes for low- and no-documentation loans and therefore underreports low-income borrowers. Low- and no-documentation loans are most prominent in the middle years of our analysis (2005 through 2007), so we are inclined to discount the analysis of low-income borrowers for those years and concentrate, where appropriate, on overall trends from 2004 to 2008. In figure 3-3, of course, that leaves only one data point (2004), and so trend analysis is impossible.

We conclude our initial analysis of the total market by assessing whether the changing distribution in the prices paid by borrowers who received loans disproportionately affected policy-targeted subpopulations. The top row of figure 3-4 provides box and whiskers plots of the APR distributions for each policy-targeted subpopulation and its complement, separately for the years 2004 through 2008. The bottom row provides the KS statistic, a metric measuring the differences in these APR distributions in each year.

The APR distributions clearly show that in each year policy-targeted subpopulations face higher APRs than nontargeted subpopulations. This relationship is consistent in each year, regardless of comparison: the fifth, twenty-fifth, fiftieth, seventy-fifth, and ninety-fifth percentiles of each policy-targeted subpopulation in each year are almost always greater than those of the complementary nontargeted subpopulation. An intriguing result is found in the second row, which provides the KS statistic: borrowers from low-income tracts and low-income and minority borrowers disproportionately tended to face higher APRs in 2008 than in 2004.[17] Simplifying a little, there appears to have been a mitigating trend in the disproportionately high APRs faced by borrowers from low-income tracts and by low-income and minority borrowers throughout a period when credit standards first relaxed and then tightened. Specifically, increased access to credit did not appear to exacerbate pricing differentials for these policy-targeted subpopulations: 2006, the clear high point of looser credit standards, is not the year when borrowers from low-income tracts and low-income and minority borrowers most disproportionately faced higher APRs. In contrast, however, there is not a strong trend for minority tracts over time, and, in particular, 2006 is the year when minority tracts disproportionately faced higher APRs. This, as shown in figure 3-10 below, seems primarily to reflect an FHA effect.

The next step in the analysis is to compare submarket (prime, FHA, and subprime) shares over time and to conduct parallel analyses to figures 3-1 through 3-4 separately for each submarket. The focus is on comparing differences across prime, FHA, and subprime mortgages and to assess how these differences may contribute to outcomes in the total market.

17. Recall that while we are not confident of our results for low-income borrowers in 2005, 2006, and 2007, we are relatively confident of them in 2004 and 2008.

Figure 3-4. *Impacts of Changes in the Distribution of Pricing on Targeted Subpopulations in the Total Market, by Origination Year, 2004–08*

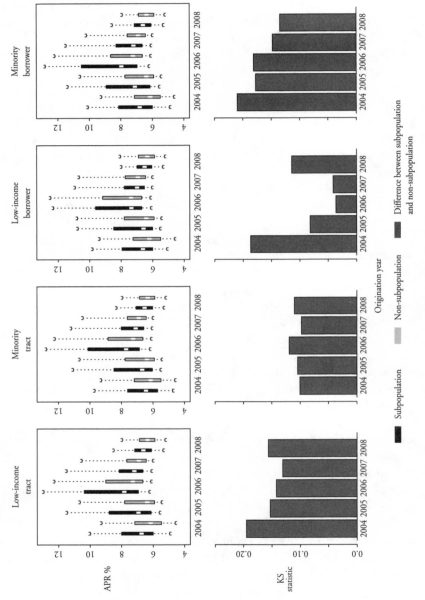

Source: Authors' calculations based on data from a sample of the top twenty lenders in 2004–08 and on HMDA data.

Figure 3-5. *Time Trends in the Share of Submarkets in the Total Market,*
by Origination Year, 2004–08

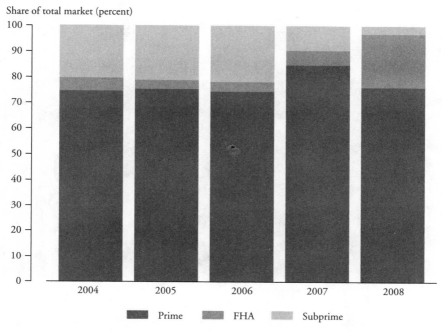

Share of total market (percent)

Prime   FHA   Subprime

Source: Authors' calculations based on data from a sample of the top twenty lenders in 2004–08 and on HMDA data.

Figure 3-5 uses stacked bar charts to show changes in the shares of prime, FHA, and subprime loans over time. The figure clearly illustrates growth in the share of subprime loans from 2004 through 2006, primarily at the expense of FHA loans. This changed dramatically in 2007, when the share of subprime loans declined more than 50 percent, resulting in growth in the share of FHA loans and disproportionate growth in the share of prime loans. The 2008 origination year saw significant further erosion in the share of subprime loans, a dramatic increase in the share of FHA loans, and a return of the share of prime loans to the level of previous years. These changes are not trivial and could have important impacts on market outcomes in the presence of significant differences across submarkets.

Figure 3-6 provides the CDR box plots for prime, FHA, and subprime originations. Given that prime loans accounted for more than 70 percent of originations during this period, it is not surprising that the distribution of CDRs on prime loans closely mirrors that of the total market. In particular, the prime submarket shows the same overall relaxation of credit from 2004 through 2006, followed by a tightening in 2007 and 2008.

Figure 3-6. *Time Trends in the Distribution of Default Risk in Submarkets,*
by Origination Year, 2004–08

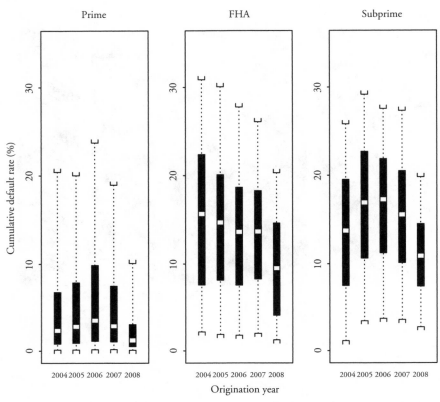

Source: Authors' calculations based on data from a sample of the top twenty lenders in 2004–08 and on HMDA data.

CDR distributions follow roughly the same trends in the subprime as in the prime submarket, with two important distinctions. First, the peak relaxation of credit in the subprime submarket occurred in 2005, a year before it occurred in the prime submarket. Second, the tightening of credit in the subprime submarket was arguably more dramatic in 2008.

More dramatic trends occurred in the FHA submarket. In particular, the FHA submarket exhibited a relatively monotonic tightening of credit standards throughout the period, with a significant tightening in 2008. However, careful interpretation of this trend is required. FHA itself does not originate mortgages, but instead guarantees mortgages that fit within its programs and meet its underwriting standards. Moreover, FHA made no obvious and significant efforts to tighten its underwriting standards over this period. Instead, the apparent tightening of standards from 2004 through 2006 likely was due primarily to the growing share of

Figure 3-7. *Time Trends in the Distribution of Pricing in Submarkets, by Origination Year, 2004–08*

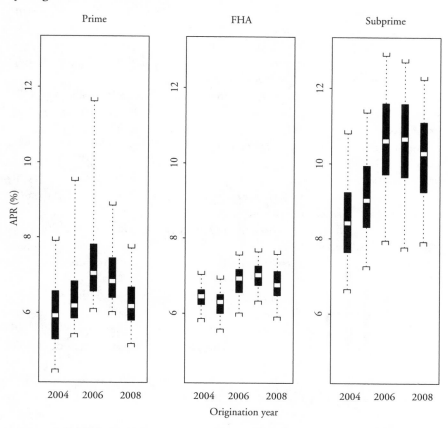

Source: Authors' calculations based on data from a sample of the top twenty lenders in 2004–08 and on HMDA data.

subprime loans, which took a disproportionately large number of higher-risk borrowers from the FHA.

The tightening in 2008 likely reflects overall credit tightening among market participants, including those originating FHA mortgages. Even with FHA's credit guarantee, loan originators are not completely free of default risk when originating an FHA mortgage. Faced with some residual risk of recourse or the loss of FHA-delegated underwriting privileges, originators likely imposed their own across-the-board tightening of credit standards in 2008 (including their FHA originations), which resulted in a reduction in cumulative default rates on FHA loans without explicit credit tightening by the FHA.

Figure 3-7 shows the box plots of APRs separately for each submarket. Again, the overall market trend is echoed in prime—APR distributions increased from

2004 through 2006 and decreased thereafter. The subprime submarket roughly followed trends in the prime submarket. Moreover, although the trend for FHA loans is less dramatic and less consistent than for either prime or subprime loans, it is roughly similar.

Four points from these data are worth noting. First, the loosening of credit in 2006, and the associated expansion of the high-end tail of the APR distribution, is arguably more dramatic for subprime than for prime loans, and the tightening of credit in 2008, and the associated decrease in the high-end tail of the APR distribution, is arguably more dramatic for prime than for subprime loans. Second, the APR distribution for FHA loans is dramatically tighter relative to either prime or subprime loans. This reflects the relatively stable pricing of FHA loans over this time period as well as the lack of any significant risk-based pricing on the part of the FHA (which is illustrated in figure 3-8). Third, generally the range of APRs for prime loans is tighter than that for subprime loans, consistent with the tighter CDR distribution evidenced in figure 3-6. Fourth, despite the overall tighter APR distribution for prime relative to subprime loans, this was not true in 2006, the year of the weakest credit standards among prime lenders. It appears, therefore, that although prime lenders significantly relaxed their credit standards in 2006, they did so while charging up for this higher risk.

This point is illustrated in figure 3-8, which uses LOESS smooth plots to illustrate the relationship between APRs and CDRs separately for each submarket. CDRs in the prime submarket are disproportionately in the range of 0–10 percent, so this is the segment of the LOESS plot on which we focus. Because of its dominant share, trends for prime loans closely mirror those for the total market. In particular, the slopes of these lines suggest that risk-based pricing increased somewhat in 2004 through 2006 and then showed a minor decline in 2007 and 2008.

The bulk of the subprime CDRs are in the 10–20 percent range, so this is where we focus in the subprime LOESS plots. There appears to be increasing reliance on risk-based pricing in subprime lending from 2004 through 2006, but unlike in prime, there is no lessening in that focus in 2007 and 2008.

FHA evidences a dramatic difference. There is no significant indication of a risk-based component to FHA pricing over this time period. As a consequence, as FHA's submarket share grew in 2007 and 2008, this growth tended to mitigate any risk-based pricing effect observed in the total market.

Figure 3-9 shows the impacts of looser credit standards (in the earlier years relative to 2008) on policy-targeted subpopulations. Prime time trends again closely follow those of the overall market. In particular, the expanding access to credit in 2004, 2005, and especially 2006 disproportionately benefited policy-targeted subpopulations. Similarly, the time trends for low-income borrowers are suspect because of concerns regarding the reporting of income for low- and no-documentation loans.

Figure 3-8. *Time Trends in Risk-Based Pricing in Submarkets, by Origination Year, 2004–08*

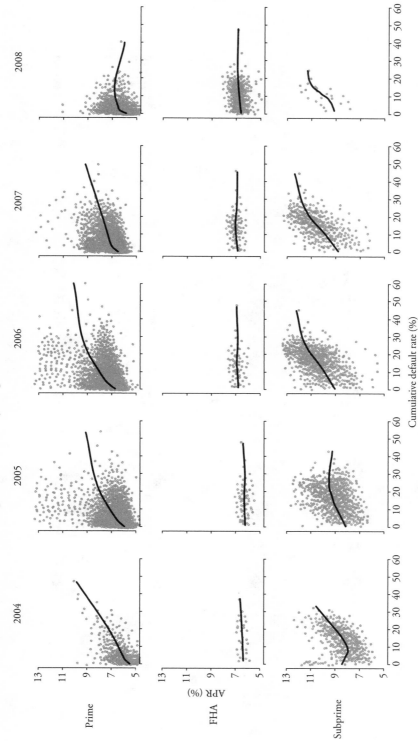

Cumulative default rate (%)

APR (%)

Prime

FHA

Subprime

2004   2005   2006   2007   2008

Source: Authors' calculations based on data from a sample of the top twenty lenders in 2004–08 and on HMDA data.

Figure 3-9. *Impacts of the Distribution of Default Risk on Targeted Subpopulations in Submarkets, by Origination Year, 2004–07*[a]

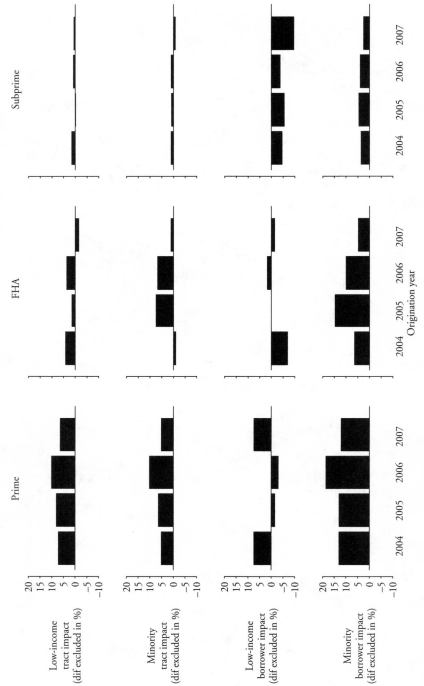

Source: Authors' calculations based on data from a sample of the top twenty lenders in 2004–08 and on HMDA data.
a. Difference relative to 2008 in the percentage excluded.

The trends in the subprime submarket, however, are dramatically different. In particular, there appears to be almost no evidence that changing credit standards had any disproportionate impact on borrowers from either low-income or minority tracts. This is consistent with the view that subprime mortgages disproportionately are push-marketed to specific neighborhoods where borrowers are more likely to be credit-impaired. A relaxation in subprime credit standards, therefore, is likely to increase loans in all "served" neighborhoods and so does not disproportionately benefit any subset of neighborhoods or tracts.

The impact of subprime loans on minority borrowers seems to follow the basic trend in the prime submarket, albeit at a lower level and with the biggest disproportionate impact occurring in 2005 rather than 2006. This latter point, again, is consistent with the observation from figure 3-6 that maximum loosening of credit occurred a year earlier in the subprime than in the prime submarket.

In general terms, the FHA results are somewhere between those of prime and subprime. However, unlike the situation for the prime and subprime submarkets, the greatest beneficial impacts on policy-targeted subpopulations do not occur when credit standards appear lowest for FHA (that is, in 2004). It is nonetheless generally true that greater access to FHA lending disproportionately seems to help borrowers from low-income and minority tracts as well as minority borrowers in particular.

The impacts of FHA loans on low-income borrowers deserve special mention. As noted earlier, anomalies with the impact on low-income borrowers in prime and subprime submarkets are expected because of issues regarding borrower overstatement of incomes for low- and no-documentation loans. However, there are fewer low- or no-documentation FHA loans, so the impacts on low-income borrowers in this submarket should be more reliable. Consistent with FHA's focus on low-income borrowers, looser FHA credit standards had no appreciable disproportionate impact on these borrowers in 2005, 2006, and 2007. The disproportionate benefits in 2004 to borrowers who were not low income are surprising, but they may reflect the more heterogeneous income mix of FHA borrowers in the time before the dramatic growth in subprime loans.

Figure 3-10 shows the differential impact of changing pricing distributions on policy-targeted subpopulations, separately for each submarket. The prime submarket shows the greatest overall disparity in the prices faced by low-income and minority neighborhoods and borrowers, but it is everywhere the case that policy-targeted subpopulations face higher APRs.[18] As in the overall market, the differentially higher APRs faced by policy-targeted subpopulations declined from 2004 to 2008.

---

18. As noted, such a differential impact should not be taken as evidence of discrimination, but likely reflects differences in the underlying distribution of credit characteristics.

Figure 3-10. *Impacts of the Distribution of Pricing on Policy-Targeted Subpopulations in Submarkets, by Origination Year, 2004–08*[a]

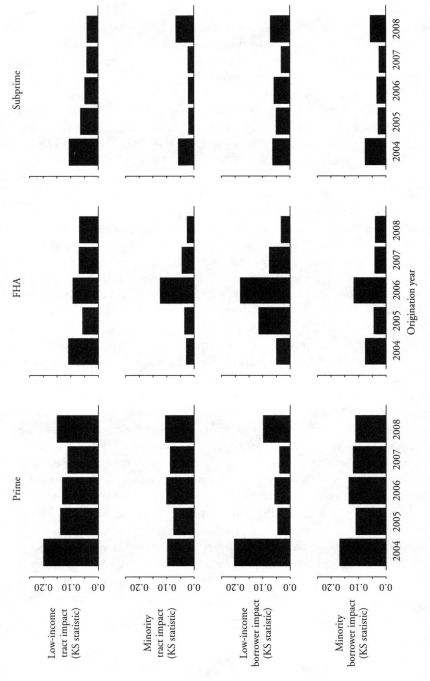

Source: Authors' calculations based on data from a sample of the top twenty lenders in 2004–08 and on HMDA data.
a. KS statistic.

The subprime submarket shows the least evidence of differential APR distributions for policy-targeted subpopulations, although here, too, low-income and minority neighborhoods and borrowers disproportionately tend to face higher APRs. The limited differential in APR distributions may reflect the subprime submarket's overall focus on higher-risk lending and therefore may indicate less systematic difference in the overall distribution of the credit characteristics of its borrower subpopulations.

FHA loans again show different time trends than either prime or subprime loans. A salient characteristic of the FHA results is that the greatest disproportionate impact appears to have occurred in 2006. Regardless, and not surprising, low-income and minority neighborhoods and borrowers disproportionately face higher prices under FHA loans, but less disproportionately than in the prime submarket.

Finally, we attempt to assess the separate impact of changing credit standards and submarket shares on the total market. We assess the effect of changing submarket shares by recalculating impacts while applying constant shares for the prime, FHA, and subprime submarkets to each year when aggregating to represent the total market (we use five-year averages). To account for changing credit standards, we apply 2008 credit standards to earlier years and reassess the impacts. Obviously, this approach makes sense when comparing pricing distributions (APRs), but not when comparing the impact of changing credit standards.

Figure 3-11 makes this assessment for CDR distributions. In this case, we can only hold constant submarket shares. To ease comparisons, the left-hand panel reproduces the observed CDR box plots from figure 3-1. The right-hand panel shows the impact of holding constant submarket shares over time. The impact of this change is very small, suggesting that changing submarket shares are not responsible for changes in the overall distribution of total market CDRs. This is not surprising because prime and subprime submarkets combine to make up the largest share of the total market and, as illustrated in figure 3-6, follow roughly the same basic time trends.

Figure 3-12 shows the more complete decomposition for APR distributions. For comparison, the first panel on the left reproduces the observed box plots from figure 3-1. The second panel shows the effects of holding submarket shares constant. In this instance there is an observable impact. In particular, while the same basic trends hold with constant submarket shares, we do see a trimming of the "box" in 2006 and a lengthening of the "whiskers" in 2007 and 2008. This is not surprising and reflects the fact that holding subprime shares constant reduces their impact in 2006, tightening the "box," while significantly increasing their contribution in 2007 and 2008, lengthening the "whiskers."

The third panel shows the effects of imposing the tighter 2008 credit standards on earlier years. By construction, therefore, the box plot for 2008 is unchanged.

Figure 3-11. *Decomposition of the Distribution of Default Risk in the Total Market, by Origination Year, 2004–08*

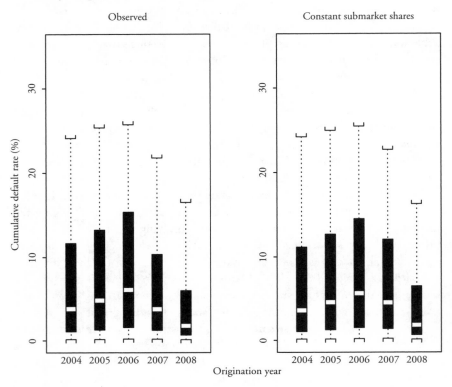

Source: Authors' calculations based on data from a sample of the top twenty lenders in 2004–08 and on HMDA data.

The box plots of earlier years again reflect the observed trend of the overall market, but in this case with tighter CDR distributions throughout.

The fourth and final panel combines the impact of both effects—holding submarket shares constant and imposing 2008 credit standards. While imposing both effects appears to mitigate the overall observed impacts, the impacts are by no means eliminated.

This is not necessarily unexpected. As illustrated in figure 3-2, the adoption of risk-based pricing was relatively unchanged throughout this period, so the remaining impacts shown in the right-most panel of figure 3-12 are due primarily to changes over time in the distribution of borrowers with CDRs below the 2008 credit cutoffs. Preliminary analysis not presented here confirms that holding these changing credit distributions constant explains most of the observed trends in the total market distribution of CDRs.

Figure 3-12. *Decomposition of the Distribution of Pricing in the Total Market, by Origination Year, 2004–08*

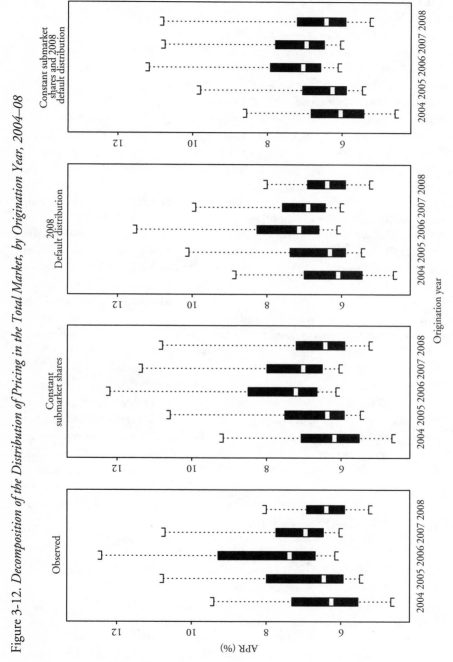

Source: Authors' calculations based on data from a sample of the top twenty lenders in 2004–08 and on HMDA data.

We conclude, therefore, that it is neither changing submarket shares nor changing credit standards per se that primarily explain the time trends in APR distributions. Rather, the impacts we are analyzing likely are subtler and more complex than they have been considered thus far. In particular, it suggests that loosening credit standards does not simply "open the doors to credit" for borrowers who were excluded, but it may also encourage borrowers to submit riskier applications even if they would previously have been included or approved. That is, a more permissive credit environment does not just encourage applications from borrowers who likely otherwise would have been denied. A more permissive credit environment also encourages the applicants who might have qualified under tighter standards to "choose" more risky mortgage characteristics (such as, for example, lower down payments or larger loan amounts). In essence, looser underwriting standards include borrowers previously excluded and also may encourage those otherwise not excluded to take out mortgages with riskier terms.

Figures 3-1 and 3-6 provide support for this contention. It is clear from the CDR box and whiskers plots that simply truncating the high-end tails of earlier years at 2008 credit boundary levels does not equate the CDR distributions across years. Not only do the CDR distributions of 2004 through 2007 have substantially higher tails than that of 2008, but their medians and interquartile ranges are also significantly higher. That is, there is a substantial upward shift to the CDR distributions in years when credit standards were looser. This observation is consistent with the view that a more permissive credit environment encourages an overall shift toward higher-risk borrowing. This analysis cannot determine, however, the extent to which this shift results from borrower or lender "choices."

Figure 3-13 examines whether holding submarket shares constant affects our assessment of the disproportionate benefit received by policy-targeted subpopulations from the loosening of credit standards. Comparing the left-hand column (observed) to the right-hand column (constant submarket shares) shows very little change. This is expected given the finding demonstrated in figure 3-11 that holding submarket shares constant has little effect on the overall distribution of CDRs. Clearly, therefore, the disproportionate benefits received by low-income and minority neighborhoods and households do not result primarily from changing subprime or other submarket shares.

Figure 3-14 decomposes the separate impacts that submarket shares and loosened credit standards have on the disproportionately high APRs paid by low-income and minority borrowers and neighborhoods. The left-hand column repeats the observed trends shown in figure 3-4. The second column holds constant submarket shares, the third column holds credit standards at the tighter 2008 levels, and the fourth column shows the impact of combining both submarket shares constant and the tighter 2008 credit standards.

The results of this exercise mirror those of figure 3-12. Specifically, neither holding submarket share trends constant nor imposing the tighter 2008 credit

Figure 3-13. *Decomposition of the Impacts of Default Risk on Targeted Subpopulations in the Total Market, by Origination Year, 2004–08*[a]

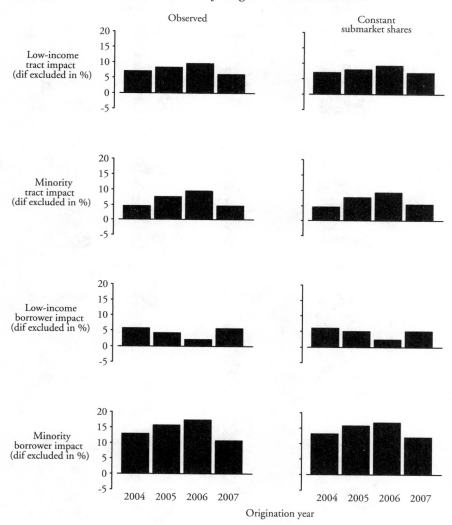

Source: Authors' calculations based on data from a sample of the top twenty lenders in 2004–08 and on HMDA data.

a. Difference relative to 2008 in the percentage excluded.

standards on earlier years fully explains the time trends in the disproportionate impact faced by low-income and minority households and borrowers. The remaining trends in the right-most column, after controlling for both shares and credit standards, necessarily must be due to changes in pricing over time or to changes in the distribution of credit risk characteristics, holding underwriting standards constant. Figure 3-8 suggests that it is more the latter than the former,

Figure 3-14. *Decomposition of the Impacts of Pricing on Targeted Subpopulations in the Total Market, by Origination Year, 2004–08*

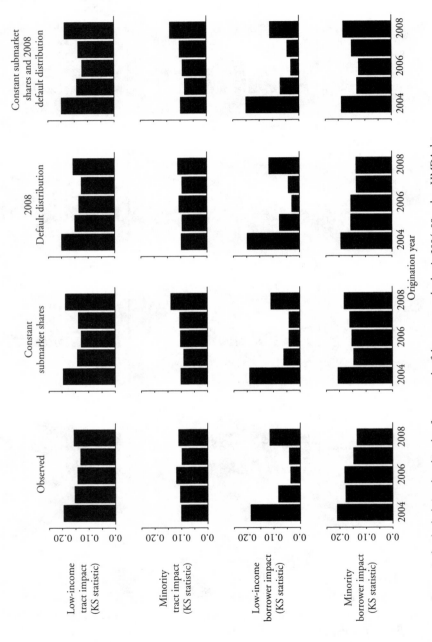

Source: Authors' calculations based on data from a sample of the top twenty lenders in 2004–08 and on HMDA data.

and, as noted earlier, this view is supported by our preliminary research, where we hold the full CDR distributions constant. This again suggests important secondary effects to relaxed credit standards: looser standards not only encourage applications from the now acceptable higher-risk borrowers, but also encourage borrowers to take a more leveraged or otherwise more risky mortgage position and encourage applications from potential borrowers in the "gray area" near the previous credit cutoff border.

Finally, a commonality in the time trends in the right-most column is the fact that disproportionate impacts on the key policy-targeted subpopulations tend to be lowest in 2006, the time of the most lax underwriting standards. With this preliminary research in mind, it is tempting to posit that the explanation for this relationship is that the loose credit standards of this period disproportionately encouraged higher-income and white non-Hispanic borrowers to take out mortgages. However, figure 3-4 does not appear to support this view.

Interpretation and Conclusions

It has been argued that the loosening of credit standards and, especially, the embracing of risk-based pricing has "democratized" credit markets by disproportionately expanding access to credit markets for low-income and minority neighborhoods and borrowers.[19] Our study of the years 2004 through 2008 strongly supports the view that these policy-targeted subpopulations benefited from the relaxing of credit standards that peaked in 2006. The role of risk-based pricing in this democratization, however, is less clear.

From a twenty-year perspective, it is plausible to argue that mortgage lending has made a significant shift from average-cost to risk-based pricing, but there is no evidence of such a trend in the overall market for the years 2004 through 2008. Instead, we see strong evidence of risk-based pricing throughout the period. The mild trend we do see—a slightly increased adoption of risk-based pricing from 2004 through 2006 followed by a slight decline—primarily reflects the changing submarket shares of subprime and FHA lending. Subprime lenders throughout this period consistently embraced risk-based pricing, but the FHA did not. The shrinking of FHA lending throughout the early years of our study period is therefore associated with an increased tendency to employ risk-based pricing in the overall market. Conversely, the dramatic shrinking in the share of subprime lending in 2007 and 2008 is associated with a slight decline in the evidence of risk-based pricing in the overall market.

Within submarkets themselves, the use of risk-based pricing remained relatively constant throughout our study period—extensive in both the prime and

19. See, for example, Gramlich (2007).

subprime submarkets and almost nonexistent in the FHA submarket. In our view, there was no dramatic change in the adoption of risk-based pricing from 2004 through 2008. For this reason, risk-based pricing does not appear to have caused the relaxation of credit standards from 2004 to 2006, although it certainly may have helped to enable them.

It is also worth noting that the expansion of credit and the adoption of risk-based pricing can have contradictory impacts on low-income and minority neighborhoods and borrowers. Because policy-targeted subpopulations tend to have higher credit risk characteristics, a relaxation of underwriting standards will disproportionately provide them with increased access to credit. At the same time, however, the higher credit risk characteristics of policy-targeted subpopulations mean that they disproportionately face higher mortgage rates in a world of risk-based pricing. So, while relaxed underwriting standards tend to provide increased access to credit disproportionately to low-income and minority neighborhoods and borrowers, they likely also aggravate the tendency for policy-targeted subpopulations to pay disproportionately higher prices for the mortgages they do obtain based on their higher default risk.

This dynamic played out in a manner that was surprising, at least to us, in the years from 2004 through 2008. Specifically, although credit standards first loosened and then tightened, and risk-based pricing was relatively constant, there was an overall decline throughout the period in the disproportionate prices that policy-targeted subpopulations paid for their mortgages. That is, we expected the credit loosening of the 2004 through 2006 period to exacerbate the differentially high APRs paid by low-income and minority neighborhoods and borrowers, but it did not.

We believe that this unexpected result reflects the complex impact that loosening credit standards can have on the overall market. Relaxed underwriting grants credit to those who previously were denied. Our analysis also suggests that a more permissive credit environment results in an overall increase in the default risk of mortgage originations, due perhaps to a greater acceptance or encouragement of higher leveraging (lower down payments) and greater "stretching" (higher debt-to-income ratios). This latter factor seems to have mitigated the differentially higher rates paid by policy-targeted subpopulations in our period of analysis.

We conclude with two broad policy implications from our analysis. First, our data suggest that there was a significant "democratization" of credit in the years 2004 through 2006. Specifically, the relaxation of underwriting standards throughout this period disproportionately increased access to credit for low-income and minority neighborhoods and borrowers, and this occurred simultaneously with a reduction in the extent to which policy-targeted subpopulations disproportionately paid higher APRs for their mortgages. This does not mean, of course, that these benefits came without costs; clearly the ex post performance of these loans raises suitability and sustainability concerns. It does suggest, however, that all policy dimensions should be considered fully when searching for causes or solutions to the recent crisis in mortgage lending.

Second, at least over this period, risk-based pricing does not appear to be the market evil that it is sometimes portrayed to be. Risk-based pricing was used relatively consistently over the 2004 through 2008 period by both prime and subprime lenders, but not at all by the FHA. Despite this difference, the time trend of impacts on low-income and minority neighborhoods and borrowers was fairly similar for all three submarkets. Arguably, in fact, the subprime, not the FHA, submarket fared the best in its overall impact on policy-targeted subpopulations. Again, of course, we have not considered either mortgage suitability or sustainability, and this could tip the balance in the other direction. Our analysis nonetheless suggests that risk-based pricing may not be the cause for concern that some believe it to be.

References

Chinloy, Peter, and Nancy MacDonald. 2005. "Subprime Lenders and Mortgage Market Completion." *Journal of Real Estate Finance and Economics* 30, no. 2: 153–65.

Collins, Michael, Eric Belsky, and Karl E. Case. 2004. "Exploring the Welfare Effects of Risk-Based Pricing in the Subprime Mortgage Market." BABC 04-8. Harvard University, Joint Center for Housing Studies (April).

Cutts, Amy Crews, and Robert Van Order. 2005. "On the Economics of Subprime Lending." *Journal of Real Estate Economics and Finance* 30, no. 2: 167–96.

Deng, Yongheng, and Stuart Gabriel. 2006. "Risk-Based Pricing and the Enhancement of Mortgage Credit Availability among Underserved and Higher Credit-Risk Populations." *Journal of Money, Credit, and Banking* 38, no. 6: 1431–60.

Gates, Susan Wharton, Vanessa Gail Perry, and Peter M. Zorn. 2002. "Automated Underwriting in Mortgage Lending: Good for the Underserved?" *Housing Policy Debate* 13, no. 2: 369–81.

Gramlich, Edward. 2007. *Subprime Mortgages: America's Latest Boom and Bust.* Washington: Urban Institute Press.

Lax, Howard, Michael Manti, Paul Raca, and Peter Zorn. 2004. "Subprime Lending: An Investigation of Economic Efficiency." *Housing Policy Debate* 15, no. 3: 533–71.

Stiglitz, Joseph E., and Andew Weiss. 1981. "A Credit Rationing in Markets with Imperfect Information." *American Economic Review* 71, no. 3: 393–409.

4

Alternative Forms of Mortgage Finance: What Can We Learn from Other Countries?

MICHAEL LEA

The U.S. mortgage finance system has gone from the envy of the world to a case study of failure in two short years. As recently as the 2003–05 period, the system generated an enormous volume of originations (nearly $4 trillion) that contributed to a record level of homeownership (69.3 percent).[1] Impressive gains were made in low-income and minority rates of homeownership. The system was characterized by low mortgage interest rates, robust competition, particularly from nonbank lenders, buoyant house prices, and low default rates. While the government role was significant, the major government-supported institutions were losing market share. There were, however, ample warning signals that this rosy picture was about to end. Affordability was falling, concerns about predatory lending abounded, delinquencies in subprime lending were rising, and numerous commentators warned of unsustainable house prices.

Fast forward to the 2007–10 time period. The homeownership rate has fallen to 67.4 percent, erasing all of the gains since 2000. House prices have been falling for three years and are off more than 30 percent nationwide. Mortgage originations are down significantly, and only prime borrowers can obtain loans. Conforming mortgage rates are historically low, but the volume of refinancing is muted. And nonconforming rates are much higher. There is reduced competition, as most nonbank lenders have failed and the large banks dominate the market. The country is experiencing record postwar default and foreclosure rates. The role

1. Joint Center for Housing Studies (2009).

of government has expanded considerably; in fact, the government backs nearly all mortgage lending. There is considerable uncertainty about when the recovery in the housing and mortgage markets will begin.

The economic recession that was sparked by the implosion of the U.S. subprime mortgage market has been global in dimension. As such, it has affected the housing and mortgage markets of many countries. Most developed countries also experienced robust growth in their housing and mortgage markets during the first half of the decade. Many countries experienced record levels of house price inflation, increased competition, and relaxed mortgage underwriting. But no major developed market has experienced the severe decline in house prices, the high rate of mortgage default and foreclosure, and the change in the mortgage finance system as have been experienced by the United States. What have these other countries done differently?

This chapter reviews the major characteristics and performance of various developed-country mortgage markets, comparing and contrasting the structure, principal features, and performance of the primary and secondary markets with those in the United States. The comparison includes the types of lender and mortgage instruments in the primary market, institutions and instruments involved in the capital market, funding of mortgages, and management of major mortgage risks (default and prepayment). The chapter then compares and contrasts the role of government in mortgage market regulation, consumer protection, and the backing of institutions and instruments through guarantees and ownership in the primary and secondary markets. Finally, it seeks to extract ideas about how the U.S. system can be reformed to improve performance and restore private capital market finance.

International Comparisons

This chapter focuses on the finance of owner-occupied housing. Figure 4-1 shows recent rates of homeownership among several Organization for Economic Cooperation and Development (OECD) countries. The United States has a relatively high rate of homeownership, but it is not the highest among major developed markets. Australia, Ireland, Spain, and the United Kingdom all have higher rates of homeownership, and Canada's rate is comparable to that of the United States. This is noteworthy because these countries provide far less government support for homeownership than the United States. Most Western European countries have lower rates of homeownership in part due to strong social rental systems. Southern European countries like Italy, Greece, and Spain have higher rates of homeownership, reflecting cultural values, discriminatory policies toward private rental housing, and relatively weak support of social rental housing.

Homeownership rates in most countries were stable in the 1999–2008 period. Canada had the largest increase in homeownership, growing from 64 to 68 percent.

Figure 4-1. *Rates of Homeownership in Select Countries, 2008, except 2006 for Japan*

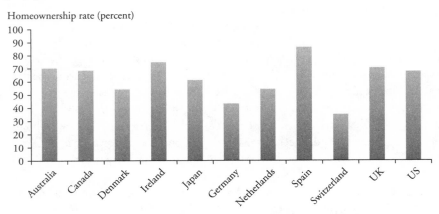

Homeownership rate (percent)

Source: Australian Bureau of Statistics, Canada Housing and Mortgage Corporation, Delft University, European Mortgage Federation, U.S. Bureau of the Census.

Homeownership in Spain, the United Kingdom, and the United States each grew 2 to 3 percentage points.

The housing boom was characterized by higher rates of housing construction in many countries. Several countries—notably Australia, Canada, Ireland, and Spain—had higher real residential investment to GDP in 2002–07.[2] Ellis points out that a major difference between the United States and other countries is that the increase in dwellings in the United States was significantly greater than the increase in households or population, which created an excess supply of houses.[3]

Figure 4-2 shows the growth in the ratio of residential mortgage debt outstanding to GDP between 1994–95 and 2008. The U.S. ratio grew from 44 to 93 percent, an impressive performance. But several other countries had a similar performance. Australia, Ireland, and Spain had greater growth, and the Netherlands had a higher ratio. All countries except Germany and Japan had significant growth in their mortgage markets.

Although the United States had an unprecedented run-up of house prices during the decade, it was not alone, as shown in table 4-1. Many OECD countries had greater house price increases between 2000 and 2006 than did the United States. Australia and the United States were the first of the bubble countries in which house prices fell; the Australian housing market has since recovered. The magnitude of the fall in U.S. house prices, as measured by the Standard and Poor's

2. IMF (2009).
3. Ellis (2008).

Figure 4-2. *Ratio of Mortgage Debt to GDP in Select Countries, 1994–2008*

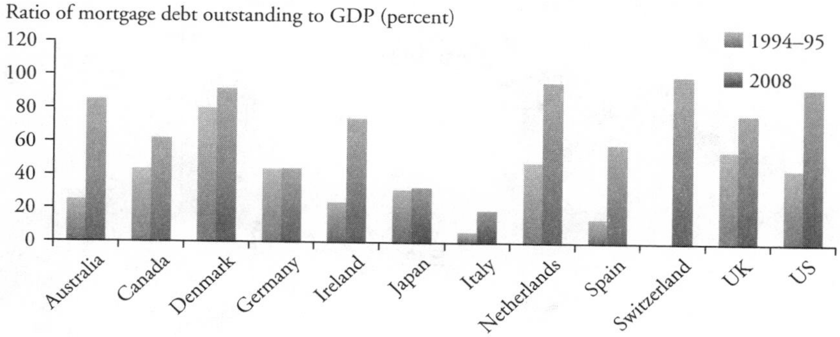

Ratio of mortgage debt outstanding to GDP (percent)

Source: Australian Bureau of Statistics, Canada Housing and Mortgage Corporation, European Mortgage Federation (various years), Federal Reserve Board, and the World Bank. Data for 1994–95 not available for Switzerland.

Case Shiller 20 metro area index, has been greater than in other countries. Research by the International Monetary Fund suggests that the housing market is more elastic in the United States than in other countries, as evidenced by a higher share of real residential investment and real variation in house prices as a result of housing demand shocks.

Mortgage interest rates in most countries declined during the decade, except in Australia (see table 4-2). The Reserve Bank of Australia raised interest rates in 2003 in part to head off a house price bubble. The rates are specific to the dominant instrument. Australia, Ireland, Spain, and the United Kingdom are predominately short-term variable-rate markets. Their mortgage rates declined more sharply than those in other countries during the crisis.

Figure 4-3 compares dominant mortgage product offerings by country in terms of interest rate variability. There is considerable difference in the types of products offered. Australia, Ireland, Spain, and the United Kingdom are dominated by variable-rate or short-term (typically one- to three-year) fixed-rate mortgages. The design of adjustable-rate mortgages (ARMs) varies. In Australia and the United Kingdom, the standard variable-rate mortgage has a rate set by the lender at its discretion. Rates are changed for all borrowers at the same time. Canada, Spain, and the United States have indexed ARMs. Recently tracker mortgages, which are indexed ARMs, have become dominant in the United Kingdom. Initial fixed-rate discounts are prevalent in Australia and the United Kingdom. The magnitudes of the discounts are less than those in the United States during the boom—typically around 100 basis points, lasting one to two years.

The United States is unusual in the high proportion of long-term fixed-rate mortgages (figure 4-3). The ARM and short-term fixed (hybrid) share in the United States grew during the boom—accounting for 30–35 percent of loans in

Table 4-1. *House Prices in Select Countries, 2000–09*

Nominal change in house price year-on-year

Country/entity	2000	2001	2002	2003	2004	2005	2006	2007	2008	2009
U.S. Federal Housing Finance Agency	7.20	7.30	6.90	7.00	10.50	11.20	4.90	-0.04	-4.30	-1.20
Japan	-3.7	-4.1	-4.6	-5.4	-6.1	-4.8	-3.0	-1.0	-1.6	-3.2
Germany	0.0	0.0	-2.8	-1.0	-1.9	-2.0	0.9	-0.7	0.0	-0.7
United Kingdom	14.9	8.1	16.1	15.7	11.9	5.5	6.3	10.9	-0.9	0.3
Canada	3.7	4.6	9.9	9.4	9.4	9.9	11.3	10.8	-1.1	2.5
Australia	8.3	11.2	18.8	18.2	6.5	1.5	7.8	11.3	4.4	12.0
Denmark	6.5	5.8	3.6	3.2	8.9	17.6	21.6	4.6	-4.5	-7.3
Spain	7.5	9.5	16.9	20.0	18.3	14.6	10.0	5.5	0.2	-6.3
Ireland	16.5	8.2	10.7	15.8	11.6	11.8	13.5	-1.0	-2.5	-18.5
Netherlands	18.2	11.1	6.5	3.6	4.3	3.8	4.6	4.2	-8.8	-5.0
U.S. CS20[a]	11.6	7.2	12.0	11.0	15.3	14.5	0.4	-8.6	-16.7	-3.1
France	8.8	7.9	8.3	11.7	15.2	15.3	12.1	6.6	1.3	-4.4
Italy	8.3	8.2	9.6	10.3	9.9	7.5	6.4	5.2	1.7	...

Source: Canada Housing and Mortgage Corporation, European Mortgage Federation, Federal Housing Finance Agency, Standard and Poor's.

a. Standard and Poor's Case-Shiller 20 metro area index.

Table 4-2. *Mortgage Interest Rates in Select Countries, 2000–09*

Percent

Country	2000	2001	2002	2003	2004	2005	2006	2007	2008	2009
Germany	6.4	5.9	5.5	5.1	4.6	4.2	4.6	5.0	4.8	4.39
Denmark	7.2	6.4	5.7	5.5	5.0	4.4	5.2	5.9	6.6	4.18
Spain	5.9	4.5	3.8	3.2	3.3	3.2	4.7	5.3	5.9	3.14
UK	7.6	5.7	5.6	5.6	6.6	6.6	5.3	6.1	5.5	4.38
Ireland	6.2	4.7	4.7	3.5	3.5	3.7	4.6	5.1	4.3	2.68
Australia	8.1	6.1	6.6	7.1	7.1	7.3	7.5	8.0	6.3	6.05
Canada	7.8	6.6	6.4	6.0	5.7	5.6	6.0	6.7	6.2	5.85
Japan	2.8	2.6	2.4	2.6	2.9	3.3	2.4	3.0	2.7	2.75
U.S. fixed rate mortgage	7.3	7.0	6.5	5.8	5.8	5.9	6.4	6.1	6.0	5.20
U.S. adjustable rate mortgage	7.0	5.8	4.6	3.8	3.9	4.5	5.5	5.5	5.2	4.70
Switzerland	4.32	4.20	3.78	3.28	3.07	2.92	3.03	3.17	3.84	3.67

Source: Central banks, European Mortgage Federation, Mortgage Bankers Association.

Figure 4-3. *Mortgage Products in Select Countries, 2009*

Share of all mortgages (percent)

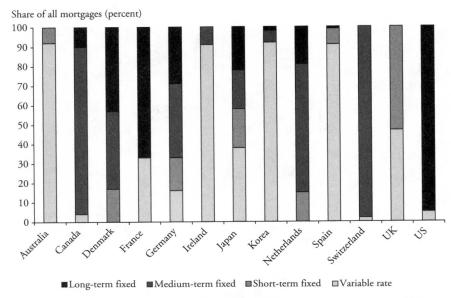

■Long-term fixed   ■Medium-term fixed   ■Short-term fixed   □Variable rate

Source: Canadian Association of Accredited Mortgage Professionals, European Mortgage Federation (various years), Genworth, Mortgage Bankers Association, Standard and Poor's.

the 2004–06 period—but the market has reverted to fixed-rate mortgages in the crisis.[4] Long-term fixed-rate mortgages used to be the dominant product in Denmark, but relatively low and falling short-term rates have led Danish borrowers to shift to medium-term (one- to five-year) fixed-rate loans in recent years. Rollover mortgages are the dominant product in Canada, Germany, and the Netherlands. These loans have a fixed rate for up to five years (ten years in Germany), with a twenty-five- to thirty-year amortization period (thirty-five years in Canada). At the end of the fixed-rate period, the rate adjusts to the new market rate. There is a substantial (as high as yield maintenance) prepayment penalty during the fixed-rate period. Canadian borrowers have responded to low short-term interest rates with a larger proportion of variable-rate loans. A high proportion of Dutch loans are interest only to maximize tax benefits. About half of Japanese loans are convertible (after the end of the fixed-rate term the borrower can select another fixed-rate period or switch to a variable rate).[5] Japanese floating-rate loans have fixed payments for five years with potential deferral and negative amortization. Some Spanish loans are part fixed and part variable rate.

4. Despite the fact that a one-year ARM is 120 basis points lower than a thirty-year fixed rate mortgage, and a 3/1 ARM is 81 basis points lower, as of September 10, 2010, according to the *Wall Street Journal*. See "Market Data," *Wall Street Journal*, September 10, 2010.
5. For more detail on Japanese mortgages, see Standard and Poor's (2009).

Figure 4-4. *Mortgage Funding in Select Countries, 2008*

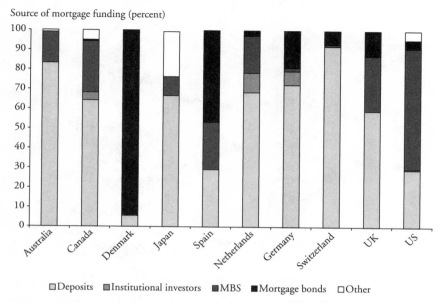

Source of mortgage funding (percent)

☐ Deposits   ◪ Institutional investors   ■ MBS   ■ Mortgage bonds   ☐ Other

Source: Central banks, Canadian Association of Accredited Mortgage Professionals, European Mortgage Federation, Federal Reserve Board, Merrill Lynch.

Mortgage funding comparisons reveal interesting differences. As shown in figure 4-4, deposit funding dominates in most countries. The United States is unique with regard to the importance of securitization. More than 60 percent of U.S. residential mortgages have been securitized; the next closest countries are Canada, Spain, and the United Kingdom, with 24–28 percent securitized. Covered bonds are a more common funding mechanism in Europe: 94 percent of Danish funding and 47 percent of Spanish funding come from this source. We comment later on the role of covered bonds and the reason for their dominance in Denmark and significance in Europe.

Mortgage lending tends to be dominated by banks and highly concentrated in most countries. The top five lenders have more than a 50 percent market share in Australia, Canada, Denmark, the Netherlands, and the United Kingdom. The top five are commercial banks, except in Denmark where they are specialist mortgage companies (which are owned by or own commercial banks).[6] Banks are the largest class of lender in Germany and Spain, but the market share of individual institutions is much smaller. Savings banks (owned by the state governments) are the largest lenders in these countries, followed by commercial banks in Spain and mortgage banks in Germany. In Europe all mortgage lenders must have a bank

6. The Nationwide Building Society is a top five lender in the United Kingdom.

Figure 4-5. *Broker Share of Originations in Select Countries, 2008*

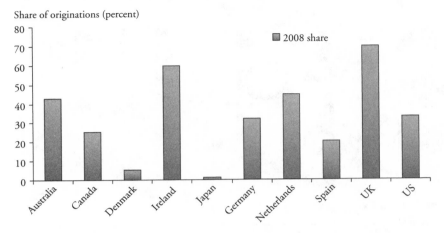

Share of originations (percent)

Source: Canadian Association of Accredited Mortgage Professionals, Europe Economics, Inside Mortgage Finance, National Australia Bank.

charter (which can be commercial, savings, cooperative, and mortgage, among others). The market in Japan is rather fragmented, but large city banks have the largest market share. As a result of the crisis, the U.S. mortgage market is beginning to look more like those in the other countries, with origination dominated by large commercial banks.

Mortgage brokers play a significant distribution role in many countries. As figure 4-5 shows, the broker share of originations varies widely across countries, from as high as 60–70 percent in Ireland and the United Kingdom to as low as 1–5 percent in Denmark and Japan. The U.S. number does not reflect correspondent lending, which accounted for 31 percent of 2008 originations. Australia and the United Kingdom have a small amount of correspondent lending as well. The broker share has fallen in the United States as a result of the crisis.

The recession has taken its toll on all mortgage markets, but more so in the United States than anywhere else. Figure 4-6 shows comparative mortgage default rates for bank portfolios in several countries. Mortgage default rates have risen but remain low in other countries.[7] The performance of bank mortgage portfolios in the United States is worse than in other countries.

Mortgage performance has been worse for securitized mortgages in those countries with significant securitization. In large part this is due to the fact that subprime or nonconforming mortgages were the collateral for these securities. Figure 4-7 shows the performance of private-label securitized loans in the United

---

7. Danish arrears (not shown) were less than 2 percent and foreclosures were 0.4 percent in 2008 (Boyce 2010). German and Japanese default rates are also quite low. Serious default rates on loans held or guaranteed by Fannie Mae and Freddie Mac were over 5.5 percent in early 2010.

Figure 4-6. *Nonperforming Loans as a Share of Housing Loans in Select Countries, 1993–2009*

Share of housing loans that are nonperforming (percent)[a]

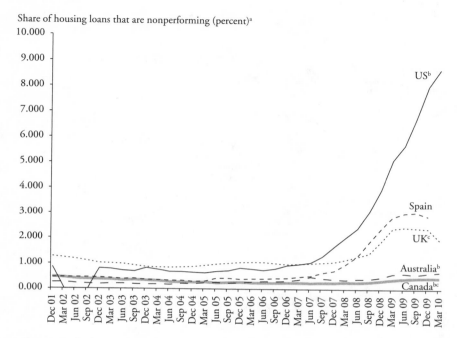

Sources: Bank of Spain; Canadian Bankers' Association; Council of Mortgage Lenders; FDIC; Reserve Bank of Australia; Australia Prudential Regulatory Authority.

a. Percent of loans by value. Includes impaired loans unless otherwise stated. For Australia, only includes ninety or more days in arrears prior to September 2003.

b. Banks only.

c. Percent of loans by number that are ninety or more days in arrears.

States. Subprime loans have extraordinarily high default rates, reflecting the decline in underwriting standards and risk layering. The recent increase in prime defaults reflects rising unemployment and falling house prices.

Figure 4-8 shows the performance of prime residential mortgage-backed securities (RMBSs) in Europe. Delinquencies on European securitized loans have increased during the crisis but remain well below those in the United States. Default rates on securitized loans are less than 1.5 percent in Australia and less than 1 percent in Canada. These results reflect the fact that subprime lending was rare or nonexistent outside of the United States. The only country with a significant share of subprime lending was the United Kingdom (a peak of 8 percent of mortgages in 2006). Subprime loans accounted for 5 percent of mortgages in Canada, less than 2 percent in Australia, and negligible proportions elsewhere. Subprime loans in Australia and Canada were more similar to U.S. Alt-A loans than to true subprime loans.

Figure 4-7. *Performance of Private-Label Securitized Mortgage Loans in the United States, 1998–2009*[a]

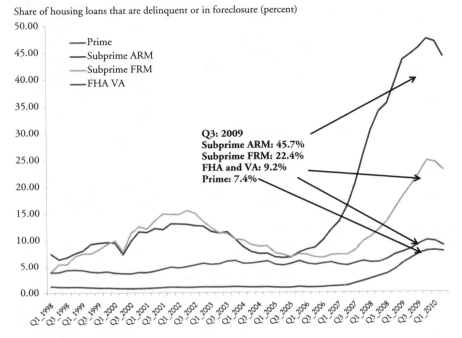

Source: Amherst Securities (2009).
a. In the third quarter of 2009, the share of loans that were delinquent or in foreclosure is the following: subprime adjustable-rate mortgages, 45.7 percent; subprime fixed-rate mortgages, 22.4 percent; Federal Housing Administration and Veterans Benefits Administration loans, 9.1 percent; and prime mortgages, 5.9 percent.

The only performance comparable to that of the United States is in U.K. non-conforming mortgages. U.K. lenders provided loans to borrowers who had both adverse credit and low documentation. Nonconforming securitized loans have high delinquency rates in the United Kingdom (see figure 4-9), but foreclosure rates are far lower than in the United States.[8]

Role of Government

Government is involved in all of the surveyed mortgage markets to varying degrees. Government involvement includes tax incentives, guarantees, government-sponsored enterprises, and regulation.

8. The U.K. Homeowners Mortgage Support Program assists unemployed borrowers with mortgage payments for up to two years, which may contribute to lower foreclosures. As in the United States, lenders have been slow to repossess houses, in part because house prices began rising at the end of 2009.

Figure 4-8. *Performance of RMBS in Select European Countries, 2000–09*

Share of residential mortgage-backed securities thirty or more days in arrears (percent)

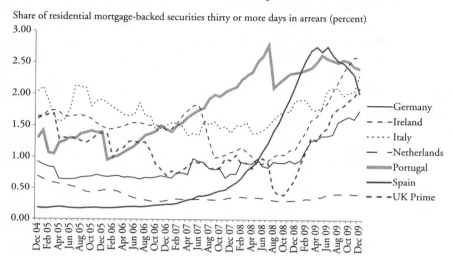

Source: Fitch Ratings.

Figure 4-9. *Performance of Nonconforming Securitized Loans in the United Kingdom at the End of 2009, by Year of Origination*

Share of nonconforming securities loans at least three months in arrears (percent)

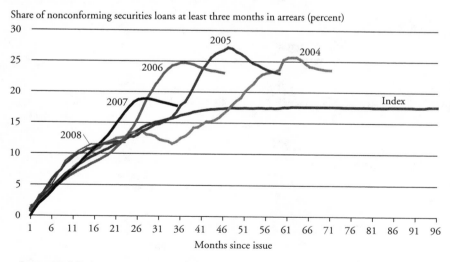

Months since issue

Source: Fitch Ratings.

Tax Treatment of Homeownership

Government can provide incentives for owner-occupied housing in many ways. Perhaps the best known is favorable tax treatment. Table 4-3 compares the tax treatment of owner-occupied housing for select OECD countries.

The tax treatment of mortgage interest is varied. Most OECD countries do not allow a deduction, and several that do cap it at low marginal tax rates. Denmark and the Netherlands have full or nearly full deductibility, although both countries tax imputed rent (albeit at low rates). Only the United States allows nearly full deductibility without taxing imputed rent. In recent years those countries with deductibility have exhibited faster mortgage growth. Ireland, the Netherlands, and the United States had the highest rates of growth in mortgage

Table 4-3. *Tax Treatment of Owner-Occupied Housing in Select Countries*

Country	Mortgage interest	Capital gains	Other
Denmark	Deductible at 33 percent maximum tax rate	Exempt if primary residence of less than 1,400 square meters	
Germany	Nondeductible	Exempt if held more than ten years	
Ireland	Deductible for seven years at 25 percent of the maximum tax rate, falling to 20 percent	Exempt	
Netherlands	Fully deductible	Exempt	Imputed income taxed
Spain	At €9,015, capped at 15 percent rate	Exempt if reinvested or sold after age sixty-five	
United Kingdom	Nondeductible	Exempt	
Australia	Nondeductible	Taxable with indexed cost base	First-time homebuyer tax credit
Canada	Nondeductible	Exempt	
Japan	Nondeductible	Taxed at 30 percent if five years or less; 15 percent if more than five years	Deduction of 1 percent of principal per year for ten years
United States	Deductible limit $1 million	Exemption of $250,000/ $500,000 for a principal residence in two out of the last five years	Temporary tax credit in 2009–10

Source: CMHC, European Mortgage Federation, Global Property Guide.

Table 4-4. *Government-Backed Mortgage Institutions in Select Countries*

Country	Government mortgage insurer	Government security guarantees	Government-sponsored enterprise
Denmark	No	No	No
Germany	No	No	No
Ireland	No	No	No
Netherlands	NHG	No	No
Spain	No	No	No
United Kingdom	No	No	No
Australia	No	No	No
Canada	CMHC	CMHC	No
Japan	No	JHF	Possible
United States	Federal Housing Administration	Ginnie Mae	Fannie Mae, Freddie Mac, Federal Home Loan Banks

Source: Author.

debt outstanding over the past fifteen years, and the Netherlands and the United States have the highest levels of indebtedness today. Countries that do not allow deductibility (Australia, Canada, the United Kingdom) or cap it (Ireland, Spain) have equivalent or higher rates of homeownership than the United States. Most countries exempt or limit the tax on capital gains on owner-occupied housing. Ellis points out that interest deductibility combined with a lack of prepayment penalties in the United States may have contributed to the growth in household leverage and mortgage indebtedness through cash-out refinance and second mortgages.[9]

Mortgage Guarantees and Institutions

The differences among countries in the presence of government-owned or -sponsored mortgage institutions are more striking. Table 4-4 compares select countries in this dimension. The United States is unusual in its use of all three types of government-supported mortgage institutions or guarantee programs: mortgage insurance, mortgage guarantees, and government-sponsored mortgage enterprises. Canada and Japan have government guarantee programs, and Canada and the Netherlands have government-backed mortgage insurance programs.[10]

9. Second-mortgage home equity lines of credit exist in other countries (for example, Australia, Canada, the United Kingdom), but in far less volume, perhaps reflecting the lack of interest deductibility. The Netherlands has a relatively high incidence of second mortgages (13 percent of borrowers in 2002), reflecting full deductibility and high marginal tax rates.

10. Australia had a government-owned mortgage insurer from 1965 to 1997, when it was sold to Genworth. For an analysis, see Lea (2009).

The market share of government-backed institutions is smaller in Canada and Japan than in the United States.[11]

The role of government in Canada is more similar to its role in the United States than in any other country. The Canada Mortgage and Housing Corporation (CMHC) is 100 percent owned by the government and enjoys an explicit guarantee of the Canadian government.[12] It provides 100 percent mortgage default insurance through its National Housing Act Program (similar to the Federal Housing Administration in the United States).[13] The CMHC also provides timely payment guarantees on securities backed by National Housing Act loans (similar to Ginnie Mae in the United States). The CMHC administers the Canada Mortgage Bond purchase program, which is a trust set up to purchase CMHC-guaranteed mortgage securities funded by the issuance of mortgage bonds. The program eliminates the cash flow uncertainty caused by mortgage amortization and prepayment through cash flow swaps executed with investment banks. The CMHC does not lend to primary mortgage institutions or invest in mortgages.

The Japan Housing Finance Agency (JHF) is a government-incorporated administrative agency.[14] It operates in a manner similar to the guarantee functions of Fannie Mae and Freddie Mac, purchasing mortgages and issuing mortgage-backed securities with its timely payment guarantee. It does not purchase loans for portfolio, although it could do so within its charter. The JHF replaced the former Government Housing Loan Corporation (GHLC) in 2007, which mainly provided loans to the public with funding from the Ministry of Finance and also securitized some of these loans. The JHF was created after the GHLC ran into asset-liability mismatch problems.

The Netherlands has a government-owned mortgage insurer, the Home-ownership Guarantee Fund (the Nationale Hypotheek Garantie, NHG).[15] The NHG provides 100 percent mortgage default insurance and a temporary mortgage payment facility. The fund is a private institution with fallback agreements with the national and municipal governments. These agreements form the basis for interest-free loans to the fund from the national and municipal governments at times when its assets are no longer sufficient to meet claims. This means that the fund is able to comply with its payment obligations at all times. As a result, the Netherlands Central Bank (Dutch De Nederlandsche Bank) considers the NHG as a government guarantee.

11. About 25 percent of Canadian mortgages are securitized through Canada Mortgage and Housing Corporation guarantees. The CMHC insures about half of mortgages through the National Housing Act program. Japan Housing Finance Agency guarantees approximately 25 percent of Japanese mortgages. Its charter allows it to purchase mortgages, but to date it has focused on guarantees.

12. See www.cmhc-schl.gc.ca/en.

13. The Canadian government also provides a 90 percent backstop guarantee for two private mortgage insurers: Genworth and United Guaranty.

14. See www.jhf.go.jp/english/about/pdf/main_1.pdf.

15. Netherlands, Ministry of Housing, Spatial Planning, and the Environment (n.d.).

Unlike Fannie Mae and Freddie Mac, none of the international, government-backed institutions has experienced exceptional loss or required government capital injections. None of these institutions has a formal affordable housing policy mandate. Also none of these institutions takes on much interest rate risk, as they have limited or no portfolio accumulation.

Regulation

Government is heavily involved in regulating the mortgage market through both consumer protection and safety and soundness regulations in all countries. A major difference between the United States and other countries is that the United States is the only country with specialized housing finance safety and soundness regulators.

Historically, building societies in Australia, Ireland, and the United Kingdom operated in a similar fashion to savings and loans in the United States. These institutions had a specialist regulator. Regulatory reform led to the creation of a single financial regulator: the Australia Prudential Regulatory Authority (1999), the Financial Services Authority (FSA) in the United Kingdom (2001), and the Financial Regulator in Ireland (2003). The building societies are regulated the same as banks in these countries. The mortgage credit institutions dominate housing finance in Denmark, regulated by the Danish Financial Services Authority. Mortgage banks are significant residential mortgage lenders in Germany. They too are regulated by the single financial regulatory agency, the Bundesanstalt für Finanzdienstleistungsaufsicht. Commercial banks dominate mortgage finance in the other countries in this survey. Thus mortgage lending is not subject to specialist regulation.[16] The United States is unique in having a fragmented regulatory structure with numerous specialized regulatory agencies.

The specialist mortgage guarantee and insurance institutions in this survey do not have specialist regulators. The Ministry of Finance in their respective countries regulates the CMHC and the JHF. The Netherlands Ministry of Housing and the Association of Netherlands Municipalities supervise the NHG. An advantage to having a single financial sector regulator is the lower likelihood of regulatory capture or regulatory arbitrage, but a disadvantage may be the lack of sector-specific expertise.

Consumer protection regulation is less clear-cut and in flux. There was significant product innovation and loosening of underwriting in most subject countries during the housing boom. Moderate versions of subprime lending appeared in Australia, Canada, and the United Kingdom during the 2000s. Documentation requirements were relaxed in those countries, creating a version of the Alt-A market. However, the extent of product innovation and underwriting relaxation

16. The mortgage managers and centralized lenders are wholesale lenders funded by securitization in Australia and the United Kingdom, respectively. They are not subject to bank safety and soundness regulation but are subject to consumer protection and business conduct regulation. Their market share has dropped significantly during the crisis.

Table 4-5. *Change in Mortgage Underwriting in Select Countries, 2007–08*

Country	Lower loan-to-value ratios	100 percent mortgages less available	Tighter loan-to-income criteria	Shorter maximum mortgage term	Interest-only loans less available	Introduction of new loan types to deal with crisis
Australia	X	X	X			
Denmark	X					
France	X	X		X		
Iceland						
Ireland	X	X	X		X	X
Netherlands		X	X		X	
Norway	X					
Poland				X		
Portugal	X		X			X
Russia	X	X	X	X		
Spain	X		X	X		
Sweden	X	X			Lower maximum LTV	
United Kingdom	X	X	X		X	
United States	X	X	X		X	

Source: Lunde, Scanlon, and Whitehead (2009).

did not approach the extent prevalent in the United States. A study by the Australian Treasury Department in 2008 notes, "The lax lending behaviour which gave rise to the sub-prime problem in the United States did not occur in Australia in part because the regulatory environment encourages a more cautious lending culture."[17]

In the current market environment, both lenders and regulators are tightening guidelines, contributing to a fall in new lending of 40–50 percent in many countries.[18] Lunde, Scanlon, and Whitehead conducted a survey in early 2009 to assess the types of mortgage tightening taking place. As shown in table 4-5, underwriting criteria have tightened in thirteen of the fourteen countries surveyed.

In light of falling house prices in most countries, lenders are requiring larger down payments, and 100 percent loan-to-value (LTV) loans, common in various countries before the crisis, have disappeared. Swedish maximum LTVs have declined from 95 percent to 85–90 percent, and the average LTV in the United Kingdom has fallen from 80 to 75 percent. Lender surveys also reveal tightening: the Netherlands reported 80 percent of lenders tightening in early 2009, and the

17. Australian Treasury Department (2008, p. 19).
18. Lunde, Scanlon, and Whitehead (2009).

United States reported 65 percent. Affordability criteria have been tightened, and all loans are now fully documented.

Most of these changes appear to be at the volition of the lenders. According to the European Mortgage Federation, regulators in several countries are mooting restrictions on products and maximum LTVs.[19] However, no new regulations have been promulgated. There is no Europe-wide mortgage regulation. The merits of a mortgage directive that would create minimum standards for all countries have been debated for several years. However, the industry has steadfastly opposed this approach and developed an industry-wide code of conduct to police transactions.[20]

The FSA in the United Kingdom has gone the furthest in Europe in contemplating tighter mortgage regulation. Its *Mortgage Market Review* of October 2009 lays out various proposals under consideration, including higher capital requirements for lenders, new quantitative liquidity standards, increased regulation of nonbank ("high-risk") lenders, and product regulation.[21] The FSA notes, however, that LTV or debt-to-income (DTI) caps are not yet warranted, pointing out that LTV or DTI caps are "a blunt approach to achieving the outcomes we want." The FSA does recommend placing restrictions on risk layering (prohibiting loans that are a mix of high-risk factors, for example, prohibiting high LTV loans to credit-impaired borrowers who have an unstable income or other similar "toxic" mixes) and requiring income verification on all mortgages. It should be noted that mortgage brokers (intermediaries) are subject to FSA regulation.

The FSA has promulgated suitability standards for mortgage lenders. Specifically, a product is considered suitable if there are reasonable grounds to conclude the following:

—The client can afford it over the repayment term.

—It is appropriate to the client's needs and circumstances.

—It is the most suitable of those available within the scope of service provided to the client.

Moreover, the lender cannot recommend the "least worst" product if it does not have access to a product that is appropriate to the client's needs and circumstances.[22] The FSA stresses that it expects a "commonsense" approach. The lender or broker is expected to document thoroughly the research on and advice given to the client.

The FSA is considering changing consumer disclosure requirements as well. Notably its October discussion paper states, "Our policy approach to date has been underpinned by a view that mortgage consumers will act rationally to protect their own interests. We believe that we need to change that approach, recognise

19. Conversation with European Monetary Fund officials earlier this year.
20. See www.hypo.org/Content/default.asp?PageID=449.
21. Financial Services Authority (2009).
22. See www.fsa.gov.uk.

the behavioural biases of consumers, and be more interventionist to help protect consumers from themselves. . . . Overall, we think that our regulatory strategy needs to change to one that relies less on disclosure as a regulatory tool and looks to influence consumer behaviour in a more sophisticated way." The FSA is signaling that consumer protection can be improved, "for example, through banning products or prohibiting sales to those consumers exhibiting multiple high-risk characteristics or limiting the amount of equity that can be withdrawn."

The FSA is not alone in contemplating fundamental consumer protection reform. Australia is also in the process of strengthening its consumer protections.[23] The Australian Uniform Consumer Credit Code has been in existence since the mid-1990s at the state level. The code empowers the courts to set aside mortgage agreements where the lender could reasonably have known that the borrower would not be able to repay the loan without causing substantial hardship. Numerous cases highlight the circumstances in which the courts have taken action to protect the interests of the borrower.

The National Consumer Protection Bill of 2009 was promulgated to create uniform nationwide legislation to replace existing (but varied) state legislation. The Australian Securities and Investment Commission was tapped to be the sole regulator of the new national credit framework and given enhanced enforcement powers. The code requires all providers of consumer credit and credit-related brokering services and advice to obtain a license from the commission. It extends the scope of credit products covered by the code to regulate the provision of consumer mortgages over residential investment properties. The bill requires licensees to assess each consumer's capacity to repay credit to ensure that the credit contract is not unsuitable for the consumer's objectives, needs, and financial circumstances. A second phase planned for 2010 will reform existing disclosures.

The Financial Consumer Agency of Canada is an independent regulatory body working to protect and inform consumers of financial services.[24] It was established in 2001 by the federal government to strengthen oversight of consumer issues and expand consumer education in the financial sector. As a federal regulatory agency, the Financial Consumer Agency of Canada is responsible for the following:

—Ensuring that federally regulated financial institutions comply with federal consumer protection laws and regulations

—Monitoring financial institutions' compliance with voluntary codes of conduct and their own public commitments

—Informing consumers about their rights and responsibilities when dealing with financial institutions

—Providing timely and objective information and tools to help consumers to understand and shop around for a variety of financial products and services.

23. See www.treasury.gov.au/consumercredit/content/publications.asp.
24. See www.fcac-acfc.gc.ca/eng/about/default.asp.

The recently passed Dodd-Frank financial reform legislation in the United States imposes significant restrictions on mortgage product design that are not present in other countries.[25] The bill bans or restricts the use of prepayment penalties, balloon payments, interest-only payments, and other features commonly offered in other countries. The bill stipulates the characteristics of qualified mortgages, which is likely to result in a greater predominance of long-term fixed-rate mortgages.

What Can the United States Learn from Other Countries?

This brief survey has shown that mortgage finance systems differ significantly across countries in structure, funding, role of government, and performance. The United States is unique, however, in several respects. It has the highest level of government involvement, the greatest use of securitization, and a product mix dominated by the long-term fixed-rate mortgage. These attributes are related. The long-term fixed-rate mortgage has been the dominant instrument in the United States since the Great Depression. Its dominance reflects consumer preferences, the ease of prepayment, past restrictions on ARMs, and emergence of the secondary mortgage market. However, it results in the federal government absorbing most or all of the mortgage credit risk, allowing investors to focus on managing and pricing the prepayment risk.

Despite the high level of government support, the mortgage finance system in the United States has performed much worse than those in other countries during the crisis. Furthermore, it does not produce higher rates of homeownership or levels of mortgage indebtedness than many other countries. It is fair to ask whether this unique system is sustainable and whether the U.S. market would be more stable and effective in meeting the needs of borrowers and lenders with a different configuration.

Four interrelated factors should be considered in evaluating a housing finance system: the product, the underwriting, the funding, and the role of government. These characteristics are so intertwined that it is difficult to evaluate them in isolation. Thus we assess the merits of four different systems: the Danish principle of balance model, the European covered bond model, the Canadian and Japanese guarantee model, and the Australian and U.K. depository model. Each of these systems has strengths and weaknesses and relevance for the United States.

The Danish Model

Denmark is the only country in the world other than the United States in which the dominant product is the long-term fixed-rate mortgage that can be prepaid without penalty. Like the United States, most of Denmark's mortgage market is funded through the capital markets. The Danish system adds several important attributes that are relevant for the United States.

25. Lea (2010).

Figure 4-10. *Ratio of Price to Yield for Various Structures of Mortgage Risk Transfer*

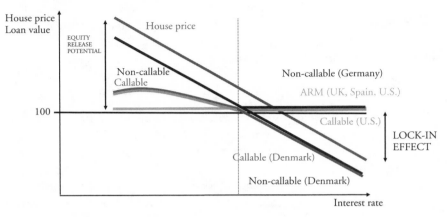

Source: Dübel (2005) as presented in Boyce (2010).

The Danish system is based on the principle of balance. When the borrower obtains a mortgage loan, the mortgage credit institution issues a bond into an existing bond series. Thus there is a one-to-one equivalence between the loan and the bond. The Danish mortgage can be canceled at the lower of the market price or par. Like borrowers in the United States, the borrower can refinance the loan at par if rates fall. But in the Danish system if rates rise, the borrower can buy the mortgage bond funding her loan at a discount and present it to the mortgage credit institution to repay the mortgage. This feature has several important benefits. It allows automatic deleveraging as rates rise and reduces the probability of negative equity. Figure 4-10 demonstrates the difference between different mortgages as rates change.

In the United States, most mortgage loans can be called at par. However, loans may not be redeemed at the market price when trading at a discount. This allows for equity release in the event of lower rates but subjects the borrower to a lock-in effect when rates rise. The Danish mortgage loan can be prepaid at par or redeemed by purchasing the bond at the market price, thus eliminating the lock-in effect. For example, if the borrower has an outstanding balance of $200,000 and rates rise, the value of the bond may fall to $180,000.[26] The borrower can go to the bond market (through the mortgage credit institution) and buy back the bond and cancel the loan. Thus the borrower saves $20,000 relative to the U.S. case.[27] Danish borrowers exercised this option in significant numbers in 2006 and

26. Svenstrup and Willeman (2006).
27. In most cases the borrower will finance the purchase with a new loan at a higher rate. If rates fall, the borrower can refinance at a lower rate, as in the United States.

2007 when interest rates were rising, which may have reduced the likelihood of negative equity when house prices fell in 2008 and 2009.

The underwriting of mortgages is more strict in Denmark than in the United States. The maximum ratio of loan to value is 80 percent, and the borrower's income is fully documented. Danish loans are recourse: in the event of a deficiency, the lender has recourse to the borrower's income and other assets. Danish borrowers have in the past been able to obtain loans over 80 percent LTV through a top-up loan system, whereby commercial banks provide unsecured loans for the amount over the mortgage.

Mortgage credit institutions in Denmark specialize in residential, commercial, and agricultural mortgage lending. The market is highly concentrated, with four institutions providing more than 80 percent of the market. There is no explicit government backing of the institutions or the bonds they issue. The mortgage credit institutions bear all of the credit risk of the mortgages they originate. However, they bear no interest rate risk due to their unique funding structure. They are required to maintain a minimum, risk-weighted capital-to-assets ratio of 8 percent. The combination of a low-risk structure and Danish Financial Services Agency and covered bond regulation results in low-risk institutions.[28]

Danish mortgages are funded through the issuance of covered bonds. Individual loans are funded by selling the loan into a larger bond series. The bond market is deep, liquid, and very efficient. The direct link established between the borrower and the bond market facilitates redemption of the bond in the future. The mortgage credit institution acts as a liability adviser, helping the borrower to obtain the lowest-cost financing. Incentives are aligned in this system in that the borrower and lender have "skin in the game" and the lender serves the needs of the borrower. Prepayments are less cyclical, as borrowers can exercise the option when rates rise or fall.

The Danish system has performed well throughout the crisis. Despite having a larger house price bubble (table 4-1), the Danish system has had far fewer defaults and foreclosures (see figure 4-11). This can be attributed to less negative equity, absence of subprime lending, borrower recourse, and strong regulation. The International Monetary Fund notes that the Danish banking system, including the mortgage credit institutions, has fared well despite a housing boom. They attribute this to conservative investments and sound regulation—in particular, tight standards of credit risk management and limited market risk.[29]

The Danish mortgage bond market has performed well. There has never been a mortgage bond default in its more than 200-year history, and the market remained open without government assistance during the liquidity crisis of October 2008. The strengths of the Danish system are incentive compatibility, efficient

28. Realkreditradet (2009).
29. IMF (2008b).

Figure 4-11. *Mortgage Delinquency and Foreclosures in Denmark and the United States, 1993–2009*

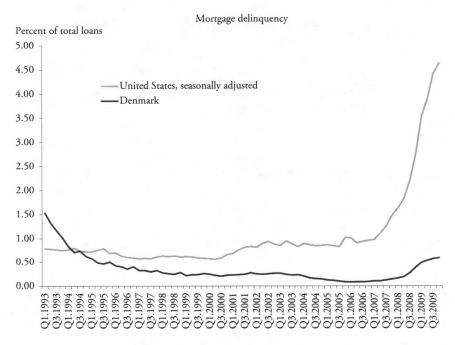

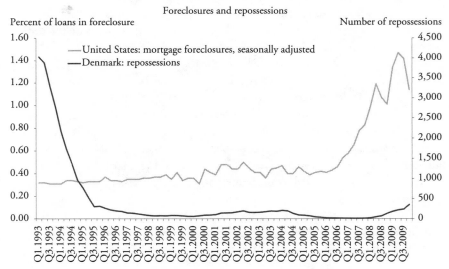

Sources: Danish Association of Mortgage Bankers; U.S. Mortgage Bankers Association.

risk allocation without government guarantees, and the potential for automatic deleveraging. The weaknesses are the need for scale to ensure efficient execution: multiple-lender issuers can create scale for smaller lenders.[30]

The European Covered Bond Model

Covered bonds in other European countries differ from those in the traditional Danish model. Mortgage covered bonds are full-recourse debt obligations of the issuing financial institution, secured by a pool of performing eligible mortgage assets (the cover pool) that remain on the balance sheet of the issuer.[31] Covered bonds are dual-recourse instruments. Investors have a priority claim on the cover pool assets in the event of an issuer default as well as a general claim on the assets of the institution. Thus the lender bears the credit risk of the mortgage. The main difference is the collateral. In the Danish model there is a one-to-one correspondence between the loan and the bond, whereas in the European model a dynamic portfolio of mortgage loans backs the bonds.

Underwriting requirements are strict in the covered bond model. The maximum LTV varies by country but does not exceed 80 percent. There are no legislative documentation requirements or debt service restrictions. As noted earlier, in most covered bond issuance countries, default rates have been low and mortgage loans are recourse obligations.

In the European covered bond model, borrowers bear potentially significant interest rate risk. Covered bonds can be backed by variable-rate mortgages (Spain, the United Kingdom) or rollover mortgages (Germany, the Netherlands, Sweden). European rollover mortgages have prepayment penalties during the fixed-rate period. For example, a common form of rollover mortgage has a twenty-five-to thirty-year amortization with a five-year fixed-rate period. During the fixed-rate period, there is a hefty penalty (typically yield maintenance) for substantial or total prepayment. Thus the borrower cannot release equity if rates fall and is locked in if rates rise (the German example in figure 4-10).

Most countries allow a partial prepayment (for example, 20 percent) without penalty. At the end of the fixed-rate period, the loan rate adjusts to the current market rate (negotiated with the lender). The borrower can manage the interest rate risk to a degree by adjusting the term of the new fixed-rate period (for example, switching from a five-year to a one-year period if rates are expected to fall).

Lenders are also exposed to portfolio interest rate risk in the European model, as outside Denmark there is not a one-to-one match. Covered bond legislation stipulates asset-liability matching requirements such as nominal balance, yield, or net present value matching. Most European covered bonds also require some over-

30. A weakness in non-U.S. models is the absence of forward-rate locks and a market for to-be-announced trades that allows efficient management of pipeline risk.

31. See European Covered Bond Council (2009) for a detailed explanation of general and country-specific frameworks.

collateralization. However, these requirements have not stopped lender failure due to asset-liability mismatch. Realkreditradet notes that the Irish, German, and Belgian governments had to step in and rescue covered bond issuers that suffered losses due to an interest rate mismatch between their mortgage loans and bonds.

By legislation, covered bond issuers must be regulated banks—commercial, savings, cooperative, or mortgage. There has been a decline in specialist mortgage banks, and in most countries covered bond issuers are lenders with a diversified mix of funding.

The European covered bond markets were stressed during the crisis. Issuance of jumbo covered bonds (minimum €1 billion) dropped to near zero in the aftermath of the Lehman bankruptcy. It was only restarted in the first quarter of 2009, after the European Central Bank announced a purchase program of up to €65 billion. One reason for the decline in issuance has been the widespread government guarantees of bank debt that have crowded out covered bonds in most countries during the crisis.[32] Unlike the U.S. Federal Reserve purchase program, which purchased more than the net new supply of agency mortgage-backed securities (MBSs) in 2009, the European Central Bank program has been limited, and private investors have returned to the market.

Secondary spreads widened dramatically during the crisis and are still well above recent historical averages (see figure 4-12). Investors differentiate among covered bond countries. Spreads are much wider in countries with weaker legislation and greater housing market turmoil (Ireland, Spain, the United Kingdom).

The strengths of the covered bond model are incentive alignment (for borrowers and lenders) and achievement of capital market access without government guarantees. The weakness is in the allocation of interest rate risk. Borrowers have substantial interest rate risk as they face unlimited interest rate change at rollover and are locked in during the fixed-rate term. The longest term is typically ten years, although there are fifteen-year fixed-rate periods in France and Germany. Lenders have suffered losses from interest rate risk, and legislative and regulatory asset-liability matching requirements have been tightened.

The Australian and U.K. Depository Model

The dominant Australian and U.K. mortgage lenders are large diversified banks that fund with deposits and MBS issuance. In recent years U.K. lenders have also used covered bonds. The dominant mortgage products in these countries are discretionary ARMs, typically with a one- to two-year initial discounted fixed-rate period. This product is ideal for depository lenders, allowing them to match assets and liabilities effectively. In the past discretionary ARMs performed in a manner

---

32. The RMBS market has been closed to new issuance, with new issues retained by lenders and repo'd with central banks. Secondary spreads have declined but remain historically high—much higher than on covered bonds.

Figure 4-12. *Covered Bond Spreads in Select Countries, 2008–10*

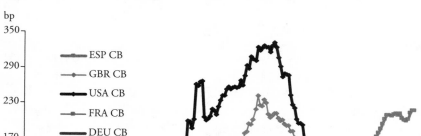

Source: BofA Merrill Lynch Global Research; our spread calculations are based on Reuters' prices. The spreads are generic spreads of 5-year Jumbos from the respective jurisdictions. Our calculation for Germany takes into account mortgage and public covered bonds.

similar to U.S. cost-of-funds–indexed loans, as lenders price mortgages at a margin over their average cost of funds. Basing interest rate changes on lenders' costs of funds does shield the borrower from some interest rate risk (relative to ARMs indexed to short-term government or money market rates), as the cost of funds is not as volatile as these rates. In recent years rate changes have followed central bank policy rate changes. Lenders in the United Kingdom have been moving to indexed or tracker ARMs, in part due to consumer complaints about the differential treatment of new versus existing borrowers. Both countries are notable in the absence of medium- to long-term fixed-rate mortgages.[33]

Although borrowers bear interest risk in this model, the use of ARMs has cushioned the downturn. Both the British Building Society Association and the Council of Mortgage Lenders attribute low rates of mortgage default to the exceptionally low mortgage interest rates. The question is how borrowers will respond to the inevitable tightening of credit and rise in interest rates. Australia has some experience, as it was the first major country to begin raising rates coming out of the crisis. House prices have been rising in Australia, and default rates remain low.

Mortgage loans predominately remain on the balance sheet of lenders in this model. Although there is no government guarantee or insurance in this model,

33. See Miles (2004).

pre-crisis securitization accounted for as much as 25 percent of mortgage debt outstanding. In Australia about one-third of mortgages have 100 percent default insurance from private mortgage insurers. Almost all Australian securitization transactions have credit enhancement (loan or pool) from a mortgage insurer. Private mortgage insurance is available, but not widely used in the United Kingdom, and credit enhancement comes primarily from structuring.

Underwriting of mortgages was more liberal in Australia and the United Kingdom than in continental Europe, but more strict than in the United States. Nonconforming loans in Australia were low-documentation or high LTV loans—very few true subprime loans were granted. The U.K. lenders provided loans to borrowers with adverse credit as well as low documentation and high ratios of loan to value. As noted earlier, default rates on nonconforming products were much higher than on bank-originated conforming loans.

The regulatory performance in these two countries has been mixed. The Australia Prudential Regulatory Authority and the Reserve Bank of Australia have been credited with cooling a house price boom in the mid-2000s. The U.K. FSA has been criticized for its oversight and resolution of mortgage lenders such as Northern Rock and Halifax Bank of Scotland.[34]

Both governments supported the market during the crisis with mortgage security purchase programs. In September 2008 the Australian government announced that it would invest A\$4 billion, which was then increased to A\$8 billion in October via its asset management arm—the Australian Office of Financial Management—to purchase AAA-rated RMBSs to shore up investor confidence in the sector and revive competition in the mortgage market.[35] The securitization market reopened in September 2009, and more than A\$6 billion in securities have been purchased by private investors since that time. The U.K. government has broadened the eligibility guidelines for central bank repurchases to include most AAA mortgage securities. Four RMBSs were issued in late 2009 and early 2010 with wider margins, significantly greater credit enhancement, and puts to the issuer.[36]

Although mortgage markets have performed better in Australia and the United Kingdom than in the United States during the crisis, it is unlikely that U.S. mortgage borrowers are going to accept adjustable-rate mortgages in high proportions. But the U.S. market may move in this direction as large banks have increasing market share. A strength of this model during the crisis was the reduction in borrower repayment burdens as interest rates fell, but a weakness is the risk of higher defaults when and if interest rates rise.

34. House of Commons (2008).
35. Bank of America Merrill Lynch (2009b).
36. Bank of America Merrill Lynch (2010).

The Canadian and Japanese Guarantee Model

The Canadian and Japanese mortgage markets have had less dislocation than the markets in most other developed countries. They have avoided the high rates of default, lender failures, and large house price declines evident in other countries. Commentators attribute this performance to more conservative lending practices, tighter regulation, and government guarantees.[37] Of course, Japan has never truly recovered from the property boom and bust of the late 1980s and has had anemic economic performance since.

The Canadian model mixes attributes of the European and U.S. models. The dominant instrument is the rollover mortgage, similar to that found in continental Europe. The maximum interest rate fixed period is five years, although a few ten-year fixed terms were offered prior to the crisis. As in Europe there are significant penalties for early repayment. Thus most interest rate risk is borne by borrowers. Japanese borrowers have somewhat greater ability to manage interest rate risk through the use of convertible and flexible-term mortgages.

Canadian borrowers have responded to falling and low short-term interest rates by switching to variable-rate mortgages. More than 45 percent of new mortgages taken out in the first three quarters of 2008 were variable rate, increasing the stock of such loans to 25 percent of the total.[38] The ability to switch between variable-rate and medium-term fixed-rate loans affords Canadian borrowers some ability to manage interest rate risk. The Canadian government did offer interest rate insurance from 1984 to 1997, but it had a very low take-up.

Lenders and the government hold credit risk in Canada. The government supports mortgage lending and funding through mortgage insurance and security guarantees, similar to the Federal Housing Authority and Ginnie Mae in the United States. Canada is unique in requiring mortgage insurance on all bank-originated mortgages with LTV greater than 80 percent. Approximately 50 percent of all bank-owned mortgages are insured, and almost all securitized loans are insured.[39] Requiring mortgage insurance has two benefits: it provides an outside review of lender practices and ensures risk capital in the origination process. CMHC guarantees have kept the MBS market functioning during the crisis. The CMHC has no quantitative affordable housing goals comparable to those of the government-sponsored entities (GSEs) in the United States. The Japan Housing Finance Agency retains credit risk on loans it purchases and securitizes (approximately 25 percent of the market).

Canadian lenders and insurers are relatively conservative in underwriting. Payment affordability criteria are similar to those in the U.S. prime market. A small

37. See Kiff (2009) for a Canadian discussion.
38. CMHC (2009).
39. There are private mortgage insurers in Canada. The government provides a 90 percent backstop on their liabilities.

Alt-A market is aimed at self-employed borrowers with difficulty documenting income. The maximum LTV is 95 percent, and all bank-owned loans with LTV greater than 80 percent are required to have mortgage insurance. Mortgages are recourse obligations. Kiff notes the differences in the relative treatment of prepayment in Canada and the United States.[40] Although Canadian lenders impose prepayment penalties, the origination (transaction) cost to the borrower is lower. His calculations suggest that the cost to refinance (penalty plus transaction cost) is comparable between the two countries. Prepayment penalties are not common in Japan, and borrowers frequently make partial prepayments.

The Canadian financial regulatory structure is widely credited with enhancing the stability of the system. The International Monetary Fund has commended the Canadians for their highly effective and nearly unified regulatory and supervisory framework.[41] Freeland notes that conservative mortgage market regulation, including the requirement that all loans over 80 percent LTV have mortgage insurance, has contributed to Canada's stable mortgage market.[42]

The government acted to support the MBS market during the crisis by committing to purchase C$125 billion of CMHC-guaranteed securities in October 2008. Issuance of CMHC-guaranteed MBSs and Canada bonds rose sharply in 2008 and 2009, reflecting the value of the guarantee and the Bank of Canada purchase program.

Conclusion

There is no ideal housing finance system. Arrangements in an individual country reflect the country's history, market structure, and government policy. However, the housing finance systems in almost all countries performed better during the crisis than the system in the United States. In examining the different systems, we can make several observations about what worked and whether it is applicable to the United States.

The Danish system offers the prospect of real improvement for the U.S. system. It retains the core long-term fixed-rate mortgage product but makes it more consumer and investor friendly by adding the option to repay the loan through the bond market if rates rise. This feature would have reduced some of the negative equity built up in the U.S. system during the crisis and the significant extension risk faced by mortgage security investors today. As discussed by Boyce, the Danish system could be implemented in the United States through the GSE cash purchase programs, which were significant during the 1980s before being largely phased out in favor of swaps and bulk purchases from individual lenders.

---

40. Kiff (2009).
41. IMF (2008a).
42. Freeland (2010).

The Danish model is also better at aligning incentives, as the credit risk remains on the balance sheet of the lender, with substantial capital requirements. In theory a Danish-style covered bond model could replace the GSE funding model. Although dropping government guarantees at the current time would be unwise and infeasible, as the crisis dissipates, the United States could move to a hybrid model in which Danish-style mortgage bonds have a backup government guarantee (for example, a Ginnie Mae wrap).[43] A model in which a private guarantor or issuer holds significant capital, combined with private mortgage insurance, would come close to achieving a similar allocation of credit risk as in the Danish system. Restricting the government role to guarantees without portfolio accumulation of mortgages would reduce the systemic risk of the U.S. housing finance system in line with the more targeted and stable Canadian system.

If the United States wants to reduce the role of government in the funding of mortgages, it could move toward a European-style covered bond model. Although less desirable than the Danish model from the perspective of interest rate risk allocation, it does align incentives and creates a liquid, simple, and low-risk security with which to fund housing. As noted, there is some flexibility for borrowers to manage interest rate risk, and insurance products could be offered to reduce the exposure of borrowers to interest rate risk even further. The rollover mortgage is a much simpler instrument than the U.S. ARM with the prospect for improved consumer disclosure and less short-term interest rate and payment volatility than a traditional U.S. ARM.

Recourse is an important feature of most developed-country housing finance systems that would reduce credit risk for lenders, investors, and the government. Research in Europe has found that the propensity to default in the face of an adverse income shock is closely related to the punishment incurred by doing so, which depends on the legal framework.[44] Recent U.S. research suggests that recourse decreases the probability of default when a borrower has negative home equity.[45]

Government policy supporting homeownership could be adjusted to focus less on mortgage debt and leverage. Many developed countries achieve similar or higher rates of homeownership than the United States without a mortgage interest deduction or government subsidies for mortgage debt (GSE support). The U.S. tax system has contributed to excessive borrower leverage and a high degree of negative equity. The First Time Homeownership Tax Credit Program of 2009 could be expanded to replace the mortgage interest deduction (which could be phased out over time through lowered maximum tax rates or deduction amounts, as was the case in the United Kingdom during the 1990s).

43. Jaffee (2010).
44. Duygan and Grant (2008).
45. Ghent and Kudlyak (2009).

The decline in underwriting standards inherent in subprime lending clearly was responsible for extending and accentuating the housing boom in the United States, worsening the housing bust, and creating the spark that triggered the financial crisis. No other country experienced a similar decline in standards. Several countries started down this road, but none created a market with as poor-quality loans as the United States. Several factors appear to be responsible. First no other country had a shadow banking system as significant as that of the United States. In all other countries there was greater regulatory oversight of mortgage lending, which may have slowed the move to lower standards. Having one financial regulator with responsibility for nonbank as well as bank lenders is an important attribute of regulation. Second, mortgage lending in most markets is dominated by large commercial banks. There is some evidence (for example, in Australia) that large lenders avoided the excesses of nonconforming lending due to concerns about reputation risk. Third, governments in other countries placed less policy emphasis on homeownership, an emphasis that many commentators suggested was responsible for part of the subprime problem in the United States. Finally, requiring lenders explicitly to consider borrower affordability, as is the case in many other countries, would have reduced the prevalence of stated-income loans and teaser ARMs.

Unlike most developed countries, the United States is still mired in a housing and mortgage crisis. Continued and expanded government support of the mortgage market is essential to its current survival. But when the recovery begins, U.S. policymakers should ask themselves whether it is desirable that most, if not all, of the U.S. mortgage market is guaranteed by the taxpayer, whether it is necessary that a majority of U.S. mortgages are securitized, and whether homeownership should receive as much emphasis and policy support as it did before the crisis. Examination of the finance of housing from other developed countries suggests that alternative arrangements with far less support from the government can achieve outcomes that are more robust than the arrangements in the United States.

References

Amherst Securities. 2009. "The Mortgage Market: Outlook and Opportunities." December.

Australian Treasury Department. 2008. "Financial Services and Credit Reform: Improving, Simplifying, and Standardising Financial Services and Credit Regulation." Green Paper. Canberra (June).

Bank of America Merrill Lynch. 2009a. "Australian RMBS Performance Update." London (October).

———. 2009b. "European Structured Finance Markets 2009–2010." London (November).

———. 2010. "The Securitisation Market: Open for Business." London (March).

Boyce, Alan. 2010. "The Danish Mortgage System Offers Some Practical Tools for the GSEs." Presentation to the Center for Study of Responsive Law, Washington, January.

CMHC (Canada Mortgage and Housing Corporation). 2009. *2009 Canadian Housing Observer.* Ottawa.

Dübel, A. 2005. "European Mortgage Markets—Conjectures on Macro Implications of Structural Idiosyncrasy." Presentation given at the DG ECFIN conference, Brussels, November 21.

Duygan, Burcu, and Charles Grant. 2008. "Household Debt Repayment Behavior: What Role Do Institutions Play?" Working Paper 08-3. Federal Reserve Board of Boston, Quantitative Analysis Unit (March).

Ellis, Lucy. 2008. "The Housing Meltdown: Why Did It Happen in the United States?" BIS Working Paper 259. Basel: Bank for International Settlements (September).

European Covered Bond Council. 2009. *Factbook 2009*. Brussels.

European Mortgage Federation. 2009a. *Hypostat*. Brussels.

————. 2009b. *Quarterly Review Second Quarter 2009*. Brussels.

Financial Services Authority. 2009. *Mortgage Market Review*. London (October).

Financial Times. 2010. "Next up for Europe: Covered Bond Catastrophe?" *Financial Times,* February 5.

Freeland, Chrystia. 2010. "What Toronto Can Teach New York and London." *Financial Times,* January 29.

Ghent, Andra, and Marianna Kudlyak. 2009. "Recourse and Residential Mortgage Default: Theory and Evidence from the United States." Working Paper 09-10. Richmond, Va.: Federal Reserve Bank of Richmond (July).

Global Property Guide. n.d. Manila. www.globalpropertyguide.com.

House of Commons. 2008. *Run on the Rock*. Fifth Report of Session 2007–08. London: Treasury Committee (January).

IMF (International Monetary Fund). 2008a. "Canada Financial Stability Assessment Update." Washington (February).

————. 2008b. "Denmark: 2008 Article IV Consultation; Update." Washington (December).

————. 2009. "The Changing Housing Cycle and Implications for Monetary Policy." In *World Economic Outlook,* ch. 3. Washington, October.

Jaffee, Dwight. 2010. "The Future Role of Fannie Mae and Freddie Mac in the U.S. Mortgage Market." Paper presented at the annual meeting of the American Economic Association and the American Real Estate and Urban Economics Association, Atlanta, Ga., January 3.

Joint Center for Housing Studies. 2009. *State of the Nation's Housing 2009*. Harvard University.

Kiff, John. 2009. "Canadian Residential Mortgage Markets: Boring but Effective." IMF Working Paper WP/09/130. Washington: International Monetary Fund (June).

Lea, Michael. 2009. "The Political Economy of Mortgage Insurance: The Australian Experience." Paper presented at the joint 2009 international conference of the Asian Real Estate Society and the American Real Estate and Urban Economics Association, Los Angeles, July.

————. 2010. "International Comparison of Mortgage Profit Offerings." Research Institute for Housing America, Washington, D.C., September.

Lunde, Jens, Kathleen Scanlon, and Christine Whitehead. 2009. "Mortgage Products and Government Policies to Help Troubled Mortgagors: Responses to the Credit Crisis." Paper presented at the international conference "Changing Housing Markets: Integration and Segmentation," European Network for Housing Research, Prague, June.

Miles, David. 2004. "The U.K. Mortgage Market: Taking a Longer View; Final Report and Recommendations." London: Her Majesty's Treasury (March).

Netherlands, Ministry of Housing, Spatial Planning, and the Environment. n.d. "Housing Funds." The Hague. www.vrom.nl/pagina.html?id=37432.

Realkreditradet. 2009. *The Traditional Danish Mortgage Model*. Copenhagen

Reserve Bank of Australia. 2009. *Financial Stability Review*. Canberra (September).

Standard and Poor's. 2009. *Japan's Residential Mortgage Loan Characteristics and Trends: RMBS Outlook for 2009*. New York (July).

Svenstrup, Mikkel, and Soren Willeman. 2006. "Reforming Housing Finance: Perspectives from Denmark." *Journal of Real Estate Research* 28, no. 2: 105–30.

Winkler, Sabine, and Alexander Batchvarov. 2009. *Global Covered Bond Markets 2009–2010*. Bank of America Merrill Lynch, November 2009.

5

The Home Mortgage Disclosure Act at Thirty-Five: Past History, Current Issues

ALLEN FISHBEIN AND REN ESSENE

This year marks the thirty-fifth anniversary of the Home Mortgage Disclosure Act (HMDA),[1] a law designed to discourage redlining in mortgage lending and to encourage reinvestment in the nation's cities by providing greater transparency and thus greater public scrutiny of lending activities. Enacted by Congress in 1975, HMDA requires most mortgage lenders to collect information about their home lending activities. Through public disclosure of mortgage data, HMDA implicitly sanctions a strong role for citizen monitors whose "regulation from below" is intended to augment enforcement efforts by the traditional regulatory agencies. A subject of controversy for much of its history, HMDA has now become an accepted part of the mortgage industry and regulatory landscape. Today there is general agreement that HMDA has helped to bring greater fairness and efficiency to the residential home loan market.

Much has changed since HMDA was enacted. In response, the act's purposes, requirements, and coverage were broadened significantly, although often not to the extent sought by its proponents. Additional data variables have allowed for more sophisticated statistical analyses of lender activities and thereby expanded HMDA's usefulness. The utility of the data is widely recognized, and the information is used for a range of purposes by community and fair lending advocates,

The views expressed in this chapter are those of the authors and do not necessarily reflect the views of the Federal Reserve Board of Governors or its staff.

1. 12 U.S.C. 2801, et seq., 89 Stat. 1125, P.L. 94-200 (1975).

economists, social scientists, the news media, government agencies, and financial institutions. Today, HMDA data are used by bank regulators and other agencies to monitor compliance with and enforcement of the Community Reinvestment Act (CRA) and the nation's antidiscrimination lending laws. Given HMDA's success, some seek to use it as a model for requiring HMDA-like disclosures for other types of credit and financial products. Others believe that, to stay relevant, HMDA will need further retooling to reflect twenty-first-century mortgage practices and address new data needs.

Proposals to expand HMDA also create questions about reconciling the law's multiple purposes. For example, HMDA serves its principal purpose by providing statistical measures of the flow of housing-related loans to neighborhoods and borrower groups. Yet most would acknowledge that the data set as presently constituted lacks key data elements that limit HMDA's utility to provide definitive proof of lending discrimination. In other words, HMDA performs more like a thermometer, providing "outcome" data, than a diagnostic tool that provides a full explanation of how those outcomes were determined. To enhance its usefulness as a tool for providing proof of lending discrimination, some believe that HMDA should include more reported variables, while others believe that it is unrealistic for HMDA to gather enough variables to definitively serve this purpose.

Tensions are increasingly evident as HMDA becomes a tool for more sophisticated research. HMDA was enacted and traditionally has served as a public-use database intended to be broadly accessible for both basic and more advanced research purposes. With the changing marketplace, the main research question has grown from "access to credit" to "access to fair credit." In response, some argue that new variables are needed to understand these changing marketplace dynamics. Several questions remain: Does the value derived from including additional data variables, thereby increasing the complexity of the data set, also result in a diminished audience for the data that are provided? Are there ways to broaden the public use, whatever information is provided?

HMDA's success as a regulatory reporting regime makes its history and evolution well worth examining. As HMDA heads into its fourth decade, this is a good time to reflect on the current issues and challenges that threaten HMDA's continuing relevancy and to investigate the possible changes to HMDA that are being advocated. While HMDA has to a great extent retained its vitality by remaining responsive to the changing economic, financial, and social environments, this paper attempts to answer the question, is HMDA still relevant, and can it remain so? The HMDA experiment to date may serve as a guide for consideration of future changes to the act and its regulations and as a model for other similar disclosure rules. This paper reviews the origins, history, and evolution of HMDA and considers the law's accomplishments and key policy questions likely to affect future changes to HMDA.

What Does HMDA Look Like Today?
Basic Reporting Requirements

Initially, HMDA pertained only to depository institutions: banks, savings institutions (savings and loans and savings banks), and credit unions. Disclosures were limited to summary totals covering originated and purchased home loans for each census tract and did not include borrower-based information, loan pricing information, or counts of applications for loans that were denied by lenders. The original legislation provided for user access to each reporting institution's loan data. It did not provide for a centralized compilation of each institution's data for the purpose of comparing different institutions' loan patterns. Instead, paper copies of HMDA reports for individual lenders were maintained for public access at a designated branch or other office within each metropolitan area where home loan credit was extended. Lenders were permitted to assess the public a reasonable charge for duplicating their HMDA report. Consequently, simply obtaining collected HMDA data was time-consuming, labor-intensive, and sometimes expensive.

To overcome this access burden, amendments to the statute made in 1980 required the Federal Financial Institution Examination Council (FFIEC), an interagency coordinating body, to compile aggregate HMDA data for every institution with a home office or branch in each metropolitan area. The FFIEC was also required for the first time to establish a nationwide system of public depositories (usually libraries) to house this information and to compile and make public aggregate reports for each individual institution in each metropolitan statistical area (MSA). The FFIEC was also required to produce tables for each MSA, aggregating the lending activity of institutions by census tract location and grouped according to location, age of housing stock, income level, and racial characteristics of the tract. These data were forwarded each year to designated, central data depositories in each MSA.

Subsequent amendments to HMDA and revisions to Regulation C, the Federal Reserve Board regulation that implements the provisions of HMDA, specified the schedule for reporting institutions to make their loan/application register (LAR) used for HMDA reporting available to the public (1993); specified the requirement for earlier public disclosure of HMDA data; required improvements to the accuracy of HMDA data; and, generally, required reporting institutions to report in machine-readable formats (1994).[2] Over the years, Congress has expanded the range of information that must be reported and disclosed and extended the reach of the law to cover a broader range of institutions. One of the more significant changes to HMDA was providing data on individual borrowers, greatly improving the data set. More recently, lending institutions have been

---

2. Federal Reserve Board's Regulation C (12 C.F.R. pt. 203)—Home Mortgage Disclosure, effective January 1, 1994. www.ffiec.gov/hmda/pdf/regulationc2004.pdf.

required to report certain price data on higher-priced loans.[3] The rules related to these pricing data were revised again in 2008 and implemented with applications taken on October 1, 2009.[4]

Combined, these changes have improved the ease of accessing HMDA data, especially for members of the public. The formatting changes enriched HMDA as an analytical tool, enhancing the ability of researchers to conduct nationwide research and to use the HMDA data set with other data sources. The application-by-application reporting has facilitated regulatory agency review of the accuracy of the reported data.

The depth of HMDA coverage today provides a broadly representative picture of home lending in the nation.[5] Current HMDA regulations apply to lending institutions of a certain asset size, including banks, savings associations, credit unions, and nondepository institutions, with offices in metropolitan areas.[6] Covering the largest loan originators, HMDA reporting is thought to capture a majority of the home loan market, usually about 80 percent of total loan volume in any given year (see table 5-1).[7] Since 2006, coverage is continuing to go down, whether as a result of the number of institutions meeting the reporting thresholds, changes in the geographic footprint of MSAs, or mergers, acquisitions, and bank failures.[8]

HMDA-reporting institutions are required to collect, report, and publicly disclose data about originations and purchases of home mortgage and home improvement loans on an annual basis. Table 5-2 lists the loan-level data that are reported, including the disposition of applications for home loans, the characteristics of loans that lenders originate or purchase during the calendar year, the census tract location of the properties related to those loans, and personal demographic

3. Avery, Brevoort, and Canner (2008).

4. Avery and others (2010a).

5. Avery and others (2010b).

6. HMDA originally covered banks, savings associations, credit unions, and their mortgage lending subsidiaries with offices in metropolitan areas in the preceding year. In 1989 HMDA was expanded to include nondepository independent mortgage companies, called independent mortgage banks (IMBs), with offices in metropolitan areas and more than $10 million in assets. For the 2008 and 2009 data, a depository must have had assets of more than $37 million. Avery and others (2010b) report that 55.7 percent of commercial banks filed 2009 HMDA data, representing 93 percent of the total mortgage dollars outstanding on commercial bank portfolios for that year. The respective percentages were 70.9 and 94.1 percent for savings institutions and 25.4 and 92.5 percent for credit unions. In 1992 the Federal Reserve Board adopted a standard that further expanded coverage to small IMBs, with an office in a metropolitan area, that meet either an asset-size test or a lending-activity test. In 2002 HMDA was expanded to include nondepository IMBs that meet criteria related to their dollar volume of mortgage lending, share of mortgage lending in their total lending, and their lending in MSAs. Avery and others (2010b) report that it remains difficult to know the scope of HMDA data coverage for IMBs because there is no comprehensive list of all IMBs.

7. Not all mortgage lenders have to provide HMDA data, such as small-asset institutions or lenders serving non-MSAs, as explained above. Not all loan types are covered by HMDA. For example, home equity lines of credit are not reported.

8. Avery and others (2010a, p. 4).

Table 5-1. *Distribution of Reporting Institutions Covered by the Home Mortgage Disclosure Act, by Type of Institution, 2006–08*

Type of institution	2006		2007		2008	
	Number	Percent	Number	Percent	Number	Percent
Depository institution						
Commercial bank	3,900	43.9	3,910	45.4	3,942	47.0
Savings institution	946	10.6	929	10.8	913	10.9
Credit union	2,036	22.9	2,019	23.4	2,026	24.2
Subtotal	6,882	77.4	6,858	79.7	6,881	82.0
Mortgage company						
Independent	1,328	14.9	1,124	13.1	968	11.5
Affiliated[a]	676	7.6	628	7.3	539	6.4
Subtotal	2,004	22.6	1,752	20.3	1,507	18.0
All institutions	8,886	100	8,610	100	8,388	100

Source: Avery and others (2010b, table 1). Except as noted, data are from the Federal Financial Institutions Examination Council or are reported under the Home Mortgage Disclosure Act (www.ffiec.gov/hmda). Components may not sum to totals because of rounding.

a. Subsidiary of a depository institution or an affiliate of a bank holding company.

and other information about the applicant, such as race or income level. These loan-level demographic data are helpful to federal financial institution regulators in examining compliance with fair lending laws and also for CRA evaluation.

The HMDA data are available to the public from individual lenders annually on March 31, when lenders report the information to the FFIEC, which is responsible for collecting HMDA data and facilitating public access to the information. On behalf of FFIEC, the Federal Reserve Board (hereafter, the Board), processes and edits the transaction-level data and also creates summary reports at the national and MSA level. The FFIEC, in turn, makes the raw data and summary reports available each September for the public to analyze for their own purposes.[9] Typically, Board economists write a *Federal Reserve Bulletin* article each year discussing market trends and providing an analysis of the previous year's data.

The HMDA statute provides the Board with some discretionary authority to carry out the purposes of the act, including requiring lenders to collect and report data as deemed necessary for supervisory purposes. Congress also has the option of amending HMDA, as it has in the past, to require additional data collection and reporting, expand coverage, specify how the data may be accessed, or in any other way Congress deems necessary.[10] In fact, the recently enacted Dodd-Frank Wall Street Reform and Consumer Protection Act shifts authority for HMDA to

9. Olson (2006).
10. GAO (2009).

Table 5-2. *The Federal Reserve Board's Regulation C Reporting Requirements for Home-Purchase Loans, Home-Improvement Loans, and Refinance Loans*

Reporting requirement	Details
For each application or loan	
Application date and the date an action was taken on the application	
Action taken on the application	Approved and originated, approved but not accepted by the applicant, denied (with the reasons for denial—voluntary for some lenders), withdrawn by the applicant, file closed for incompleteness
Preapproval program status (for home-purchase loans only)	Preapproval request denied by financial institution, preapproval request approved but not accepted by individual
Loan amount	
Loan type	Conventional, insured by the Federal Housing Administration, guaranteed by the Department of Veterans Affairs, backed by the Farm Service Agency or Rural Housing Service
Lien status	First lien, junior lien, unsecured
Loan purpose	Home purchase, refinance, home improvement
Type of purchaser (if the lender subsequently sold the loan during the year)	Fannie Mae; Ginnie Mae; Freddie Mac; Farmer Mac; private securitization; commercial bank, savings bank, or savings association; life insurance company, credit union, mortgage bank, or finance company; affiliate institution; other type of purchaser
For each applicant or co-applicant	
Race	
Ethnicity	
Sex	
Income relied on in credit decision	
For each property	
Location	By state, county, metropolitan statistical area, and census tract
Type of structure	One- to four-family dwelling, manufactured home, multifamily property (dwelling with five or more units)
Occupancy status	Owner occupied, non-owner occupied, or not applicable
For loans subject to price reporting	
Spread above comparable Treasury security	
For loans subject to the Home Ownership and Equity Protection Act (HOEPA)	
Indicator of whether loan is subject to the HOEPA	

Source: For the most up-to-date information on Regulation C, go to www.ffiec.gov/hmda/RegC.htm.

the newly created Consumer Financial Protection Bureau (hereafter the CFPB) beginning after July 21, 2011.[11]

The Conceptual Underpinnings of HMDA

It would be difficult to comprehend why HMDA looks and operates the way it does today without understanding some basic background about the law. The story of HMDA's origins and history is a fascinating one. The impetus for HMDA grew out of public concern in the 1970s about mortgage "redlining" and the effects of disinvestment on the nation's older urban neighborhoods. Many took the view that neighborhood decline encouraged urban flight and created extra barriers to the rehabilitation of deteriorating urban areas. Community leaders from these areas blamed the lack of credit availability on mainstream financial institutions— banks and savings and loans—the source of most mortgage originations at the time. The perception was that these financial institutions were deliberately disinvesting in certain geographic areas by accepting deposits from households within certain neighborhoods but failing to reinvest that money in the form of loans to those same areas, notwithstanding the presence of creditworthy borrowers and sound lending opportunities. The lack of credit availability was thus seen as contributing to the deteriorating condition of the nation's cities, particularly in lower-income and minority neighborhoods.

Discriminatory mortgage lending practices had deep historic roots in mortgage industry practices, including some that were directly attributable to the policies and practices of the federal government. The term "redlining" refers to the practice of systematically deeming certain neighborhoods as ineligible for credit due to demographic factors or age of the housing stock. Evidence of the practice appears to go back to at least 1935, when the Federal Home Loan Bank Board (FHLBB) asked the Home Owners' Loan Corporation to designate geographic areas considered to be the riskiest for lending, including many neighborhoods that were then predominately African American or populated with other people of color. Such areas were color-coded in red on area maps—hence the term "redlining." Private lenders reportedly used similar maps to determine credit availability and loan terms.[12]

With the deterioration of urban neighborhoods caused in part by historic redlining, community organizations from these neighborhoods were the principal supporters of HMDA's enactment. The leaders of these organizations hoped that the new, standardized reporting required by the federal mandate would provide statistical support to back up their complaints about the prevalence of lender

11. Dodd-Frank Wall Street Reform and Consumer Protection Act, P.L. 111-203, 111 Cong., 2 sess. (July 21, 2010), §113(a)(1).

12. Bernanke (2007).

redlining in their communities. Opposition to HMDA came chiefly from the mortgage industry, which argued that it was being singled out unfairly as the culprit for deteriorating neighborhood conditions. Mortgage lenders objected to what they anticipated would be the increased regulatory burden that HMDA would entail. Federal bank regulators also expressed reservations, warning that it would lead to unfair credit allocation and other undesirable ends.

The rationale for HMDA is therefore embedded in three main purposes. Congress specified two of these in the HMDA statute: to provide the public with information that will help to show whether or not financial institutions are serving the housing finance needs of their communities, and to help public officials to target public investments, and those from the private sector, to areas of need. A third purpose emerged as a result of the 1989 amendments to HMDA: to enhance the enforcement of laws prohibiting discrimination in lending by requiring the collection and disclosure of data about applicant and borrower characteristics.[13]

Bringing Mortgage Data into the Sunlight

The decision to use transparency and public disclosure as tools to improve private market conduct was not a new idea at the time of HMDA's enactment in 1975. The philosophical underpinnings for the use of public disclosure as a corrective to certain market practices can be traced back to at least the early part of the twentieth century. As expressed in the oft-quoted maxim of Justice Louis B. Brandeis, "Sunlight is . . . the best of disinfectants." Brandeis had recommended new transparency laws to require private sector companies to disclose their profits and losses in order to deter insider deals that deceived investors. His maxim also reflected the theory behind an even earlier law, the 1906 Pure Food and Drug Act, which required the listing of ingredients on food products, as an example of government-mandated "sunlight" to reduce public risks. For Brandeis, "sunlight" was intended to achieve more than just providing the public with better information about products or practices. It also served as an incentive to the disclosing party to discontinue its socially harmful behavior or risk public embarrassment and reputational harm.[14]

Fung and coauthors note that President Franklin D. Roosevelt would echo Brandeis's words two decades later, in urging Congress to establish new corporate financial disclosure rules in the wake of the stock market crash of 1929. The Securities Act of 1933 and the Securities Exchange Act of 1934 required publicly traded companies to disclose their assets and liabilities at regular intervals and in a standardized format. Corporate financial disclosure, as required by those laws, remains central to U.S. securities policy and still serves as a leading example of targeted transparency policy. Since then, targeted "sunlight" measures have been

13. McCoy (2007).
14. Fung, Graham, and Weil (2007).

used to require the disclosure of many types of information to the public, such as the presence of toxic pollutants released by manufacturers, the ingredients and nutrients contained in various food products, and the mortality rates for hospital patients undergoing specific medical procedures.

Transparency policies of this nature have common characteristics, even though the problems they seek to address may vary considerably. Each arises out of a desire by a public body to address a perceived market imperfection or failure that is contrary to the social good. Disclosure theorists find that the common characteristics for targeted transparency and disclosure laws include the following:[15]

—Mandated public disclosure by private companies

—Standardized, comparable, and disaggregated information regarding specific products or practices

—Furthering a defined public purpose

As a public disclosure law, HMDA was intended to provide "sunlight" on private sector mortgage lending practices as a deterrent to employing policies that resulted in the redlining of neighborhoods. HMDA seeks to achieve this objective by providing public, standardized disclosures in the form of mortgage loan data made available to users on a disaggregated loan-level basis. The disclosed data can then be tailored to serve a variety of research needs and purposes.

HMDA thus fits squarely into the tradition of using targeted transparency policies to address perceived market gaps and failures that lawmakers determine are operating in a manner contrary to the broader social good. In many respects, the political environment in favor of transparency and public "right to know" laws was never greater than it was during the time of HMDA's enactment. During the decade of the 1970s, Congress enacted the Truth in Lending Act (TILA) requiring consumer disclosures regarding the cost of loans.[16] Federal lawmakers also strengthened the Freedom of Information Act, with its presumption of openness in government, during this period. Nevertheless, the decision by Congress in 1975 to use public disclosure as a means to address perceived discrimination in mortgage lending was controversial and hotly debated.

"Regulation from Below" to Fill the Gap

The lawmakers' willingness to experiment with public disclosure and "regulation from below," as embodied in HMDA, evidenced their displeasure with the slowness of the regulatory response to redlining.[17] According to the report accompanying the 1975 House bill, the lack of data reporting created a "compelling necessity"

---

15. Fung, Graham, and Weil (2007).

16. The TILA prescribes uniform methods for computing the cost of credit, for disclosing credit terms, and for resolving errors on certain types of credit accounts. See www.federalreserve.gov/bankinforeg/reglisting.htm.

17. McCluskey (1981).

for action on HMDA, since the FHLBB, which at the time supervised the savings and loan industry, was unwilling to require such disclosures by regulation.[18]

Subcommittee on Financial Institutions Supervision, Regulation, and Insurance, Chairman Fernand J. St. Germain: All they want to know is what institutions have a commitment to the neighborhoods from whence they are getting their deposits. Are they making a fair reinvestment in these neighborhoods? Now, doesn't the [FHLBB] have the necessary authority to require this information?

FHLBB Chairman Thomas R. Bomar: Mr. Chairman, our attorneys tell me that *we do have the authority to require it.* We have not required it. [emphasis added][19]

Indeed, federal regulators' resistance to data collection for fair monitoring purposes continued even after HMDA's enactment. Finally, in 1976 the National Urban League and other national civil rights organizations brought suit against the regulators for the alleged failure to adopt fair lending regulations.[20] Settlement agreements with three agencies were reached in 1977 (the suit against the Federal Reserve was dismissed due to lack of standing by the plaintiffs) and resulted in an agreement to establish internal data collection and analysis that provided more detailed information than was available at the time through HMDA. After HMDA was expanded in 1989 to include data on individual loan applicants, the agencies' fair lending databases were phased out.[21]

Even more so than CRA, mortgage lending disclosure is firmly rooted in the grassroots activism that was occurring at the time of HMDA's passage. This view is reflected in the House report on the original HMDA legislation:[22]

The withdrawal of private investment capital for home mortgage loans and rehabilitation loans from an increasing number of geographic areas, principally within the nation's major metropolitan centers, exacerbates the problem of providing public sector investments to stabilize and rehabilitate essentially older neighborhoods within our cities, and adds to the frustration of millions of Americans denied access to credit at reasonable rates of interest for the sale, improvement, and rehabilitation of residential housing.

The process had led to the introduction of the word "redlining," which increasingly has served to polarize elements of our society in a manner where the dialogue has become entirely destructive, rather than constructive. As

---

18. Kolar and Jerison (2005).
19. H.R. no. 94-561, at 2302, 2312.
20. *National Urban League et al.* v. *Office of the Comptroller of the Currency, et al.* 1977.
21. Goering and Wienk (1996).
22. H.R. no. 94-561, at 4.

polarization intensifies, neighborhood decline accelerates. The purpose of this title is, by providing facts, [to] bring to an end to more than a decade of "redlining" charges and countercharges.

In fact, community organizing against redlining and bank disinvestment had begun well before HMDA's enactment. Activist neighborhood groups, such as those led by the Chicago community leader Gale Cincotta, sometimes used confrontational tactics. At other times, they employed more collaborative approaches to get the attention of lenders and bank regulators. These groups had long sought to document their allegations of redlining by using information sources available prior to HMDA.[23] They engaged in laborious searches of public records to demonstrate the lack of mainstream financial institution lending. The information contained in property records varied from county to county, was difficult to replicate, and had other limitations. These deficiencies left the results of such research open to criticism.

HMDA's Final Passage

The anti-redlining movement found a champion in Senator William Proxmire (D-Wisc.), who ascended to chairmanship of the Senate Banking Committee in 1975. In the same year, Chairman Proxmire introduced a bill calling for public disclosure of loan data collection. Yet HMDA proved controversial, and opposition to its passage was considerable. The lending industry, along with federal regulators, staunchly opposed its adoption. Congressional critics charged that HMDA would inevitably distort the mortgage market and create unnecessary regulatory burdens and compliance costs for lenders.[24]

By successfully portraying HMDA as in the tradition of other popular consumer right-to-know laws, Senator Proxmire and his counterpart in the House of Representatives, Fernand St. Germain (D-R.I.), chair of the Subcommittee on Financial Institutions Regulation, obtained the necessary political support to prevail over the opposition. After legislative compromises to attract the necessary votes scaled back some of the bill's provisions, Congress ultimately approved HMDA, but only with the inclusion of a five-year "sunset" provision and by a narrow margin in both the Senate (47 to 45) and the House (177 to 147).[25]

HMDA remained highly controversial and politicized even after its enactment. Opponents sought to terminate the act or otherwise narrow its data collection requirements as the sunset period neared. The act was extended near its termination date, but only through a series of temporary extensions. At one point, it even

---

23. Immergluck (2004).
24. Fishbein (1993).
25. 121 *Congressional Record* 34, 581 (1975); 121 *Congressional Record* 27, 3623 (1975).

lapsed for a brief interval. However, HMDA was eventually reauthorized in 1980 after a series of very close votes and only for another five years. The act would eventually become permanent in 1987, twelve years after its original enactment.

Some proponents were disappointed that the HMDA legislation that passed Congress in 1975 was significantly more limited in scope than originally sought. Community organizations supporting the legislation had hoped to include reporting on small business credit in addition to mortgage loans. Original drafts of the bill had also included reporting on consumer deposit account data. The bill as introduced had included nondepository mortgage lenders as well as depository institutions, reporting for both urban and rural areas, and disclosures indicating the race and income of loan applicants.[26] All of these proposed inclusions were dropped prior to final passage. Some of them, such as the characteristics of individual applicants and the expansion to include reporting of loans made by independent mortgage lenders, would be added to HMDA in later years. Other provisions, such as the inclusion of rural loans by rural lenders, have never been added.[27]

HMDA's Public Disclosures Are Enhanced by Other Laws

HMDA is designed to promote its purposes through public disclosure instead of through the establishment of substantive mandates or prohibitions. As mentioned, HMDA was adopted in 1975 to "provide citizens and public officials of the United States with sufficient information to enable them to determine whether depository institutions are fulfilling their obligation to serve the housing needs of the communities in which they are located."[28] The law acknowledges that financial institutions had sometimes contributed to the decline of older urban and racially diverse neighborhoods by failing to provide adequate home financing to qualified applicants on reasonable terms and conditions.

HMDA does not set forth lending standards or establish any lender responsibilities, other than reporting. In contrast, the 1977 Community Reinvestment Act established an affirmative obligation on the part of certain banks and thrifts to help meet the credit needs of the communities in which they operate and linked community reinvestment records to the approval of mergers and other expansion applications. Unlike some fair lending laws, such as the Equal Credit

26. Immergluck (2004).

27. HMDA does pick up nonmetropolitan lending by lenders that have offices in MSAs. Those lenders with both rural and metropolitan offices would be included, while nonmetropolitan lending by lenders who have offices solely in nonmetropolitan areas would not. Because the HMDA statute itself focuses on metropolitan areas, some have argued that a congressional change to the statute may be needed to cover all rural lending.

28. One of the stated purposes of HMDA, section 302 of Title III of the Act of December 31, 1975 (P.L. 94–200; 89 Stat. 1125), effective June 28, 1976. www.fdic.gov/regulations/laws/rules/6500-3030.html#6500hmda1975.

Opportunity Act (ECOA) and the Fair Housing Act,[29] HMDA does not authorize private lawsuits based on HMDA violations or otherwise prohibit or restrict any lending practices.[30] Yet the existence of companion laws, like CRA and ECOA, has had synergistic effects with HMDA. Since HMDA does not provide a necessary context for understanding a lender's restraints on extending credit, mortgage lenders might face undue pressure if appropriate standards for lending are not established through other statutes or policy means.[31]

Even more so than CRA, mortgage lending disclosure is firmly rooted in the grassroots activism that was occurring at the time of HMDA's passage. HMDA was one of several laws passed during the 1970s intended to reduce credit-related discrimination, expand access to credit, and shed light on lending patterns. Enacted two years after HMDA in 1977, the CRA set forth the standard that commercial banks and savings and loan associations, as insured depository institutions chartered to serve the convenience and needs of the local communities in which they operate, also have affirmative obligations to serve local credit needs and otherwise encourage lending to previously neglected lower-income communities.[32] Congress also amended ECOA in 1976 to prohibit discrimination based on race, national origin, and other criteria. Passage of HMDA and CRA with their emphasis on citizen action also reflected a congressional disenchantment at the time. The prevailing congressional view was that the traditional regulatory apparatus was insufficiently engaged in efforts to deter redlining, and consequently more vigorous action was needed through elevation of the role of citizen monitors— "regulation from below."[33]

Notwithstanding congressional support for legislation to curb redlining, the detailed reporting required by HMDA for home loans—even in HMDA's initial form—are typically not required for other types of consumer financial loan products. Public reporting of important mortgage loan data seems to have

29. ECOA prohibits creditors from discriminating against credit applicants on the basis of race, color, religion, national origin, sex, marital status, age, and use of public assistance or for exercising their rights under the Consumer Credit Protection Act, www.usdoj.gov/crt/housing/housing_ecoa. php. The Fair Housing Act (Title VIII of the Civil Rights Act of 1968), as amended, prohibits discrimination in the sale, rental, and financing of dwellings and in other housing-related transactions, based on race, color, national origin, religion, sex, familial status, and disability; www.hud.gov/ offices/fheo/FHLaws.

30. Olson (2006).

31. Barr (2005, p. 632).

32. The CRA was enacted by Congress in 1977—12 U.S.C. 2901(b)—and is implemented by Regulation 12, *Code of Federal Regulations,* parts 25, 228, 345, and 563e; www.federalreserve. gov/bankinforeg/reglisting.htm. The CRA sought to encourage depository institutions to invest in community development ventures and lending to small businesses and low- and moderate-income people and neighborhoods in areas where the institution maintained banking operations, consistent with safety and soundness principles.

33. Fishbein (1993).

reflected the judgment that access to home loans was vital, not just for individual loan seekers, but also for the health and well-being of the broader community.

Continued Improvements to HMDA: HMDA's History and Evolution

HMDA's history and evolution can be grouped into three major periods: the period between HMDA's enactment until the 1989 Financial Institutions Reform, Recovery, and Enforcement Act (FIRREA) amendments; the post-FIRREA amendments period up to 2001 during which HMDA was expanded; and the period that began in 2002 with the adoption of the Board's changes to HMDA that required the reporting of loan pricing data for some mortgage originations. Changes in mortgage lending and market structure, as well as emerging concerns about new aspects of market conduct, prompted HMDA's continued evolution in the years since its enactment.

Classic HMDA Period: Events Leading to the 1989 HMDA Expansion

The new data that became available after HMDA's passage in 1975 were intended to be used to help document patterns of redlining and disinvestment in the nation's cities. Indeed, the availability of the early HMDA data precipitated a torrent of redlining research during much of the 1980s, mostly conducted by local community groups and academic researchers assisting these organizations.[34] Typically, HMDA data were analyzed to show the geographic distribution of mortgage extensions during a given period. These loan data were matched with census tract demographic and economic information from the U.S. decennial census to analyze differences in lending activity by census tract characteristics.

These studies almost always found that substantially fewer mortgage loans were originated in census tracts with a high proportion of minorities and lower-income households. This empirical research, in general, was not viewed by federal banking agencies as conclusive evidence of redlining.[35] The available HMDA data at that time could not (and were not intended to) provide absolute evidence of discrimination against individual applicants. What these studies helped to reveal, however, was what community leaders had long alleged: mortgage credit was not flowing into many older urban neighborhoods in the nation's cities.[36]

With the passage of CRA in 1977, HMDA was often the primary statistical tool used by community groups and others challenging bank merger and branch expansion requests pending before federal regulators. CRA authorizes regulators to sanction financial institutions with weak community reinvestment records by

34. Goldstein (2008).
35. Canner (1982).
36. Goldstein (2008).

denying these requests, although relatively few have been denied over the years. While HMDA is unlikely to be the sole basis for denying applications, the data have helped bank supervisors to establish general community reinvestment standards for these institutions. These HMDA-enriched studies were also used by local groups as the basis for discussions with lenders about local community needs and to provide an objective data source for monitoring lending commitments resulting from these CRA challenges.

The quality of HMDA research during this early period was enhanced greatly after the emergence of computerized loan data in the late 1980s. Computerized HMDA data opened the door to more sophisticated analyses of mortgage lending patterns. Using statistical techniques such as cross-tabulation and regression analysis, researchers could better measure the influence of neighborhood demographic factors and income characteristics on lending patterns. Despite the increasingly sophisticated methods used by researchers, the early HMDA redlining research was often criticized for failing to take into account the demand for credit and the fact that not all lenders were part of the data set. The absence of data variables associated with lender underwriting was also cited as a limitation to research that relied only on HMDA data.[37]

A breakthrough in the methodological impasse regarding HMDA's application beyond just redlining occurred in 1988 with publication of the *Atlanta Journal-Constitution*'s remarkably influential investigative series entitled "The Color of Money," written by Bill Dedman.[38] This Pulitzer Prize–winning series almost single-handedly shifted the public discussion beyond redlining to concerns about discrimination against individual loan applicants, thereby setting the stage for the important changes made to HMDA the following year. Using a variety of quantitative and qualitative sources, the *Atlanta Journal-Constitution* uncovered evidence indicating the existence of racial disparities in home mortgage lending in the Atlanta area. As part of the research, the newspaper compared mortgage lending activity for comparable white and minority census tracts (for example, similar income levels). This comparison revealed that mortgage lending in predominately white middle-income census tracts occurred at a rate five times higher than in comparable black middle-income neighborhoods.

At about the same time as the *Atlanta Journal-Constitution* series, the *Detroit Free Press* published its own series on mortgage lending in the Detroit area. Comparing minority and nonminority census tracts in Detroit, the *Detroit Free Press* found that mortgage lending in white tracts occurred at three times the rate in similarly situated African American neighborhoods.

The results of a third major study conducted by the Federal Reserve Bank of Boston were released in January 1989. The widely publicized Boston Fed study

37. Canner (1982).
38. Dedman (1988).

documented differences in lending patterns across neighborhoods grouped by racial composition. Portions of the study were first obtained by a local newspaper, and the results of the full study eventually were published. The study's authors concluded the following:[39]

> Lower mortgage originations in black neighborhoods cannot be explained away by lower levels of income and wealth, lower rates of housing development, or other neighborhood differences. Even after taking these factors into account, one still finds a substantial discrepancy between mortgage originations relative to the housing stock in white and black neighborhoods.

The collective impact of this research sparked new controversies as to whether or not lenders were discriminating against prospective home loan borrowers based on their race and income, creating doubts about the fairness of home loan decisionmaking. HMDA, at the time, did not collect or report information that could be used to analyze comparative treatment of individual loan applicants by race, income, or other factors. HMDA proponents believed that this new research provided the "smoking gun" needed to make the case for further changes to HMDA and the need for enhanced emphasis on fair lending enforcement.

The value of data on the race of the individual loan applicant was highlighted further through a follow-up study by the *Atlanta Journal-Constitution,* published in January 1989, a year after its original series.[40] This second study relied on more detailed mortgage information obtained as a result of a Freedom of Information Act request to the FHLBB. The information obtained by the newspaper came from the federal regulator's fair lending data collection system and was not ordinarily available to the public. Such data included information on loan rejection rates by thrift institutions sorted by borrower characteristics. The analysis revealed that African American mortgage applicants, on average, were rejected twice as frequently as white applicants, with disparities in some cities as high as ten to one.[41]

In its original form, HMDA provided, at the individual lender level, the number and dollar amount of loans by census tract or county (in the case of small-population counties located in metropolitan areas). These data were designed for the sole purpose of permitting the public and regulators to determine the geographic areas in which an institution was making—and not making—residential mortgage loans.[42] Publication of the 1989 *Atlanta Journal-Constitution* study helped to convince HMDA proponents in Congress that the time was right to seek legislative changes to HMDA requiring additional loan reporting requirements for lenders.

---

39. Bradbury, Case, and Dunham (1989, p. 31).
40. Dedman (1989).
41. Dedman (1989).
42. Gramlich (2002).

Savings and Loan Crisis Contributes to HMDA Expansion

Joseph Kennedy (D-Mass.) and House Banking Committee Chairman Henry Gonzalez (D-Tex.) co-sponsored expanded HMDA reporting requirements in an amendment to the House Financial Institutions Reform, Recovery, and Enforcement Act of 1989, legislation aimed at addressing the savings and loan crisis.[43] Although the measure was defeated initially in committee, the amendment ultimately passed the House by a narrow vote. This amendment to HMDA required mortgage lenders to include information on the race and income of mortgage loan applicants as part of their disclosure reports. While the Senate version of the bill did not contain a provision comparable to the Kennedy-Gonzalez amendment, the House provision was adopted by Senate conferees with only slight modification. The additional information required by the Kennedy-Gonzalez FIRREA amendment helped to transform HMDA into a significantly more useful tool for detecting discriminatory lending patterns.[44]

The passage of FIRREA, and the resulting amendments to the HMDA statute, required reporting on a transaction-level basis, fundamentally altering how HMDA data were structured. These amendments authorized reporting changes to permit loan-level analysis revealing denial rates and information on the race, ethnicity, income, and gender of mortgage applicants, leading to the period of HMDA expansion from 1989 to 2001.

Post-FIRREA HMDA Expansion

The new data variables and the application-by-application disclosure format provided by the FIRREA amendments allowed new and more sophisticated HMDA research, which was supplemented with other data sources and prompted new concerns about disparities in denial rates for minority loan seekers. This new research drew public attention to the questions of lending discrimination and the basic fairness of loan decisionmaking.

In late 1991, Federal Reserve Board economists analyzed the first year of data with information on applications, disposition, borrower income, race, and ethnicity and published an extensive analysis of the expanded HMDA data set mandated by the 1989 FIRREA amendment. The data showed that minorities were rejected two to three times more frequently than nonminorities of similar income levels.[45] Public disclosure of the expanded HMDA data triggered a spate of newspaper reports analyzing individual lending institutions. Federal Reserve Governor John LaWare characterized the disparities in rejection rates as "worrisome," but

---

43. Financial Institutions Reform, Recovery and Enforcement Act of 1989, H.R. 1278, 103 Stat. 183, P.L. 101-73 (1989).

44. Fishbein (1993); Brown (1991).

45. Immergluck (2004).

emphasized that the data were not dispositive proof of discrimination and cautioned against false conclusions.[46]

The mortgage industry also was critical of attempts to conclude that disparities revealed by the new data demonstrated illegal discrimination. The American Bankers Association commissioned a white paper to elaborate on the limitations of HMDA data and to develop a critique of HMDA as a tool for detecting lending discrimination.[47] Notwithstanding these criticisms, the release of the new data renewed the public debate over the existence of lending discrimination. Numerous studies followed, and the large differences in denial rates drew considerable media attention. Attention to race-based differences in denial rates was arguably an important factor in the increased focus on expanding lending and increasing the rates of homeownership for minorities in the early 1990s. Furthermore, federal regulators and other enforcement agencies announced that they were using the new HMDA data to augment their fair lending monitoring and enforcement procedures and issued an "Interagency Policy Statement on Fair Mortgage Lending Standards" in 1992.[48]

Concerns about large disparities between minority and white borrowers with similar incomes, as demonstrated by the data, prompted the Federal Reserve Bank of Boston to undertake yet another study in 1992. The Boston study was one of the first to focus on pricing variables, instead of just denials, to better understand the level of fair lending compliance. This study represented the first major attempt to supplement new HMDA data with a variety of traditional underwriting variables (absent from all other studies) in order to determine whether or not critics were correct in asserting that racial differentials in denial rates represented possible lending discrimination or could, instead, be the result of legitimate underwriting considerations regarding the riskiness of the loan. The authors of the study reported that, even controlling for relevant financial risk factors, African Americans were rejected for loans 56 percent more frequently than whites.[49]

The challenge with these findings is that many economists will argue that this finding is a "smoldering gun" and that it is impossible to add enough criteria to make a definitive statement about discrimination. Other researchers point to the fact that, even after controlling for a relatively detailed list of variables, African Americans still appear to be more likely than whites to receive higher-priced loans.[50] Still others, including some legal scholars, argue that the "smoldering gun" points to areas that may need more targeted examination and is therefore critical

46. LaWare (1991).
47. Galster (1991).
48. See www.federalreserve.gov/bankinforeg/interagencystatement.htm.
49. Munnell and others (1992).
50. Apgar, Bendimerad, and Essene (2007).

to the success of companion laws such as ECOA and CRA. This debate may never be entirely resolved.

Another key finding of the Boston Federal Reserve study provided new insight into how bias can enter into loan decisionmaking. The study found that the majority of loan applicants—both white and minority—had some flaw in their credit credentials and that in many cases these flaws were overlooked. Yet as the authors found, whites seemed to enjoy a general presumption of credit-worthiness not extended to blacks and Hispanics, with lenders more willing to overlook the flaws of white than of minority applicants.[51] The results of the study and the methodology employed were the subject of considerable research itself. Despite criticism, the study's main findings generally confirmed the observed racial disparity.[52]

With hindsight we know now that publication of the expanded HMDA data, revealing disparities in denial rates between minority and nonminority loan applicants, was as shocking to many in the mortgage lending industry as it was to those outside the industry. Industry representatives continued to maintain that the disparities found could not be said to indicate the presence or absence of discrimination because key underwriting variables were not part of the HMDA data set. However, the disparities prompted considerable introspection by the mortgage industry and led many to review their underwriting criteria and loan processes and to improve their employee fair lending training programs.

The public disclosure of the expanded HMDA data in 1991 also triggered greater emphasis on government enforcement of the Fair Housing Act and ECOA. For example, in 1992, the Justice Department filed suit against the Decatur Federal Savings and Loan Association,[53] the first case ever filed accusing a depository institution of engaging in a pattern and practice of mortgage lending discrimination under the department's twenty-four-year-old authority to bring these actions. The Justice Department filed twelve other pattern and practice cases against mortgage lenders over the next five years. During this period, the Justice Department also brought suits against lenders for price discrimination, charging that minority borrowers were frequently charged higher rates than white borrowers with similar credit profiles.

The federal banking regulatory agencies also made fundamental changes to their fair lending examination procedures, adopting an approach more in line with the findings from the Boston Fed study. Until 1992, the banking regulatory agencies examined loan files of individual minority applicants to determine if the denials were based on legitimate underwriting or credit-based reasons. The new

---

51. Munnell and others (1992); Goldstein (2008); Brown (1991).

52. Goering and Wienk (1996); Carr and Megbolugbe (1993).

53. *United States of America* v. *Decatur Federal Savings and Loan Association,* 1-92 CV2198 (N.D. Ga., September 17, 1992).

procedures compared the application files of minorities and whites to see if they were treated comparably.[54]

Concerns about Disparities in Subprime Lending and 2002 Changes to HMDA

With the exception that HMDA coverage was extended to IMBs in 1992, HMDA reporting requirements remained largely unchanged in the decade following the 1989 FIRREA amendments. Yet the slew of new studies also raised new concerns: Did mortgage credit always reflect the lender's risk or cost? Was it being tied in any way to the race, ethnicity, or gender of the borrower? Was it otherwise connected to predatory lending practices that some at the time contended were prevalent in subprime lending?

Beginning in 2002, this period was focused on the substantial changes in the marketplace and concern over the concentrations of subprime lending to minorities and lower-income households and communities. Analyses of mortgage pricing based on HMDA data were not possible during this period, due to the absence of reported variables on loan pricing. Nevertheless, many studies during this period examined whether certain borrower groups were disproportionately served by subprime lenders.[55] The resulting revisions to the HMDA rules in 2002, discussed later, were aimed at permitting enhanced monitoring of pricing variations for subprime loans.

Significant changes in mortgage lending facilitated by automated underwriting, deregulation, and other financial innovations facilitated the rapid growth of the subprime mortgage market. Views differed during this period as to whether or not the growth of the subprime market represented a healthy development for borrowers. Subprime lenders and many analysts argued that the expanded access to mortgage credit as a result of subprime loans was a boon for minorities, lower-income, and other historically underrepresented households with traditionally limited access to prime mortgages. However, expansion of subprime credit also led to an increasingly complex market. Throughout the period of subprime growth, there were frequent warnings by consumer and community advocates, in particular, that abusive and predatory practices were stripping borrower equity and leading to unusually high default rates.

Subprime mortgages were, in general, priced significantly above the rates charged for prime loan products, regardless of whether or not the borrowers possessed prime-level credit scores. This prompted concerns that borrowers were being steered to more expensive products and were not necessarily obtaining the best-priced loans for their needs. Concerns were also expressed that price variations in the subprime market reflected discrimination against borrowers by race, ethnicity, income, and gender and were not a result of legitimate risk-based

54. Marsico (1999).
55. Fishbein and Bunce (2000).

pricing factors. The fact that subprime loans appeared to be disproportionately concentrated in communities of color and made to African American and Latino borrowers also provided indication of concerns with regard to fair lending.[56]

Recognizing the need for a better understanding of the pricing of subprime loans and for greater oversight in this area, in 2002 the Board adopted new HMDA rules that added information on the pricing of certain mortgage loans. Lenders for the first time were required to report on the spread to the comparable-maturity Treasury for first-lien mortgages with an annual percentage rate (APR) 3 percentage points over the Treasury benchmark and for junior liens with an APR 5 percentage points over the benchmark. Mortgages with a reported spread were called "higher-priced loans" and were generally intended to be a proxy for subprime.[57] The relative nature of this measure was thought to enable comparisons over time, regardless of changes in the level of interest rates.

Before the APR rate spread data were added to HMDA, researchers commonly labeled a loan in the HMDA data as subprime if it was originated by a lender on the list of subprime and manufactured home lenders maintained by the Department of Housing and Urban Development (HUD). The list identifies lenders that specialize in subprime or manufactured home lending and was designed to be used as a companion to the HMDA data.[58] The list, named after the HUD employee who developed it, was used as a proxy for subprime in many of the HMDA studies developed during the decade of 1990s. Yet the Scheessele list was thought to underestimate the size of the subprime market, since only those lenders "specializing" in subprime were listed.[59]

The first analysis of the 2004 pricing data revealed pricing disparities between minority and nonminority borrowers for higher-priced loans.[60] This research found significant gaps between borrower groups even after the data were adjusted to reflect differences in income, loan size, and property location. Board staff authoring this research cautioned that there could be other possible explanations for the racial and ethnic disparities revealed in the pricing of mortgages. It was suggested again that credit risk of the borrowers, loan-to-value ratios, and a variety of other cost factors can all contribute to price variation for borrowers and that these variables are not part of the HMDA data set. To examine the additional risk factors that could explain these disparities, the authors referenced other research that attempted to control for several important risk factors, such as credit scores and loan-to-value ratios, not part of HMDA's disclosure requirements. This analysis examined data from eight unnamed subprime lenders. There are different

56. HUD and Department of Treasury (2000).
57. Avery, Canner, and Cook (2005); Avery, Brevoort, and Canner (2006).
58. Mayer and Pence (2008).
59. Bradford (2002).
60. Avery, Canner, and Cook (2005).

opinions about the conclusions that should be drawn from this research. The authors concluded that controlling for the additional credit-related factors not included in the data can make a difference, fully accounting for the racial or ethnic differences found for some products. Others concluded, however, that the disparities between African Americans and whites and Latinos and whites, while reduced, still persisted.[61]

The initial public focus was once again on the higher incidence of higher-priced lending among minorities (particularly African Americans) compared to non-Hispanic whites. In response, the Board developed statistical screens using the new pricing data, which were used for supervisory purposes, to identify mortgage lenders with significant pricing disparities by race and ethnicity. This list of lenders was then shared with other federal and state agencies. The initial analysis found that about 2 percent of lenders (or 260 institutions) covered by HMDA had statistically significant disparities in either the amount of rate spread or the incidence of higher-priced lending. Of this number, IMBs accounted for almost half of the list, although as a group these lenders account for only about 20 percent of all HMDA data reporters.[62] This analysis, since 2005, has led the federal banking regulatory agencies to refer more than 100 lenders to the Justice Department for further investigations of potential fair lending violations, as required by ECOA.[63]

What HMDA Data Can and Cannot Reveal about Discrimination

For a long time, differences in denial rates across various borrower groups provided a useful means for regulators to target areas of potential discrimination in the mortgage market. The advent of new loan products, especially over the past decade, has meant that this limited measure has become less useful as the focus has shifted away from access to credit and more toward comparing access to fairly priced credit. By providing new information on loan prices beginning in 2005, HMDA data offered an opportunity to test for potential discrimination via pricing differentials. Loan pricing data are crucial for understanding more precisely what can and cannot be determined about discrimination in this new marketplace.

As in the case of information on denials, pricing data may provide an indication of whether or not discrimination is occurring through differentiation, but this information alone is limited in its utility to provide definitive proof. There are other factors that bear on the price of a home loan. While HMDA reporting today captures some of these factors such as lien status of the property, many more factors are not identified in the data. For example, some of the most pertinent measures of a borrower's credit risk are not reported under HMDA, including a borrower's

---

61. Apgar, Bendimerad, and Essene (2007); Goldstein (2008).
62. Avery, Canner, and Cook (2005); GAO (2009).
63. GAO (2009).

credit score and debt-to-income ratio. Additionally, there is a consensus that many important factors related to the property are omitted from HMDA, such as the ratio of the loan amount to the value of the property (loan-to-value ratio) and whether home prices in the neighborhood are rising or falling. Furthermore, HMDA does not include information about a lender's costs, including those associated with loan origination, default, and prepayment risk. While it would be helpful for the public and regulators to have access to these and other pricing factors, lawmakers and the Board must weigh the benefit of such information against the burden of the additional data collection reporting for lenders.

Without these additional pricing and underwriting factors, it has been the judgment of federal banking and other enforcement agencies that use of the HMDA data alone cannot determine definitively whether lenders are engaged in discriminatory lending activity. However, the data do provide an initial means for screening for the potential presence of discrimination in mortgage lending. Should a particular pattern of pricing or other disparities be revealed from the HMDA data for particular lenders, loan products, or geography, regulators can decide if the matter warrants deeper investigation. In such cases, depository institution regulators can and do review actual loan application files, which include many of the pricing and other factors discussed above, to seek to determine the cause of the disparity. HMDA data also enable regulators to monitor broader trends in loan pricing within the higher-priced home loan market.[64]

What Has HMDA Accomplished?

It is generally acknowledged that the experience under HMDA over the past thirty-five years has led to constructive outcomes. But what are the appropriate metrics for determining the effectiveness of pure disclosure laws such as HMDA? Transparency laws are viewed as effective if the disclosures have significantly affected the behavior of most users and resulted in disclosers moving closer to the intention of the overarching public policy the transparency law seeks to achieve. In contrast, an ineffective disclosure law is thought to be one that has failed to change the behavior of users or disclosers appreciably or has changed behavior in directions other than those intended by the policy.[65]

HMDA seems to meet the first test of an effective disclosure law. HMDA's history demonstrates how the simple disclosure of mortgage loan data can affect enforcement practices (users) and market conduct (disclosers). However, some argue that the conclusions drawn from HMDA data may sometimes lead to unfair accusations about discrimination. Where institutions are accused unfairly of discrimination, reputational costs to institutions can be real.

---

64. Afshar (2005).
65. Fung, Graham, and Weil (2007).

Congress thought that requiring lenders to disclose information about their mortgage lending records would motivate them to increase their lending in red-lined neighborhoods rather than face embarrassing publicity and reputational risk. It was hoped that the "sunlight" of disclosure would assist community groups and other data users to identify institutions with poor lending records and thereby encourage those institutions to devise strategies to curtail redlining and promote reinvestment.[66]

HMDA also would appear to meet the second test for determining the effectiveness of a public disclosure law: the disclosures provide an incentive for behavior consistent with the law's public purpose. In the case of HMDA, the purpose is to promote fairer and more efficient mortgage lending. Available evidence suggests that HMDA has met this purpose by exposing "low-roader" practices[67] that are potentially discriminatory. In fact, the scale of initiatives by financial institutions in response to HMDA disclosures suggests that this law, in conjunction with CRA and other antidiscrimination laws and policies, has spurred changes in market behavior.

Yet research in this area has had difficulty distinguishing the effect of HMDA and CRA apart from other policy and market changes. Nevertheless, HMDA proponents often cite the increase in lending to minority borrowers in the years immediately after 1991 as evidence that expanded HMDA reporting contributed to this outcome.[68] For example, the disclosure of data showing that the applications submitted by African Americans and Latinos were denied significantly more frequently than comparable applications submitted by whites generated considerable public attention. Community leaders viewed these disclosures as pivotal to shifting the focus back to the mortgage lending industry to explain why the disparities in rejection rates did not reflect bias in loan decisionmaking.

HMDA plays an integral role in connection with the determination of lenders' compliance with federal laws, such as CRA, ECOA, and the Fair Housing Act. The Federal Reserve and the other federal banking agencies that supervise insured depository institutions use these data as part of the compliance examinations they conduct on a scheduled basis. Further, after 1991 federal banking regulators strengthened their CRA enforcement efforts, denied a greater number of expansion applications, and initiated enforcement actions against banks based on CRA, HMDA, and fair lending concerns more frequently than they had prior to 1991.[69] By providing more detailed information that exposed differential lending patterns, disclosure of HMDA data seems to have played a significant role in driving this expanded activity.

66. Marsico (1999).
67. Kennedy (2004).
68. Marsico (1999).
69. Marsico (1999).

Increased attention to federal oversight of fair lending continued for most of the rest of the decade. In 1993 the federal banking agencies initiated a rulemaking process that resulted in strengthening the CRA regulations to emphasize an institution's lending performance to a greater extent than under the previous rules. Furthermore, in 1994 nine federal agencies adopted a joint policy statement on lending discrimination.

The Expanding Demand for HMDA Data

Myriad users rely on HMDA data to help identify whether disparities do or do not exist in lending, including researchers, media, community groups, regulatory agencies, and the lenders themselves. The data are used to focus attention on both the records of individual lenders and in the aggregate, to assist bank regulatory agencies with CRA and fair lending compliance examinations and enforcement, and to monitor local mortgage lending patterns. They are also used to document CRA challenges to bank expansion requests, to direct public sector investments in ways that would improve the environment for private investment, to provide information for news reports on a variety of mortgage lending and lending discrimination topics, and to otherwise provide a better understanding of the housing finance market. HMDA data are also used to estimate the size of the mortgage market for purposes of establishing affordable housing lending goals for the government-sponsored housing enterprises: Fannie Mae and Freddie Mac.

Notwithstanding HMDA's past value, rising choruses of users complain of the diminished utility of these data resulting from changes in mortgage lending over the past decade. In particular, these critics point to the increasing importance of pricing factors in determining fairness in mortgage lending and the lack of variables that explain pricing variations for higher-priced loans. HMDA usage has also been affected by greater reliance on loan data provided by fee-based private proprietary database providers.

The attractiveness of these proprietary databases is that they often include data variables not featured in the HMDA database. Private providers collect loan-level mortgage data from individual financial institutions and those servicing loans and then repackage the data for consumption by other lenders, analysts, academics, and government agencies. Some large nonprofits are able to buy this information, but most cannot because the cost is out of reach. The attractiveness of these proprietary databases is understandable. One expert sums up the situation this way: "HMDA is a limited data set for groups without financial resources to pay for better information."[70]

70. Rust (2009).

Did Expanded HMDA Data Result in Expanded Lending?

Only a few studies have attempted to isolate HMDA's influence on mortgage lending.[71] This research mostly examines lending trends for the decade after release of the expanded HMDA data, when the race, ethnicity, and income of individual applicants were publicly disclosed for the first time. Data for this period invariably showed significant increases in mortgage lending for previously underrepresented borrower groups. One typical analysis, for example, found that from 1993 to 1999, the number of home purchase loans made to Hispanics increased 121.4 percent; to Native Americans, 118.9 percent; to African Americans, 91 percent; to Asians, 70.1 percent; and to whites, 33.5 percent. Over that period, the number of home purchase loans extended to applicants with income under 80 percent of the median increased 86.2 percent, a much higher rate of growth than for any other income group.[72] Yet isolating the independent effects of HMDA has proven difficult, and no doubt many other factors—for example, the impact of other regulations, a relatively low interest rate environment, good economic conditions, the advent of automated underwriting, and other new technologies—contributed to the surge in lending to these borrower groups during this period.

Similarly, until the FIRREA changes to HMDA were made, it was difficult to obtain a quantitative sense of CRA's impact on overall lending markets.[73] This research has tended to show that CRA has had positive effects on lending to lower-income households. One comprehensive study investigating CRA's impact on mortgage lending examined differences in prime lending between bank and nonbank institutions and found that CRA-covered institutions and their affiliates made more loans to lower-income geographies and households in areas that were scrutinized in CRA evaluations.[74] In this same vein, the HMDA data have been a central element in research challenging the assertion by some critics that the CRA contributed to the subprime crisis. For example, a Federal Reserve Board staff analysis using HMDA data found that of all the higher-priced loans issued in 2006, only 6 percent were made by depository institutions to low- and moderate-income borrowers or neighborhoods in their CRA assessment area, with the major portion of these loans issued by non-CRA-covered mortgage companies.[75]

71. Marsico (1999).
72. Barr (2005).
73. Immergluck (2004).
74. Apgar and Duda (2003).
75. Bernanke (2008); Kroszner (2009). About 17 percent of the higher-priced loan originations were made by CRA-covered lenders or their affiliates to lower-income populations in areas outside the banking institutions' local communities.

A combination of factors led many more financial institutions to improve their lending practices to minorities and lower-income communities in the 1990s. HMDA proponents contend that the shift resulting at least in part from HMDA's expanded reporting requirements contributed to the impetus for stronger enforcement of fair lending and CRA, as well as increased citizens' activism and recognition by financial institutions that community reinvestment requirements were less burdensome than initially anticipated, and they fostered new opportunities for profitable lending.

Increased Public Awareness and Engagement

Perhaps the broadest area of agreement about HMDA's impact is that annual disclosure of loan information helps to promote heightened public awareness about lending discrimination and market fairness concerns. In this sense, public disclosure plays a valuable role in shaping efforts to promote fair lending practices. Few could have anticipated that annual release of this data set would generate the news stories and public exposure that it often does. This attention ultimately has contributed to improving fairness in lending and stimulating stepped-up efforts by lenders to expand housing finance opportunities and address apparent market failures. In contrast, HMDA's critics might contend that the annual disclosures draw more heat than light. But even these critics—those who believe the reported data are too limited to be of much use—acknowledge that the data are useful for providing additional insights about mortgage market activities. Furthermore, release of the 1991 expanded HMDA data is viewed as having increased community activism, as reflected in the increase in challenges to bank expansion requests and the surge in lending agreements and commitments by banks that occurred over the next decade.[76]

The annual release of HMDA data helps to shine the public spotlight each fall on any lending disparities that the data reveal. Industry and community stakeholders now anticipate the data's annual release, with many issuing press releases or otherwise making themselves available to the press to offer their insights and commentaries on the significance of the just released data set.[77] One likely byproduct of the public's scrutiny is that it provides incentives for lenders to try to manage their reputational risk by paying attention to the distribution of their originations, particularly in regard to their lending to lower-income and minority consumers and communities. In this sense, HMDA works better than its original sponsors likely ever imagined. Moreover, it has been argued that this public focus also produces a certain prophylactic effect, discouraging discriminatory lending and encouraging lenders to reexamine potential barriers to credit.[78]

76. Marsico (1999, p. 501).
77. Bostic and Surette (2004).
78. Bostic and Surette (2004).

The Need for Periodic Updating of HMDA

While the changes to HMDA can be described as evolutionary, no one would dispute that the process of revising HMDA has often been quite difficult and arduous to achieve. The arc for changing HMDA usually follows a similar protracted process: HMDA proponents, mostly community, civil rights, and other advocacy organizations, seek the support of federal lawmakers to expand HMDA in some way, such as expanding the reported data variables or addressing gaps in coverage for lenders. Representatives from the mortgage industry voice opposition to the proposed expansions sought by advocates. Industry opposition frequently centers on estimations of additional reporting costs and regulatory burdens. More recently, mortgage trade groups have also expressed concerns about potential infringements on their proprietary interests and threats to consumer privacy.[79]

Consequently, changes to HMDA sometime give the appearance of happening in spurts. However, major changes to HMDA are more evolutionary than spasmodic. In fact, expansions to HMDA often lag behind new developments in mortgage lending and new concerns about market conduct and fairness resulting from these developments. This sometimes lengthy gestation period reflects the difficulties that often exist in reconciling these different points of view about whether or how HMDA should be expanded. The resolution of these differences, therefore, usually requires the expenditure of considerable political capital by lawmakers and other decisionmakers. Many of the most important changes to HMDA were decided by the slimmest of margins on one side or the other. The fact that making changes to HMDA has proven so difficult and time-consuming poses an ongoing challenge to keeping the law up to date with changing circumstances.

Updating transparency laws, like HMDA, and engaging in periodic review are generally considered necessary. Yet the HMDA statute itself does not provide for any formal periodic review by Congress. However, the Board, as the agency responsible for HMDA rulemaking, does undertake regulatory reviews on a periodic basis.

This chapter has shown how different market developments and new concerns have led to the expansion of HMDA's purposes, requirements, and coverage. Almost without exception, these changes have improved the law's utility and been regarded as positive by the user community. In fact, it is difficult to conceive of HMDA continuing to provide any particular value if the reporting of race and income of individual applicants, the reporting by nonbank mortgage lenders, or the centralized reporting and processing by the Board had never occurred.

HMDA in its original form was of value as long as the principal concern was redlining and the data could be used to illustrate gross patterns of geographic disinvestment. However, it was not until fifteen years after passage of HMDA that

79. Duncan (2006).

the law was amended to address concerns about the fairness of loan decisionmaking. By then, the issue was whether minority borrowers were denied mortgage loans more frequently than white borrowers and whether those disparities reflected discrimination in mortgage lending. The public disclosure of some pricing information under HMDA occurred via rulemaking more than thirteen years after the 1989 amendments.

Would HMDA have benefited from more frequent congressional oversight, as some have suggested?

Challenges to HMDA's Continuing Relevancy

Since the last significant changes were made to HMDA seven years ago, much has changed in the world of mortgage lending. The development of risk-based pricing increased the complexity of mortgages, while credit-scoring technology allowed for faster desktop processing of loans. Yet HMDA does not capture these loan and borrower characteristics. While these variables are collected to some extent by private data collectors, the lack of relevant public data during the boom may well have contributed to the difficulty of regulators and mortgage market analysts in identifying the toxic trends that were emerging. As subprime lending ballooned from a relatively small percentage of mortgage lending to a significant one, new concerns arose about the fairness of pricing and marketing of loan products, not just the availability of loans. After the bust, concerns about access to credit have reemerged, as the most recent HMDA data reveal the impact of lending patterns resulting from tighter mortgage credit conditions and the growth of government-backed mortgages as a share of the origination market. Regulators and mortgage market analysts are now focused on the issues of both fairness and access to credit. Notwithstanding these recent trends, many HMDA proponents continue to advocate for additional data variables to ensure HMDA's ongoing relevancy. One community advocacy organization describes the situation this way: "Originally HMDA helped regulators and community groups to paint a vibrant picture of lending, but now that picture is sketchy and out of focus."[80] While acknowledging the limitations of the present database to provide information about underwriting and pricing decisions, major financial trade groups have opposed the expansion of HMDA data collection and cautioned Congress not to "chill the innovation" in the mortgage markets.[81]

With the Dodd-Frank Wall Street Reform and Consumer Protection Act signed into law on July 21, 2010, HMDA reporters will also be required to collect and report new data variables. These new variables include additional borrower and loan characteristics, loan origination information, property information, loan

80. National People's Action (2009).
81. Duncan (2006, p.11).

Table 5-3. *New Information That the Dodd-Frank Wall Street Reform and Consumer Protection Act Requires Financial Institutions to Report*[a]

Area for which information is required	New information required
For each application or loan	Loan term, rate spread (for all loans); total points and fees (per HOEPA); prepayment penalty (term); introductory rate period; negative amortization; origination channel; loan originator unique identifier (SAFE Act); and universal loan identifier
For each applicant or co-applicant	Age; credit score information
For each property	Parcel number; property value

Source: Authors. For a complete version of the Dodd-Frank act's amendments to HMDA, see section 1094: www.gpo.gov/fdsys/pkg/BILLS-111hr4173ENR/pdf/BILLS-111hr4173ENR.pdf.

a. Financial institutions must report the following new data and any other information that the Consumer Financial Protection Bureau may require.

identification numbers, at the option of the CFPB, and any other information the CFPB deems necessary (see table 5-3). The act also transfers HMDA rule-making authority from the Board to the new CFPB as of the transfer date of July 21, 2011. The CFPB will have similar authority to the Board's current authority to prescribe rules regarding the method of submitting HMDA data and the format for disclosure as well as to require modifications of HMDA data prior to public disclosure.

The Dodd-Frank act also establishes a new public Default and Foreclosure Database that will be established and maintained jointly by the Bureau and HUD, in consultation with other relevant federal regulators. The Bureau and HUD will collect and distribute information about foreclosures and defaults on one- to four-unit residential properties. Available at the census-tract level, this database will require banks and financial institutions involved in mortgage lending and servicing to report the number and percentage of delinquent mortgage loans both thirty and ninety days late, mortgage loans in foreclosure, properties that are real estate owned, and mortgage loans that are underwater, that is, where the value of the property is less than the amount of the mortgage. In creating the database, the Bureau and HUD are to take steps to ensure the confidentiality of personally identifiable information and to ensure data security and integrity.

Changes to other consumer protection laws, such as the Truth in Lending Act, in the Dodd-Frank act may also affect HMDA. For example, there is a new definition in TILA for a "qualified mortgage" that, among other things, addresses a lender's compliance with the new ability-to-pay provisions. Some have suggested adding a data field to HMDA to capture information on loan originations meeting the "qualified mortgage" criteria as well as for some other newly mandated TILA definitions.

Beyond the changes due to Dodd-Frank, the Federal Reserve Board of Governors' Division of Consumer and Community Affairs, as part of a regulatory review of Regulation C, held a series of public hearings on HMDA in the summer and fall of 2010 to solicit feedback from interested stakeholders on possible revisions to the HMDA rules.[82] Until the transfer date, the Board retains full authority to propose and enact changes to HMDA. If changes to HMDA are made during that time, the CFPB would inherit the amended HMDA rules. If rule changes have been proposed for public comment but have not yet been finalized by the date of transfer, the CFPB would inherit the proposed changes and move forward on its own accord.

Proposals for Keeping HMDA Current

In addition to the pending congressional changes to HMDA, stakeholders have proposed additional data variables and suggested revisions to HMDA. Some of these are intended to add underwriting criteria that are not presently part of the HMDA database. Others would permit the tracking of new features in mortgages, including characteristics of higher-priced loans. Still others include information pertaining to the full life cycle of an originated loan, including its performance. Many are intended to support fair lending enforcement and consumer protection and to otherwise promote the usefulness of and access to the HMDA database. The suggestions generally include the following:

—*Variables pertaining to borrower characteristics.* The Dodd-Frank act requires the inclusion of the loan applicant's age and credit score information.[83] The reporting of other variables used for loan underwriting, such as household debt-to-income ratio, loan-to-value ratio, and combined loan-to-value (including the first and second lien) have also been suggested.[84]

—*Variables pertaining to loan characteristics.* The Dodd-Frank act requires many additional variables related to the mortgage, including the total points and fees, rate spread (measured against a benchmark rate to be determined by the CFPB),

---

82. Audio files and transcripts of the hearings are on the Board's website: www.federalreserve.gov/communitydev/hmda_hearings.htm.

83. Obtaining the credit score when there are multiple credit-scoring companies with different scoring methodologies can cause methodological problems and could raise privacy concerns. One suggestion for addressing both concerns is to use "buckets" of top 20 percent, bottom 20 percent, and so forth or to have the lender report where the individual ranks compared to the population distribution.

84. "Missing" data on a borrower's characteristic, like race or income, can also challenge researchers. Missing data on race or ethnicity were a growing problem, up to 28 percent in 2002. Reporting rules for the 2003 data required lenders to ask about race in telephone applications, and these missing variables fell to 16 percent by 2005 (Avery, Brevoort, and Canner 2007). However, the challenge remains.

duration of the prepayment penalty, length of the introductory-rate period, presence of negative amortization features, and the term to maturity. Some have called for additional mortgage criteria, including certain information regarding the type of loan product (for example, adjustable rate, fixed rate, balloon, interest only), down payment, the presence of a piggyback loan, private mortgage insurance, originator compensation, and the transaction costs for closing, among others.

—*Variables pertaining to loan purpose.* Variables intended to distinguish between mortgages taken out by borrowers for cash-out refinances, home equity loans, and home equity lines of credit; currently, credit card debt that is rolled into a mortgage loan is captured by HMDA, but home equity lines of credit and reverse mortgages are not.

—*Variables pertaining to loan origination information.* The Dodd-Frank act calls for the origination channel to be identified along with the originator identification number, as set forth in the Secure and Fair Enforcement for Mortgage Licensing (SAFE) Act, at the option of the Bureau. The use of separate coding would help to distinguish between the channel used by a lender to originate the loan; that is, mortgage broker, retail branch, or correspondent channel.

—*Variables related to the property.* The Dodd-Frank act calls for the collection of the property value and a parcel identification number, at the option of the Bureau. The use of a unique property identifier would enable the linking of HMDA data to other property-related databases, such as local property transfer records that contain information on foreclosure starts, linking junior-lien loans to their first-lien counterparts to determine combined loan-to-value ratio or loan performance.

—*Establishment of a unique loan identification number.* More sweeping changes have been proposed to allow links with other loan-level databases, such as the new Default and Foreclosure Database that will be established by the CFPB and HUD featuring information about individual loan performance. The Dodd-Frank act calls for the collection of a universal loan identification number, at the option of the Bureau. This will necessitate the establishment of a unique identification number for every loan originated.[85]

—*Customized HMDA reports.* At present, customized reports can only be realized through the purchase of the raw data set from the FFIEC, which requires the user to have fairly detailed technology and research capabilities. Many stakeholders called for the availability of more user-friendly and more timely online reports that can be individually crafted, like census bureau reports.

---

85. Howell Jackson, in his chapter in this volume, argues for greater loan-level disclosures as securitized transactions are compiled to improve the transparency of loan pricing, allow for policing of loan abuses and discriminatory practices in loan origination, facilitate loan modifications, and reduce foreclosures. This would include all materially important information on loan and borrower characteristics with a unique loan identification code that could be linked to HMDA.

Other Considerations for Determining Expansions to HMDA Reporting

At least three additional considerations are necessary for determining the expansion of HMDA: considering the increased regulatory burden, addressing consumer privacy concerns, and addressing the public-use objectives of an increasingly complex database.

Enhanced HMDA disclosures may improve the data's utility, but lawmakers and regulators will need to balance the purported public benefits of each new data element against the estimated increased marginal costs of reporting and compliance burdens for reporting institutions. Certainly technological developments have eased the compliance costs and timelines for gathering data, yet challenges remain. While concerns about costs are warranted, it has been difficult to gather data on the marginal increased cost of specific additions to HMDA. Often, lenders purchase software from HMDA data vendors who may be unwilling to share the actual cost of these additions. The annual format may also cause timeliness challenges, and one solution could be quarterly electronic submissions, with allowance for later data corrections.

Before a decision is made regarding possible expansions to HMDA, rule writers have been instructed by Congress to weigh the potential consumer privacy concerns posed by additional data collection and reporting. When considering these questions in 2002, the Board signaled that these concerns warranted close attention, particularly where data fields are susceptible to matching with other information that may reveal the identity of individual borrowers or loan applicants. Congress, too, has indicated similar concerns going as far back as 1989, when it directed the Board to withhold from public disclosure certain calendar-specific loan application information at the transaction level.

Thus far Congress and the Board have not heard much from consumers regarding possible compromises to their privacy posed by HMDA disclosures. Part of the reason for this is that considerable information already exists, whether as property records in the public domain or as a result of data collection from lenders facilitated by private vendors. However, this dynamic could change should HMDA data be expanded to include reporting on potentially consumer-sensitive items, such as borrower creditworthiness or basic metrics regarding a borrower's likely ability to repay a mortgage loan.

Some possible options have been suggested for resolving the conflict between the privacy interests of individual consumers and the legitimate public interest in ensuring that HMDA is a robust database. One possibility suggested by Engel and McCoy would be to require lenders to limit access to certain data variables deemed as "sensitive" to individual consumer privacy. In such cases, the Federal Reserve Board, or another federal agency, could be designated to analyze the data and provide aggregate reports to the public. Another option would require the development of procedures to provide access to sensitive data variables only to certified researchers who meet appropriate criteria. Such a method is in place at the Bureau of the Census, which has established research data centers in which carefully screened researchers sign confidentiality agreements in order to gain access to individual-level census data.[86]

Nature of Public Use

An important question is whether providing a more comprehensive database poses a conflict with the objective of providing a broadly accessible public-use database and whether this conflict can be reconciled. One possible way to greatly enhance the use of HMDA, while addressing privacy concerns, would be to provide additional customized HMDA reports within set parameters. An example is the Census Bureau's "American FactFinder," where users can create maps and use drop-down tabs to access population, housing, economic, and geographic data. Users of Census Bureau data can also have custom tabulations created on a cost-reimbursable basis, which is useful for those who need more information than the standard data products provide. While making such information available would certainly entail substantial costs to government, it could improve data transparency. However, it would also create the challenge of helping the average data user to understand the statistical underpinnings of summary charts, such as the need to do regression analysis for borrower characteristics to control for multiple variables. To improve the public use and ensure timely analysis of the mortgage market, policymakers may also need to address the time lag between the collection and the public release of data.

Lessons from Proprietary Databases

One of the greatest strengths of HMDA is the demographic and geographic loan data that are collected and reported in a disaggregated form. Yet HMDA is also a limited data set, in that it does not provide loan performance, provides only limited pricing data, and excludes other important variables helpful for distinguishing the reasons behind lending disparities for different borrower groups. These types of variables are not publicly available but are gathered by private companies and sold to researchers and government entities with contractual agreements about the use of these data.

Two national, proprietary and fee-driven databases are CoreLogic, previously known as First American LoanPerformance or LP, and Lender Processing Services (LPS) Applied Analytics, formerly known as McDash. At least until recently, the LP database captured about 70 percent of the subprime securitized mortgage market, with limited coverage of the prime market. The data are collected from the administrative records of large mortgage servicers, are originated by a wide variety of institutions, and include both prime and subprime loans. The database

---

86. Engel and McCoy (2009).

includes all mortgages purchased or guaranteed by Fannie Mae or Freddie Mac and also includes nonagency securitized loans. It is assumed that securitized mortgages are likely overrepresented in the LP data. The LPS database includes eighteen large servicers (nine of the top ten) as of September 2008. It does not include portfolio loans and may be missing smaller servicers that may disproportionately service the prime market. LPS claims to cover 57 percent of the market, with greater shares in some marketplaces.

Both data sets have limitations, including limited demographic information in the manner provided under HMDA. Academic and regulatory researchers who have purchased the data have had some success in matching HMDA with these proprietary data sources in order to get a clearer picture of the mortgage market. One example is the successful match between HMDA and LPS data used for a recent Federal Reserve Bank of San Francisco study.[87] This research created a crosswalk between zip codes and census tracts using HMDA census data, used loan characteristic variables for matching, and then added lender variables from HMDA. The combination of variables provides a clear picture of the mortgage market. For example, the Ladermann and Reid study found that borrower characteristics, loan terms, and original channel had an effect on loan performance. Center for Responsible Lending researchers also matched loan data from HMDA and a proprietary database that includes variables pertaining to loan risk at origination and reached similar conclusions.[88]

More recently, Bank of America Merrill Lynch analysts Vipul Jain and Tim Isgro used matching to understand the dynamics of underwater borrowers and to determine which borrowers have a low probability of default. They matched new data provided by credit bureau Equifax with LP data, not by identifying borrowers or addresses but by using complex matching algorithms.[89] By matching original loan amount, zip code, and other data items in the LoanPerformance loan-level security database to Equifax data, the researchers were able to ascertain if the borrower had other first-lien or second-lien mortgages (both closed end and home equity lines of credit), the extent of other credit lines and revolving debt, and current delinquent status on other debt.

While marrying the HMDA and proprietary data sets seems to hold promise for researchers, policymakers, and regulators, combining such data may create conflicts with proprietary interests. Some private vendors reportedly have cautioned that such matches are in violation of their contract terms and have asked paid subscribers and researchers to refrain from using their data in such a fashion. These actions are perhaps understandable from the perspective of the data providers who may be providing other services, such as risk management, to their clients—

87. Laderman and Reid (2009).
88. Bocian, Ernst, and Li (2006).
89. Lowell (2010).

that is, the lenders and servicers who provide the data. These lenders and servicers could be concerned about providing data to a firm that could potentially be used as evidence in fair lending disputes. Often, these lenders provide data to the firm in order to manage their lending risks.

Conclusion

As we have seen, transparency and public disclosure regimes, such as HMDA, begin as imperfect compromises and must evolve to stay abreast of changing markets and new political priorities. Yet keeping pace is not a simple proposition. New developments alter the competitive playing field and change the benefits and costs to disclosers. Making changes in a timely manner is difficult, given the rapidity of changes in market conditions.

It is the contention of this chapter that as effective as HMDA has been over its thirty-five-year history, its continued relevancy as a data tool for detecting problems with market conduct is far from assured. The focus on HMDA has shifted over time from a concern with depository institutions that were not lending to communities in which they received deposits, to a more general inquiry into whether lenders of all types were discriminating, to the more recent emphasis on whether vulnerable population groups, including minorities, are being targeted for unfavorable rates and products. This shift in emphasis generally reflected market trends and new concerns about market fairness. The challenge in light of current market conditions is to anticipate data needs for a market that still is emerging in the wake of the present mortgage crisis.

Mortgage lending was highly localized in 1975 when HMDA was enacted, but it has become a nationwide industry dominated by a relative handful of very large mortgage originators, and this consolidation continues in the industry. Changes have been made to HMDA in response to some aspects of the changing mortgage market, but not to others. However, past changes to HMDA may not provide sufficient information to analyze the constantly evolving mortgage lending market.

With future changes to HMDA, one issue that needs to be considered is whether the HMDA database should only provide information to screen and identify patterns that warrant closer view. Another view is that the database should become a more effective tool for proving discrimination, by collecting data elements that are needed to present a prima facie case of lending discrimination. Clearly, policymakers will need to grapple with determining the highest and best use of HMDA data when deciding whether and which variables may need to be added. Policymakers will also need to consider how best to implement the goal of improving public access to the data, whether by addressing the time lag issues or the format of the public data.

Another challenge to the relevancy of HMDA is the effect of the increasing reliance on loan data purchased from private proprietary sources. These private data sets include important variables not presently part of the HMDA data set, but they do not obviate the need for HMDA. HMDA's comparative advantage is the size of the database and the unique combination of variables, such as those for race, gender, income, and census-tract location, that are not commonly featured in the proprietary data sets. The virtue of HMDA, therefore, still rests on the premise that the data remain accessible to a broad audience at a comparatively inexpensive cost. In view of this, future decisions to expand the HMDA data set should consider the effect of such changes on HMDA's continuing usefulness as a valuable data source for the broadest possible public use.

References

Afshar, Anna. 2005. "New HMDA Data: Intent, Interpretation, and Implications." *Communities and Banking Journal* (Spring): 19–23. www.bos.frb.org/commdev/c&b/2005/Spring/HMDA.pdf.

Apgar, William, Amal Bendimerad, and Ren Essene. 2007. *Mortgage Channels and Fair Lending: An Analysis of HMDA Data.* Harvard University, Joint Center for Housing Studies. www.jchs/harvard.edu/publications/finance/mm07-2_mortgage_market_channels.pdf.

Apgar, William, and Mark Duda. 2003. "The Twenty-Fifth Anniversary of the Community Reinvestment Act: Past Accomplishments and Future Regulatory Challenges." *Economic Policy Review* 9, no. 2: 169–91.

Avery, Robert, Neil Bhutta, Kenneth P. Brevoort, and Glenn B. Canner. 2010a. "The 2009 HMDA Data: The Mortgage Market in a Time of Low Interest Rates and Economic Distress." Draft forthcoming in the *Federal Reserve Bulletin* 96: n.p. www.federalreserve.gov/pubs/bulletin/2010/pdf/hmda2009.pdf.

Avery, Robert, Neil Bhutta, Kenneth P. Brevoort, Glenn B. Canner, and Christa N. Gibbs. 2010b. "The 2008 HMDA Data: The Mortgage Market during a Turbulent Year." *Federal Reserve Bulletin* 96: A169–211. www.federalreserve.gov/pubs/bulletin/2010/pdf/hmda08 final.pdf.

Avery, Robert, Kenneth P. Brevoort, and Glenn B. Canner. 2006. "Higher-Priced Home Lending and the 2005 HMDA Data." *Federal Reserve Bulletin* (September 28): A123–66. www.federalreserve.gov/pubs/bulletin/2006/hmda/bull06hmda.pdf.

———. 2007. "Opportunities and Issues in Using HMDA Data." *Journal of Real Estate Research* 29, no. 4: 351–80. www.business.fullerton.edu/finance/journal/papers/pdf/past/vol29n04/02.351_380.pdf.

———. 2008. "The 2007 HMDA Data." *Federal Reserve Bulletin* 94 (December): A107–46. www.federalreserve.gov/pubs/bulletin/2008/pdf/hmda07final.pdf.

Avery, Robert, Glenn B. Canner, and Robert E. Cook. 2005. "New Information Reported under HMDA and Its Application in Fair Lending Enforcement." *Federal Reserve Bulletin* (Summer): 344–94. www.federalreserve.gov/pubs/bulletin/2005/summer05_hmda.pdf.

Barr, Michael S. 2005. "Credit Where It Counts: The Community Reinvestment Act and Its Critics." *New York University Law Review* 80, no. 2: 513–52.

Bernanke, Ben S. 2007. "The Community Reinvestment Act: Its Evolution and New Challenges." Speech at the Community Affairs Research conference, Washington, March 30.

———. 2008. "Letter to the Honorable Senator Menendez." menendez.senate.gov/pdf/11258 ResponsefromBernankeonCRA.pdf.

Bocian, Deborah Gruenstein, Keith Ernst, and Wei Li. 2006. *Unfair Lending: The Effect of Race and Ethnicity on the Price of Subprime Mortgages.* Durham, N.C.: Center for Responsible Lending. www.responsiblelending.org/mortgage-lending/research-anlaysis/rr011-Unfair_Lending-0506.pdf.

Bostic, Raphael W., and Brian J. Surette. 2004. "Market Forces or CRA-Induced Externalities: What Accounts for the Increase in Mortgage Lending to Lower-Income Communities?" Working Paper 2004-1013. Los Angeles: Lusk Center for Real Estate (December).

Bradbury, Katharine, Karl Case, and Constance Dunham. 1989. *Geographic Patterns of Mortgage Lending in Boston, 1982–1987.* Federal Reserve Bank of Boston.

Bradford, Calvin. 2002. *Risk or Race? Racial Disparities and the Subprime Refinance Market.* Washington: Center for Community Change.

Brown, Jonathan. 1991. *Community Benefit Requirements for Banking Institutions: The U.S. Experience.* Washington: Essential Information Banking Research Project.

Canner, Glenn. 1982. *Redlining: Research and Federal Legislative Response.* Washington: Board of Governors of the Federal Reserve System (October).

Carr, James, and Isaac Megbolugbe. 1993. "The Federal Reserve Bank of Boston: Study on Mortgage Lending Revisited." *Journal of Housing Research* 4, no. 2: 277–314.

Dedman, Bill. 1988. "The Color of Money." *Atlanta Journal-Constitution,* May 1–4. www.powerreporting.com/color/.

———. 1989. "Blacks Turned Down for Home Loans from S&Ls Twice as Often as Whites." *Atlanta Journal-Constitution,* January 22. powerreporting.com/color/53.html.

Duncan, Douglas. 2006. "Testimony on Behalf of the Mortgage Bankers Association." Testimony before the Subcommittee on Financial Institutions and Consumer Credit of the Committee on Financial Services, U.S. House of Representatives, June 13.

Engel, Kathleen, and Patricia McCoy. 2009. "HMDA Reporting of Credit Scores." Posted on "Credit Slips: A Discussion on Credit and Bankruptcy," February 11. www.creditslips.org/creditslips/2006/12/hmda_reporting_.html.

Fishbein, Allen. 1993. "The Ongoing Experiment with Regulation from Below: Expanded Reporting Requirements under HMDA and CRA." *Housing Policy Debate* 3, no. 2: 601–36.

Fishbein, Allen, and Harold Bunce. 2000. *Subprime Market Growth and Predatory Lending.* Washington: HUD.

Fung, Archon, Mary Graham, and David Weil. 2007. *Full Disclosure: The Perils and Promise of Transparency.* New York: Cambridge University Press.

Galster, George. 1991. "A Statistical Perspective on Illegal Discrimination in Lending." White Paper. Washington: American Bankers Association.

GAO (Government Accountability Office). 2009. *Fair Lending: Data Limitations and the Fragmented U.S. Financial Regulatory Structure Challenge Federal Oversight and Enforcement Efforts.* Washington.

Goering, John, and Ron Wienk, eds. 1996. *Mortgage Lending, Racial Discrimination, and Federal Policy.* Washington: Urban Institute Press.

Goldstein, Ira, with Dan Urevick-Ackelburg. 2008. *Subprime Lending, Mortgage Foreclosures, and Race: How Far Have We Come and How Far Have We to Go?* Philadelphia: Reinvestment Fund.

Gramlich, Edward M. 2002. "CRA at Twenty-Five." Remarks at the Consumer Bankers' Association Community Reinvestment Act conference, Arlington, Va., April 8.

HUD (Department of Housing and Urban Development) and Department of Treasury. 2000. *Joint Report 2000: Curbing Predatory Home Mortgage Lending.* Washington. www.huduser.org/publications/hsgfin/curbing.html.

Immergluck, Dan. 2004. *Credit to the Community: Community Reinvestment and Fair Lending Policy in the United States.* Armonk, N.Y.: M. E. Sharpe.

Kennedy, Duncan. 2004. "Cost Benefit Analysis of Debtor Protection Rules in Sub-Prime Market Default Situations." Building Assets, Building Credit Working Paper 04-22. Cambridge, Mass.: Joint Center for Housing Studies, Harvard University.

Kolar, Joseph M., and Jonathan D. Jerison. 2005. "The Home Mortgage Disclosure Act: Its History, Evolution, and Limitations." *Consumer Finance Law Quarterly Report* 59 (Fall): 189.

Kroszner, Randall. 2009. "The Community Reinvestment Act and the Recent Mortgage Crisis." In *Revisiting the CRA: Perspectives on the Future of the Community Reinvestment Act.* Federal Reserve Bank of Boston and Federal Reserve Bank of San Francisco.

Laderman, Elizabeth, and Carolina Reid. 2009. "CRA Lending during the Subprime Meltdown." In *Revisiting the CRA: Perspectives on the Future of the Community Reinvestment Act.* Federal Reserve Bank of Boston and Federal Reserve Bank of San Francisco.

LaWare, John. 1991. "Press Statement." Washington: Board of Governors of the Federal Reserve System (October 21).

Lowell, Linda. 2010. "Who, in the End, Will Default?" *Housing Wire,* April 9. www.housing wire.com/2010/03/01/who-in-the-end-will-strategically-default/.

Marsico, Richard D. 1999. "Shedding Some Light on Lending: The Effect of Expanded Disclosure Laws on Home Mortgage Marketing, Lending, and Discrimination in the New York Metropolitan Area." *Fordham Urban Law Journal* 27, no. 2 (December): 481–532.

Mayer, Chris, and Karen Pence. 2008. "Subprime Mortgages: What, Where, and to Whom?" Finance and Economics Discussion Series 2008-29. Washington: Federal Reserve Board, Divisions of Research and Statistics and Monetary Affairs.

McCluskey, Orin L. 1981. "The Community Reinvestment Act: Is It Doing the Job?" *Banking Law Journal* 100: 33–57.

McCoy, Patricia A. 2007. "The Home Mortgage Disclosure Act: A Synopsis and Recent Legislative History." *Journal of Real Estate Research* 29, no. 4: 391–98.

Munnell, Alicia, Lynn Browne, James McEneaney, and Geoffrey Tootell. 1992. "Mortgage Lending in Boston: Interpreting HMDA Data." Working Paper 92-7. Federal Reserve Bank of Boston. Subsequently published in the *American Economic Review* 86, no. 1: 25–53.

National People's Action. 2009. "Public Statement on Modernizing the Home Mortgage Disclosure Act." Chicago.

Olson, Mark W. 2006. "Home Mortgage Disclosure Act." Testimony to the Subcommittee on Financial Institutions and Consumer Credit, Committee on Financial Services, U.S. House of Representatives June 13.

Rust, Adam. 2009. "A Principle-Based Redesign of HMDA and CRA Data." In *Revisiting the Community Reinvestment Act: Perspectives on the Future of the Community Reinvestment Act.* Federal Reserve Bank of Boston and Federal Reserve Bank of San Francisco.

6

Loan-Level Disclosure in Securitization Transactions: A Problem with Three Dimensions

HOWELL E. JACKSON

T he securitization of residential mortgages and other forms of consumer credit has become a subject of intense national interest and debate. Many have questioned the wisdom of the originate-to-distribute model of loan underwriting, and others have focused on the conflicts inherent in the role of investment banks assembling securitization pools and then marketing them to their institutional clients. The capacity of credit-rating firms to rate accurately the securities backed by securitization pools has been roundly criticized in many quarters. Still others have identified as problematic the manner in which borrowers were encouraged to obtain mortgages that they were unlikely to be able to repay without refinancing or reselling the underlying property at an inflated price. These concerns and others have led to a series of regulatory proposals as well as a number of provisions in the recently adopted Dodd-Frank Wall Street Reform and Consumer Protection Act.

In this essay, I focus on a different aspect of the securitizations: loan-level information on assets assigned to securitization pools. Limitations on this information came to the fore when the financial crisis unfolded in 2007 and 2008, as investors began to question the value of interests in securitization pools and found themselves unable to obtain sufficient information about underlying mortgages to ascertain the current value of their investments. While the relationship between inadequate loan-level disclosures and the valuation of toxic assets has received the most attention in the academic literature, there are at least two other dimensions of public policy on which loan-level information has been found wanting. One is in the area of mortgage renegotiations. While an array of institutional barriers inhibits the renegotiation of underwater mortgages, one aspect of the problem is uncertainty as to the fair market value of loans held in securitized pools and the terms on which comparable loans have been renegotiated or sold in other market transactions. Another dimension on which the value of securitized loans comes into play is in disputes over the fairness of the origination of loans that were transferred into securitization pools. The amount by which originators "marked up" mortgages above the price at which those mortgages were sold into securitization pools offers critical evidence of the presence of unfair origination practices as well as violations of the Equal Credit Opportunity Act and other consumer protection statutes. While economists have developed techniques to estimate excessive markups and discriminatory impacts from other sources of data, the preservation of data regarding prices at which individual mortgages were purchased by securitization pools as well as contemporaneous data on loan and borrower characteristics would offer a more accurate source of information with which public officials could police the fairness of the origination process.

This chapter proceeds in three sections. First, I review the debate over loan-level information for the purpose of improving the pricing of interests in securitization pools, discussing both problems that emerged in the recent financial crisis and steps that are being taken to address those concerns, as reflected in federal financial reform legislation and best practice standards being developed under the American Securitization Forum's Project RESTART. The principal elements of these reforms include the following:

—The development of consistent disclosure requirements for loans assigned to securitization pools

—The imposition of periodic updating requirements for loan-level disclosures for outstanding securitization transactions

—The development of model representations and warranties for loan sales into securitization pools

—Various efforts to improve the transparency and efficiency of loan modifications.

I then review the emerging literature on barriers to the renegotiation of underwater mortgages and explain how the availability of better loan-level data on securitization pools, if supplemented with additional information on loan sales and renegotiations, may help to facilitate both private renegotiations and also possibly government purchase programs. Among other things, this analysis emphasizes the following:

—The supply of updated loan-level information contemplated under current reform proposals to assist investors in securitization pools could also assist in loan renegotiations.

—More aggressive forms of government intervention, including loan purchases or write-downs of loans in bank examinations, could also make use of such loan-level data from securitization pools.

Finally, I discuss the role that the loan-level data from securitization pools might play in policing the fairness of loan originations, both as offering a metric against which to measure loan markups and also as providing a more precise instrument for detecting discriminatory lending practices. The following are the key points:

—Whereas securitization pool investors and loan renegotiators are critically concerned with the value of loans over the life of the pool, borrowers are interested in the value of the loan when it was transferred to the pool, that is, the price the pool paid to purchase the loan.

—Borrowers (or regulators acting on behalf of borrowers) can use information on the origination purchase price to ascertain the markup the originator earned on the pool as well as any potentially problematic variations in pricing based on impermissible categories.

The chapter concludes with a short review of other proposals to reform the securitization of financial assets—particularly those designed to require loan originators to retain additional "skin in the game"—and a consideration of how these reforms might interact with efforts to improve the transparency of loan-level disclosure. The form of "skin in the game" can affect the usefulness of loan-level pricing information on all three dimensions discussed above. In particular, retaining originator risk in individual loans reduces loan-level transparency, whereas allocating securitization pool interests to the originating firm does not. I also raise the question of whether loan-level disclosure requirements should be extended to portfolio lenders and government-sponsored entities (GSEs) as well as securitization pools. Finally, the conclusion touches on privacy concerns raised by loan-level disclosure requirements and considers briefly the options for limiting disclosure of loan-level information to regulatory authorities and rating agencies, but not the public markets.

Loan-Level Information and the Pricing of Mortgage-Backed Securities

Throughout the past few decades, an increasing share of U.S. residential mortgages were financed through securitization transactions. By year-end 2004, roughly 45 percent (or $4.8 trillion) of the $10.7 trillion in outstanding mortgages were held in mortgage pools or trusts.[1] Just three years later at year-end 2007, the share of securitized mortgages approached 51 percent (or $7.4 trillion) on $14.6 trillion of outstanding mortgages. While government-backed pools remained the dominant share of securitized mortgages, growth in private securitizations in the mid-2000s (some 102 percent between year-end 2004 and year-end 2007) greatly outpaced overall growth in mortgages outstanding during the same

1. Unless otherwise noted, the figures in this paragraph are available at the following link: www.federalreserve.gov/econresdata/releases/mortoutstand/mortoutstand20090331.htm.

period (36 percent) and contemporaneous growth in government-backed securi-tization pools (32 percent). As a result, private mortgage securitizations accounted for nearly 40 percent of total mortgage securitizations by year-end 2007 and more than 20 percent of all mortgages outstanding. As the vast majority of the loans placed into private securitization pools constituted subprime or Alt-A origina-tions,[2] these investment vehicles were peculiarly vulnerable to the bursting of the U.S. housing bubble and the ensuing economic downturn that engulfed the global economy in 2008.

By 2009 government officials, policy analysts, and industry representatives were converging on a package of reform proposals designed to address the prob-lems of mortgage securitization and structured financing more generally. The Obama administration's proposal for financial regulatory reform, unveiled in June 2009, identified strengthening the supervision and regulation of securitization markets as a key plank of regulatory reform and included five basic components:

1. Federal banking agencies should promulgate regulations that require orig-inators or sponsors to retain an economic interest in a material portion of the credit risk of securitized credit exposures.

2. Regulators should promulgate additional regulations to align compensation of market participants with longer-term performance of the underlying loans.

3. The Securities and Exchange Commission (SEC) should continue its efforts to increase the transparency and standardization of securitization markets and be given clear authority to require robust reporting by issuers of asset-backed securities.

4. The SEC should continue its efforts to strengthen the regulation of credit-rating agencies, including measures requiring firms to have robust policies and procedures that manage and disclose conflicts of interest, differentiate between structured and other products, and otherwise promote the integrity of the ratings process.

5. Regulators should reduce their use of credit ratings in regulations and super-visory practices, wherever possible.[3]

For purposes of this chapter, the third of the administration's priorities—increased transparency and standardization in securitization markets—is of most relevance, and I return to that aspect of the Treasury Department's recommen-dations in a moment. But it bears noting that the Obama administration reforms also include two other important components. The first, reflected in the first two components of the reform proposal, is that the administration contemplated mandatory requirements that originators and sponsors retain "skin in the game" and accept compensation packages that align their incentives with the interests of both borrowers and investors in securitization pools. Reforms of this sort respond

---

2. See Ashcraft and Schuermann (2008).
3. Department of Treasury (2009).

to widespread criticisms of existing originate-to-distribute business models and the associated agency problems that these arrangements have generated, such as high-risk loans, which have proved detrimental to both borrowers and investors as well as burdensome for the broader economy as a result of what have proved to be substantial negative externalities. The second component of the administration's securitization reform proposal addresses credit-rating agencies and contemplates (a) increased regulation of these agencies to improve the usefulness of ratings for investors in structured products and (b) reduced reliance on ratings for supervisory purposes, thereby encouraging more direct market discipline (and fewer regulatory safe harbors and incentives) for rated securities. Implicit in these proposed reforms of credit-rating agencies is a greater reliance on investors to police securitization transactions, thus indirectly linking credit-rating reforms with greater transparency of securitization pools.

Returning now to the central component of the administration's reform proposal—transparency and standardization in securitization transactions— several points bear emphasis. First is the regulatory body to which the proposal is addressed: the Securities and Exchange Commission. What the Obama administration contemplated in these recommendations is the improvement of SEC disclosure requirements for securitization transactions, building on specialized rules that the commission adopted in the 1990s.[4] In a brief textual summary, the administration's proposal noted four distinct areas for improvement. First was the need for loan-level information in SEC filings, including information about the identity of the broker or originator associated with each loan and information regarding the compensation structures and risk exposures of the sponsor and other

---

4. Several SEC requirements touch on securitization transactions. In terms of disclosure requirements, the provisions of the Securities Act of 1933 apply to public offers of securities. In Regulation AB, the SEC has codified its registration and disclosure requirements for asset-backed securities. See SEC Final Rule on Asset-backed Securities, 70 Fed. Reg. 1506 (January 7, 2005). These requirements do not apply to securitization transactions that are privately placed (as opposed to publicly offered) or otherwise exempt from the SEC reporting requirements, including mortgage-backed securities underwritten or guaranteed by government-sponsored agencies like Fannie Mae and Freddie Mac. In general, when a corporation issues securities to the general public, the issuer will have ongoing periodic reporting obligations under the Securities Exchange Act of 1934. These obligations, however, expire if a sufficient number of investors do not hold the issuer's securities. Under section 15(d) of the 1934 act, deregistration from the periodic reporting requirements is available when an issuer has fewer than 300 holders of securities, and most private securitization transactions currently qualify under this standard. Accordingly, their continuous reporting obligations typically expire within two years of their initial offering. A final set of SEC exemptions for securitization transactions concerns the Investment Company Act of 1940. As pools of financial assets, securitization transactions are presumptively subject to regulation under the 1940 act. As the requirements of the act are strict and inconsistent with the structure of most securitization pools, transactions are invariably designed to conform with the exemptions, such as 3(c)(1) and 3(c)(7), which are available to privately placed securitization, or another exemption promulgated under SEC rulemaking authority and available to publicly sold securitizations that receive sufficient credit ratings and meet other standards. See Rule 3(a)(7) under the 1940 act. See Coates (2009). For certain securitization transactions, the Trust Indenture Act of 1939 also applies.

key parties to the securitization. The second area of reform addressed the updating of information over the life of the securitization; under current SEC requirements, while extensive disclosures were mandated at the time of initial offering of interests in securitization pools, the interests were typically exempt from periodic reporting requirements under the Securities Exchange Act of 1934, as the number of holders typically fell beneath thresholds established under section 15(d) of the act. Third, the administration called for standardization of legal documentation for securitization transactions both to make it easier for investors to value interests in securitization pools and to facilitate loan modifications. This last aspiration moves beyond disclosure and standardization into the imposition of mandatory terms that would increase the discretion of loan servicers to modify mortgages if the modification would benefit the trust as a whole. Finally, the Obama blueprint addressed the need to improve electronic trade–reporting databases for asset-backed securities.

While the Obama administration's proposals for securitization reform were sketchy and conceptual, the administration drew up its recommendations in response to several more detailed studies of the problems facing investors in securitization transactions during the market disruptions of 2008 and 2009. The most comprehensive of these studies can be found in the Committee on Capital Markets Regulation (CCMR) May 2009 report titled "The Global Financial Crisis: A Plan for Regulatory Reform."[5] The CCMR study is instructive because it presents an empirical study of the actual loan-level data available for a sample of major private mortgage securitizations in 2006, the height of the housing boom. Measured against the 165 fields of data that the rating agencies had identified as required or recommended to assess the creditworthiness of loan pools, the CCMR research found that many of the fields were not available in the majority of transactions, often including fields that investors deemed of critical importance. The study also documented systemic failures on the part of securitization sponsors to update loan-level data on a monthly basis or to present the loan-level data in a form that permitted effective evaluation of downstream products, like collateralized debt obligations. Criticizing the laxness of SEC Regulation AB, which defines the disclosure requirements for asset-backed securities distributed in public offerings, the CCMR report paints a disconcerting picture of loan-level disclosure practices in the mid-2000s, but one that is fully consistent with the difficulties that investors and government officials encountered in their efforts to value "toxic assets" in the fall of 2008, as the widespread deterioration of housing markets became apparent and the level of mortgage defaults skyrocketed above historical averages and model assumptions.

Reform of loan-level disclosure requirements has now proceeded on four distinct, but related, tracks. On the congressional front, legislative proposals in both

---

5. CCMR (2009). www.capmktsreg.org/pdfs/TGFC-CCMR_Report_%285-26-09%29.pdf.

the House and Senate included securitization reform provisions, and these proposals were melded into Subtitle D—Improvements to the Asset-Backed Securitization Process of Title IX of the Dodd-Frank Wall Street Reform and Consumer Protection Act.[6] Section 942 of the Dodd-Frank act addresses the issue of loan-level losses in two ways. First, subsection 942(a) amends section 15(d) of the Securities Exchange Act of 1934 to prevent issuers of asset-backed securities from discontinuing periodic disclosures relatively soon after a public offering is complete (which is generally permitted for classes of securities with fewer than 300 holders, as is typically the case with securitization offerings) and grants the SEC authority to adopt specific rules for allowing the discontinuation of periodic reporting requirements for asset-backed securities.[7] Second, subsection 942(b) instructs the SEC to amend its disclosure requirements for asset-backed securities to mandate additional loan-level data, which would facilitate investor comparisons across different securities and permit investors to perform their own due diligence regarding both the underlying loans and their origination process, including compensation arrangements for originators and risk retention provisions.[8]

The legislation also includes fairly extensive provisions establishing risk retention requirements for assets financed through asset-backed securities, contemplating a presumptive risk retention requirement of 5 percent but allowing lower amounts of retention for qualified mortgages and full or partial exemptions for certain asset classes.[9] Unlike the Dodd-Frank act's disclosure requirements for asset-backed securities, which fall within the exclusive jurisdiction of the SEC, the risk retention provisions are to be implemented through joint rulemaking among

6. Conference Report 111-517 to Accompany H.R. 4173, 111 Cong. 2 sess. §§ 941–57 (June 29, 2010). These legislative reforms deal with the full gamut of asset-backed securities and in certain respects establish different rules for different asset classes. In this chapter, I focus primarily on asset-backed securities based on residential mortgages.

7. Id. §942(a). The bill would also eliminate an exemption from the Securities Act of 1933 for certain notes secured by real estate. Id. §944. While presumably designed to increase the application of the SEC public offering rules, it is not clear how significant this reform would be in practice, as the remaining exemption for private placements typically exempts offerings of securities sold exclusively to institutional investors.

8. The exact language reads as follows: "(c) DISCLOSURE REQUIREMENTS.—

(1) IN GENERAL.—The Commission shall adopt regulations under this subsection requiring each issuer of an asset-backed security to disclose, for each tranche or class of security, information regarding the assets backing that security.

(2) CONTENT OF REGULATIONS.—In adopting regulations under this subsection, the Commission shall—(A) set standards for the format of the data provided by issuers of an asset-backed security, which shall, to the extent feasible, facilitate comparison of such data across securities in similar types of asset classes; and (B) require issuers of asset-backed securities, at a minimum, to disclose asset-level or loan-level data, if such data are necessary for investors to independently perform due diligence, including (i) data having unique identifiers relating to loan brokers or originators; (ii) the nature and extent of the compensation of the broker or originator of the assets backing the security; and (iii) the amount of risk retention by the originator and the securitizer of such assets." Id. §942(b) (to be codified at 15 U.S.C. §77g).

9. See id. §941.

the commission, the federal banking agencies, and in some instances also the Department of Housing and Urban Development and the Federal Housing Finance Agency. The responsibility for coordinating joint rulemaking under the risk retention provisions is assigned to the chair of the Financial Stability Oversight Council, who is the secretary of the Treasury.[10]

The act also directs the SEC to improve disclosures regarding the terms of representations and warranties governing the contracts under which loans are transferred to securitization pools. Most notably, with respect to asset-backed securities transactions, credit-rating agencies will be required to report on the quality of representations and warranties as compared with industry standards.[11] In addition, the commission will have to establish aggregate disclosure requirements with respect to "fulfilled and unfulfilled repurchase requests across all trusts aggregated by the securitizers, so that investors may identify asset originators with clear underwriting deficiencies."[12] The act also mandates two separate studies on risk retention: one focusing on potentially negative effects of risk retention requirements on the availability of credit, to be conducted by the Federal Reserve Board (working in conjunction with federal banking agencies and the SEC),[13] and another focusing on positive macroeconomic effects of risk retention requirements in reducing asset bubbles, to be conducted by the chair of the Financial Services Oversight Council.[14] A separate title, addressing the reform of credit-rating agencies, includes another provision targeted specifically at securitization transactions: one mandating an SEC study of the feasibility of establishing a system for assigning credit-rating agencies to securitization transactions, to be followed, if appropriate, by SEC rulemaking to implement such a system.[15]

While the final legislation is generally consistent with the Obama administration's June 2009 proposals and responsive to the defects revealed in the CCMR study, the statutory language is still vague, especially with respect to precise loan-level disclosure requirements, and much is left to the SEC for implementation. Details are being worked out at the industry level. The American Securitization Forum (ASF), an industry group, launched in July of 2008 Project RESTART, which has evolved into a multifaceted effort to address weaknesses in securitization practices.[16] Among other things, the ASF project includes a model disclosure package for residential mortgage-backed securities including 135 data fields for

10. Id. §941(h).
11. Id. §943(1).
12. Id. §943(2).
13. Id. §941(c).
14. Id. §946.
15. Id. §939F. Elsewhere in the Dodd-Frank act is a provision adding a new section 27B to the Securities Act of 1933 and establishing special conflict-of-interest rules for the sale of asset-backed securities. See section 621 of the Dodd-Frank act.
16. For an overview of the project, see www.americansecuritization.com/restart.

pool- and loan-level information, an associated periodic reporting template that would specify fields of loan data for monthly updating, and coding protocols to establish unique numbers for individual loans, which would permit investors to track individual loans notwithstanding changes in ownership or servicing.[17] The ASF work also entails the development of standards, representations, and warranties for securitization transactions and includes various types of information that would be helpful in facilitating and tracking loan modifications.[18]

Another somewhat surprising and parallel line of securitization reform is taking place at the Federal Deposit Insurance Corporation (FDIC). The FDIC has long had an indirect role in the regulation of securitization transactions; in 2000 it issued a regulation clarifying that the FDIC, as receiver, would not seek to recover assets from a securitization transaction undertaken by an insured bank that later becomes insolvent provided the transaction was structured in compliance with the sale accounting treatment under generally accepted accounting principles.[19] This ruling was of critical importance to the development of securitization markets because investors and rating agencies needed assurance that securitization vehicles would be "bankruptcy remote" from sponsoring banks. Without the FDIC regulations, the capacity of insured depository institutions to transfer loans into securitization pools could be called into question. In the summer of 2009, however, the continued viability of the FDIC regulation became uncertain when the Financial Accounting Standards Board revised its rules on loan transfers for reporting periods beginning after November 15, 2009. The new rule would likely require consolidation for accounting purposes of securitization vehicles that were previously considered off balance sheet.[20]

To resolve the uncertainty raised by changes in generally accepted accounting standards, the FDIC issued an interim rule in November 2009 grandfathering its current regulatory safe harbor for securitization pools assembled and financed before March 31, 2010. Shortly thereafter, the FDIC released an advance notice of proposed rulemaking dealing with the structure of a proposed new safe harbor for future securitizations.[21] Unlike the 2000 safe harbor, the FDIC's advance

17. For a good analysis of both existing loan-level disclosure practices and ASF reform proposals, see Peppet (2009).

18. For example, AFS literature notes that its model disclosure packages address "significant expansion of public and investor reporting of loan modification activity by mortgage servicers nationwide; disclosure standards for securitization or resecuritization of mortgage loans that have previously been modified in the loss mitigation process; uniform national standards for the secondary market definition of a full-documentation loan; proposed mechanism for owners of first-lien mortgages to immediately know a second-lien mortgage has been originated on the subject property; methods to address higher rates of fraud in new originations and in modifying loans; and recommendations for universal loan identification system for mortgage and consumer loans." Peppet (2009).

19. See 12 C.F.R. §360.6 (2009).

20. See 74 Fed. Reg. 59, 066 (November 17, 2009).

21. 75 Fed. Reg. 934 (January 7, 2010).

notice contemplated a highly prescriptive set of rules governing many aspects of the structure of securitization transactions, including disclosure requirements. Under the draft regulatory provision, the FDIC would mandate an extensive list of loan-level information, including all of the information that the SEC Regulation AB requires for public asset-backed securities offerings even if the transactions were structured as private placements and thus formally exempt from Regulation AB.[22] Perhaps not surprising, the FDIC's initiative prompted swift and vehement objections from industry representatives, including the ASF,[23] although others have endorsed the FDIC's efforts and even advocated more stringent daily updating of loan-level data.[24] Notwithstanding initial criticisms, the FDIC moved forward to the next stage of the rulemaking process. A notice of proposed rulemaking was released on May 17, 2010, largely tracking the FDIC's previous announcement with respect to disclosure requirements and including extensive provisions regarding compensation, capital structure, and risk retention for securitization transactions.[25]

The final participant in the reform of securitization disclosure requirements is the SEC itself. On May 3, 2010, the SEC released its own notice of proposed rulemaking involving extensive revisions of Regulation AB, which governs disclosure requirements for asset-backed securities.[26] The SEC proposal includes elaborate new requirements for loan-level disclosures both at the time of offering and on an ongoing basis. The proposal includes a host of ancillary reforms designed to ensure that information is available in machine-readable formats and to slow down shelf offerings so that investors can review disclosures before making investment decisions.[27] The SEC proposal draws explicitly on the work of the ASF in its Project RESTART as well as several other sources of standardized terms for loan-level disclosures.[28] In addition, it includes periodic reporting requirements focused on loan modifications and renegotiations.[29] Finally, like the FDIC proposal, the SEC's

22. Id. at 940.

23. www.americansecuritization.com/uploadedFiles/ASFFDICCommentLetterreSafeHarbor 010409.pdf.

24. www.fdic.gov/regulations/laws/federal/2010/10c02AD55.pdf.

25. 75 Fed. Reg. 27, 471 (May 17, 2010).

26. 75 Fed. Reg. 23, 328 (May 3, 2010). In a speech in October 2009, Chair Mary Shapiro announced that the SEC might seek additional statutory authority to provide more comprehensive and substantive oversight of asset-backed securities, perhaps modeled on the Investment Company Act of 1940, from which the securitization transactions are currently exempt under safe harbor rules adopted many years ago. www.fdic.gov/regulations/laws/federal/2010/10c02AD55.pdf. Such a reform would constitute a reversal of the SEC's current practice of providing fairly generous 1940 act exemptive relief to securitization transactions. These proposed reforms were not incorporated into the Dodd-Frank act and are not reflected in the SEC's proposed amendments to Regulation AB.

27. The SEC proposal includes two new schedules: Schedule L (asset-level information), to be codified at 17 C.F.R. §229.1111A, and Schedule L-D (asset-level performance information), to be codified at 17 C.F.R. §229.1121A.

28. 75 Fed. Reg. at 23, 356; 23, 360.

29. 75 Fed. Reg. at 23, 368–70.

new rules would extend to privately placed asset-backed securities offerings, imposing for the first time extensive mandatory disclosure obligations on an important class of privately placed securities.[30]

In sum, the debate over loan-level disclosures in securitization transactions is a quadrille with many partners, not all of whom are dancing to the same music. Building on the Obama administration's June 2009 proposal, the Dodd-Frank act contemplates SEC implementation of expanded loan-level disclosure standards to be imposed on a periodic reporting basis at least on securitization financings sold to the general public, complemented with risk retention rules to be implemented by the SEC working in conjunction with other agencies. The SEC's May 2010 proposal, while antedating passage of the Dodd-Frank act, offers an extensive system of loan-level disclosure, building on the Obama administration's framework and incorporating the prior work of the ASF and its working groups. The FDIC initiative covers similar ground, but at this stage seems out of step with intervening developments. With regard to loan-level disclosures, the most striking feature of the FDIC's proposal is the extension of SEC disclosure obligations for public securitization transactions to privately placed offerings sponsored by insured depository institutions. With its May 2010 proposal, the SEC would impose a similar requirement on all privately placed securitization transactions, effectively superseding this aspect of the FDIC's proposal and arguably also going beyond the contours of the relevant provisions of the Dodd-Frank act, which seem limited to public offerings of asset-backed securities.[31] The other significant aspect of the FDIC initiative—its proposal on risk retention—does not track the legislative compromises incorporated into the Dodd-Frank act, which include exemptions for certain asset classes, and it remains an open question whether the FDIC will choose to proceed with a distinctive set of risk retention rules for insured depository institutions when Congress has mandated another set of risk retention rules for general application.

While this chapter focuses on the evolution of the loan-level disclosure requirements for securitization transactions, one cannot help but be struck by the tension evident in the range of reform initiatives seeking to move beyond mere disclosure and into more intrusive mandatory requirements. Even in the Obama administration's initial proposals, this tension was apparent with the inclusion of

---

30. 75 Fed. Reg. at 23, 393–99.

31. While it is beyond the scope of this chapter, the SEC's proposal to impose substantial disclosure obligations on privately placed securities offerings raises some interesting questions of agency authority. Traditionally, the section 4(2) securities act exemption for private placements has been understood to be self-executing—that is, operating without any need for SEC implementing regulations. While the SEC has broad statutory latitude to add additional exemptions, the authority of the agency to limit the private placement exemption for offerings to institutional investors—the primary purchasers of asset-backed securities—may be susceptible to legal challenge, notwithstanding the strong public policy arguments in favor of the SEC's proposal.

"skin in the game" requirements that have evolved into legislative provisions setting 5 percent credit retention as a presumptive standard. The FDIC-proposed
rulemaking pushed even further into mandatory terms, dictating not just credit
retention but also dealing with permissible capital structures and potentially even
loan terms. And the Dodd-Frank act itself mandates both enhanced disclosure and
extensive provisions regarding risk retention. While understandable, this turn of
events is modestly ironic, as the securitization of financial assets initially emerged
as a way of escaping the mandatory requirements imposed on banks and other
highly regulated financial intermediaries.[32] These more intrusive reform initiatives
attempt to replicate those regulatory requirements in a new and specialized form
applied directly to the securitization vehicles themselves. The logic of enhancing
the substantive content of securitization oversight as well as the disclosure obligations is understandable in light of the profound problems that securitization
transactions have imposed on the rest of the economy in the recent financial crisis. As the next part of my analysis explores, however, one complexity of implementing this expanded regulation of securitization transactions is that the agency
primarily responsible for the oversight of securitization transactions is the Securities and Exchange Commission, and it is not at all clear that the commission's
expertise is well suited to the task of taking into account all of the collateral ram-
ifications of large-scale asset securitizations.

Other Potential Public Uses of Loan-Level Disclosures

At root, the debate over loan-level disclosure in securitization transactions
recounted above centers on two different points of disclosure: the initial disclosure of information at the launching of the securitization vehicle, when funds
are raised in the capital markets, and then continuous updating of information
while the securitization is outstanding. The debate touches on many issues of
implementation—Which kinds of offering are covered: only public offerings
or also private placements? How long should the continuous reporting obligations
continue? What is the appropriate content of the disclosure requirements?—but
the essence of the matter consists of offering disclosure under the 1933 act and
continuous disclosures under the 1934 act. Because the debate is framed largely
as a matter of securities regulation and thus within the regulatory bailiwick of the
SEC, the issue is generally evaluated in terms of investor protection. What information do investors need to properly value interests in securitization pools and
derivative products? Certainly investor protection is the bread and butter of SEC
oversight, and groups such as the ASF are concerned primarily with the interests
of investors, if not for the purposes of protecting investors themselves, then at least

---

32. See Bryan (1988), an early work propounding securitization as a more efficient form of
financing credit.

for the purposes of restoring sufficient confidence in the securitization process to allow the market to begin operations again. Even when the reform proposals extend to the standardization of representations and warranties or disclosures regarding compensation arrangements and loan modification terms, issues of transparency and investor confidence remain the primary focus.

However, other public uses of loan-level disclosure information should also be factored into any mandatory rules for securitization transactions. Loan-level disclosures broadly construed could play a helpful role in facilitating loan modifications and reducing foreclosures and resultant economic and personal dislocations. Loan-level disclosures, particularly at the offering stage, could also prove useful in policing loan abuses and discriminatory practices in loan origination. Consideration of these uses might well factor into a fully informed public debate over mandatory loan-level disclosure requirements.

Loan Modifications and Disclosures

As is well documented in this volume and elsewhere, one of the great public policy challenges of the subprime crisis and subsequent bursting of the housing bubble has come from the difficulty borrowers have encountered in their efforts to renegotiate lending transactions and seek meaningful modifications of principal balances. As with any negotiation, one of the chief barriers to settlement is disagreement over the value of contractual commitments and fair terms for renegotiation. While the SEC proposal specifically addresses the issue of loan modifications, the SEC's disclosure requirements focus on providing useful information to investors seeking to value interests in securitization pools. The commission's proposals are not concerned principally with the potential value of loan modification for borrowers and lenders with mortgages held in other forms, such as portfolio holdings or government-sponsored securitization pools.

With relatively modest adjustments in structure and content, however, one could imagine loan-level disclosure requirements in securitization transactions playing an important role in facilitating private renegotiations of other loans. Particularly important would be information on the settlement terms accepted by securitization services for loans in specific markets with specific underwriting characteristics. The beauty of mandatory continuous disclosure of terms for securitization transactions is that mandatory disclosure would produce current data about loan characteristics. Such current data could be extraordinarily useful for others seeking to renegotiate loan terms or for the government if it were to initiate a program of loan purchases, as I and others have advocated.[33]

While the technical task of broadening the scope of loan-level disclosures to facilitate loan renegotiations is not particularly challenging, the institutional barriers may be more severe. As enacted, the Dodd-Frank bill vests the SEC with the

---

33. See, for example, Jackson (2008a).

power to develop loan-level disclosure requirements. And, in practice, it seems likely that the ASF and other industry groups would likely play a valuable (indeed indispensable) role in formulating the final rules. The expertise of these organizations does not, however, extend to loan renegotiations. Indeed, to the extent that enhanced bargaining power for borrowers and their representatives might impose costs on investors and the securitization industry, one might imagine that these groups would have some resistance to broadening access to loan-level disclosures. Accordingly, public policy concerns may well justify broader access and slightly more transparent and extensive loan-level disclosure obligations than investors would themselves demand. Accordingly, in finalizing its reforms of Regulation AB, the commission should consider whether its disclosure requirements provide sufficient access to borrowers and their representatives seeking to gain a better understanding of the terms on which individual loans in particular markets are being modified.[34]

Abusive and Discriminatory Origination Practices

Again other chapters in this volume address in considerable detail the problems of policing abusive and discriminatory origination practices in residential mortgage originations.[35] As is explained in those chapters, one of the complexities of effectively policing these practices has been the inability of regulators and aggrieved parties to control for risk characteristics of mortgages at the time of origination. One could imagine expanding upon the Home Mortgage Disclosure Act (HMDA) disclosure requirements (as Allen Fishbein and Ren Essene discuss in their chapter in this volume). Or one could leave it to private litigants and government enforcement officials to collect and reconstitute relevant risk factors through discovery and other litigation techniques. But here again loan-level disclosures in securitization transactions offer a potentially efficient and highly accurate source of supporting data.

For these purposes, the relevant source of information is at the offering stage of securitization transactions. As contemplated in the Dodd-Frank act and the SEC proposal, sponsors of securitization transactions would be required to assemble all materially important information on loan and borrower characteristics with a unique loan identification code. As long as these codes were linked up to the associated HMDA disclosure data set, regulatory authorities (and potentially litigants) would have a ready-made resource for all relevant risk controls.[36] With a

34. The disclosure provisions of the Dodd-Frank act—section 942(b)—amend section 7 of the Securities Act of 1933, which allows the SEC, in establishing disclosure obligations for registration statements, to require such information "as the Commission determines necessary or appropriate in the public interest or for the protection of investors." This grant of authority allows the commission to look beyond investors' interests in appropriate cases.

35. See Fishbein and Essene's chapter in this volume.

36. In an earlier paper, I explore the usefulness of individual loan transfer prices for policing origination abuses. See Jackson (2008b).

few modest refinements—adding in links to the Real Estate Settlements and Procedures Act Housing and Urban Development 1 forms and providing an allocated price for each loan transferred to the securitization pool—loan-level disclosures could revolutionize the manner in which mortgage originations are policed in the United States.

Again, expansion of disclosure obligations along these lines is unlikely to be the kind of amendment that the SEC or investor groups would propose on their own initiative. The agencies charged with policing abusive lending practices—currently the Federal Reserve Board and, in the future, presumably the new Consumer Financial Protection Bureau—would be more plausible proponents, and perhaps their views can be factored into SEC deliberations as it revises its May 2010 proposals. But clearly the possible benefits of loan-level disclosures for policing loan originations should be part of the debate.

Further Thoughts and Extensions

In this final section, I offer a few thoughts and possible extensions of the foregoing analysis. One concerns the relationship between proposals for mandatory credit retention and loan-level disclosures. A second touches on the appropriate scope of loan-level disclosure proposals beyond securitization transactions. And finally I flag very important issues of individual privacy and possible limitations on the scope of loan-level disclosure.

Credit Retention and Loan-Level Disclosures

As explained earlier, both the Obama administration's initial recommendations and the Dodd-Frank act require loan originators and securitization sponsors to retain credit risk on loans transferred to securitization pools, presumptively 5 percent of total credit retention, subject to various statutory exemptions. While this retention could be structured in various ways, much of the statutory language points toward either an actual retention of interests in the loan or some sort of loss coverage for loans assigned to a securitization pool.[37] While an understandable response to concerns that the originate-to-distribute model fueled the subprime crisis, this approach to credit risk retention has several drawbacks. To begin with, leaving the securitization pool with fractional interests in loans complicates the valuation exercise for investors, thereby reducing transparency and also complicating interpretation of the loan modification terms or the value of loan originations. In addition, requiring at least two parties to have an interest in each loan assigned to a loan pool could also complicate loan renegotiations themselves. An

---

37. As a technical matter, the SEC and other agencies responsible for implementing the Dodd-Frank act risk retention rules appear to have some latitude in how the requirements are satisfied, and certain classes of assets—most notably qualified mortgages—will be exempt from these requirements. See section 941 of the Dodd-Frank act.

alternative approach would be to force originators and sponsors to retain interests in the securitization pool itself (either in the most junior tranche or perhaps a pro rata share in all tranches). This approach, which is similar to the direction that European reforms are taking,[38] allows for greater transparency as to loan values and also more directly aligns the interests of originators and sponsors to pool investors. To be sure, in cases where securitization pools contain loans originated by multiple parties, agency problems may emerge. But at least for the immediate future, securitization sponsors will be keenly attuned to such matters and can use other mechanisms, such as deferred compensation arrangements, to safeguard against opportunistic behavior.

Appropriate Scope of Loan-Level Disclosure Requirement

The remit of this chapter has been loan-level disclosures in securitization transactions, and so far I have been reasonably faithful to that assignment. But if one considers the primary goal of imposing mandatory rules in this area—to improve transparency of loan values so as to improve the pricing of interests in securitization pools—one may quite reasonably ask whether similar information should not be retained and updated for loans held in institutional portfolios or on the books of government-sponsored entities and the securitization pools those GSEs guarantee, where the vast majority of residential mortgages were still financed even at the height of the subprime boom. After all, the loan-level disclosure movement is premised on the assumption that this information is essential for valuing pools of mortgages. Regulatory officials charged with policing the solvency of financial institutions and also GSEs should be keenly interested in precisely the same information. Indeed, one wonders what the argument would be for such regulators not to demand the retention and updating of this information once the SEC and market participants conclude that it is essential for securitization pools. After all, if investors need this information to evaluate securitization pools, regulators must also need it to oversee institutional balance sheets.[39] And, of course, the public benefits of retaining this information to facilitate loan modifications and policing of origination abuses and discrimination are equally applicable to loans held on institutional portfolios and on GSE balance sheets. Finally, a broader application of loan-level disclosure requirements would prevent the promulgation of these rules from favoring some forms of loan financing over others.

Privacy Concerns and Loan-Level Disclosures

Finally, let me offer a word on loan-level disclosures and privacy concerns. As Allen Fishbein and Ren Essene recount in their chapter in this volume, privacy

---

38. See Allen & Overy (2010).

39. To be sure, the costs of collecting loan-level data may be unduly burdensome for smaller institutions with relatively limited exposures, and so mandatory collection rules would likely be appropriate only above some asset threshold.

concerns have already been identified as a problem in the area of HMDA disclosures, and Scott Peppet has recently written a quite helpful paper discussing the not-inconsiderable privacy issues presented by the ASF's preliminary proposals on loan-level disclosure.[40] Clearly, these are serious issues. However, the logic of loan-level disclosure is that this information needs to be provided to the broader market in order to obtain accurate pricing. Limiting disclosures to a narrow group of parties—like credit-rating agencies—defeats the purposes of the proposals and was itself thought to be one of the sources of the subprime crisis. Similarly, to the extent that loan-level disclosures are being used to facilitate third-party loan renegotiations, public access is essential. To be sure, some information might be kept out of public hands. For example, the key connecting unique loan codes to HMDA data need not be disclosed to the general public. Rather, access to this information could be limited to regulatory officials conducting fair lending reviews and private litigants conducting discovery under court-supervised conditions. But, in large part, loan-level disclosure should be public disclosure, and the complexities of privacy protections are simply one more issue that public officials will need to address.

References

Allen & Overy LLP. 2010. "ECB Eligible Collateral Framework." January 15. www.allen overy.com/AOWEB/AreasOfExpertise/Editorial.aspx?contentTypeID=1&itemID=54420 &prefLangID=410.

Ashcraft, Adam B., and Til Schuermann. 2008. "Understanding the Securitization of Subprime Credit." Staff Report 318. Federal Reserve Bank of New York (March).

Bryan, Lowell L. 1988. *Breaking up the Bank: Rethinking an Industry under Siege.* Homewood, Ill.: Irwin Professional.

CCMR (Committee on Capital Markets Regulation). 2009. "The Global Financial Crisis: A Plan for Regulatory Reform." Cambridge, Mass. (May). www.capmktsreg.org/pdfs/TGFC-CCMR_Report_%285-26-09%29.pdf.

Coates, John C. 2009. "Reforming the Taxation and Regulation of Mutual Funds." *Journal of Legal Analysis* 1, no. 591: 663.

Department of Treasury. 2009. "A New Foundation: Rebuilding Financial Supervision and Regulation 43-46." Washington (June). www.financialstability.gov/docs/regs/FinalReport_web.pdf.

Jackson, Howell E. 2008a. "Building a Better Bailout." *Christian Science Monitor,* September 25.
———. 2008b. "Enlisting Market Mechanisms to Police the Origination of Home Mortgages." Harvard University, Joint Center for Housing Studies (November).

Peppet, Scott. 2009. "Smart Mortgages, Privacy, and the Regulatory Possibility of Infomediation." University of Colorado Law School (August 19). papers.ssrn.com/sol3/papers.cfm?abstract_id=1458064.

40. See Peppet (2009).

7

The Regulation of Consumer Financial Products: An Introductory Essay with a Case Study on Payday Lending

JOHN Y. CAMPBELL, HOWELL E. JACKSON,
BRIGITTE C. MADRIAN, AND PETER TUFANO

Recent economic events have focused attention on the financial decisions made by consumers and the practices of retail financial institutions. Many argue that consumer confusion in the increasingly complex mortgage market contributed to the subprime market meltdown of 2007, which in turn triggered the global financial crisis. More generally, there is widespread concern that consumers are being asked to take increasing responsibility for their own financial well-being in retirement and that many households are ill prepared for this task.

While consumer financial regulation has always been an important element of public policy, it has received much greater emphasis recently. One of the first actions of the 111th Congress under the new Obama administration was passage of the Credit Card Accountability, Responsibility, and Disclosure Act of 2009, which banned retroactive fee changes and required consumers to opt in to over-the-limit fees, among other features.[1] A far more comprehensive approach to the protection of consumers is embodied in the new Consumer Financial Protection Bureau (CFPB) established with passage of the Dodd-Frank Wall Street Reform and Consumer Protection Act. The CFPB is charged with establishing, implementing, and enforcing rules that ensure that "all consumers have access" to financial services and that markets for these services be "fair, transparent, and compet-

---

Portions of this chapter appear in an article to be published in the *Journal of Economic Perspectives*.
   1. For details, see www.whitehouse.gov/the_press_office/Fact-Sheet-Reforms-to-Protect-American-Credit-Card-Holders.

itive." In particular, the act enumerates the following objectives. With respect to consumer financial products and services,

(1) Consumers are provided with timely and understandable information to make responsible decisions about financial transactions.

(2) Consumers are protected from unfair, deceptive, or abusive acts and practices and from discrimination.

(3) Outdated, unnecessary, or unduly burdensome regulations are regularly identified and addressed in order to reduce unwarranted regulatory burdens.

(4) Federal consumer financial law is enforced consistently, without regard to the status of a person as a depository institution, in order to promote fair competition.

(5) Markets for consumer financial products and services operate transparently and efficiently to facilitate access and innovation.

While its jurisdiction does not extend to insurance or investment products and other agencies at both the state and federal level will retain important and independent roles, the bureau is poised to become the premier authority for safeguarding consumer financial products and services in the United States.

Officials at the CFPB and at other government agencies responsible for policing other areas of consumer finance need a framework within which to set rules and regulations. Our goal in this chapter is to explain the *economic basis* for consumer financial regulation. We begin by briefly describing the functions, scope, and scale of consumer financial markets. We then survey the justifications for government intervention into consumer financial markets. While regulation in this field is often framed in terms of "transparency, simplicity, fairness, accountability, and access," we relate these concepts to various market failures that may impede economic efficiency or create unacceptable distributional outcomes. We then review the structure of consumer financial regulation in the United States and the most common regulatory mechanisms that are used to police consumer financial markets.

To illustrate how many of the themes in the chapter apply to consumer financial markets, we explore a case study on payday loans, a controversial financial product that has been subject to a variety of regulatory regimes.[2] Finally, we outline the types of future research (and their data requirements) that would be most useful in informing the optimal regulation of consumer financial markets. By clarifying the economic foundations of consumer financial regulation, we hope to define the metrics for evaluating the success or failure of regulatory reform. In short, without knowing the goals for reform, it is impossible to assess whether we have succeeded in creating a "better" financial system.

---

2. In an expanded version of this chapter, we include additional case studies on retirement savings, mortgage lending, and mutual funds. See Campbell and others (2010).

A Brief Overview of Consumer Financial Markets

To understand the role of regulation of consumer financial products, it is useful to consider first the functions of the consumer financial system and the economics of consumer financial markets.

Functions of the Consumer Financial System

While consumer finance could be defined by reference to specific institutions (banks or insurance companies) or products (deposits or life insurance), we follow Merton and Bodie as well as Tufano in positing that financial systems can be best understood in terms of the *functions* they perform, including the following:[3]

—*Payments.* The financial system must provide a mechanism for transferring money and payments for goods and services. In the consumer sector, the payments function includes cash, checks, debit cards, credit cards, prepaid cards, postal and private money orders, wire transfers, remittances, barter, online funds transfer tools like PayPal, Automated Clearing House (ACH) transactions, payroll systems, and the infrastructure supporting all of these activities. These products are delivered by many different organizations, including the government (such as money and post offices), banking institutions, nonbanks (such as check-cashing stores), data processors, online businesses, and others.

—*Managing risk.* There are many mechanisms for mitigating the financial risks faced by consumers, such as insurance (health, life, property and casualty, disability), financial products (put options to protect against portfolio declines), precautionary savings, social networks, and government welfare programs. The organizations that perform this function range from the family and local community to insurance companies and government disaster relief plans. From the perspective of businesses that serve consumers, risks are managed by applying credit-scoring models and credit risk practices as well as by assembling a diversified portfolio or securing insurance against default.

—*Borrowing: advancing funds from the future to today.* The function of household credit encompasses short-term unsecured borrowing (credit and charge cards, banking overdraft protection, and payday loans), longer-term unsecured borrowing (student loans, person-to-person lending), and secured borrowing (auto loans, mortgage loans, and margin loans). The provision of credit takes place in the formal sector, in the informal sector (friends and family), and through various hybrid organizations (person-to-person lending websites). In addition to explicit borrowing, implicit borrowing is built into various derivative products, including options and forwards, as well as commercial structures (rent-to-own schemes).

---

3. Merton and Bodie (1995); Tufano (2009). In prior work, advice and resolution of conflicts of interest have also been included as financial functions. In this chapter, we characterize these activities as solutions to problems of asymmetric information or incomplete contracts.

—Saving and investing: moving funds from today until a later date. Investing or savings functions are embodied in a host of products and services, including bank products (savings accounts and certificates of deposit), mutual funds, variable annuities, workplace retirement programs, and Social Security. These products vary based on the intended time horizon, level and type of risk borne by the investor, tax treatment, and other factors.

The Economics of Consumer Financial Businesses

To understand the regulation of consumer financial markets, it is useful to get some idea of the economics of this sector, which is both very large and quite small. In aggregate, households held $68.2 trillion in assets at year-end 2009, with 34 percent ($23.1 trillion) of these funds in tangible assets (mostly real estate) and 66 percent ($45.1 trillion) in financial assets.[4] On the other side of the balance sheet, households held $14.0 trillion in liabilities, mostly home mortgages ($10.3 trillion) and consumer credit ($2.5 trillion, primarily in credit cards). In sheer size, the household sector dominates the corporate sector. Total corporate debt, for example, is only about half the size of household debt ($7.2 trillion).

Balance sheet numbers alone belie the full magnitude of the consumer finance sector. Visa and MasterCard, for instance, report combined annual transaction volume exceeding $6 trillion.[5] While easy to focus on such aggregates, this sum comprises a staggering number of small transactions: more than 70 billion a year. Similarly, while total mutual fund industry assets exceed $10 trillion, the Investment Company Institute reports that the median investor has $100,000 in fund assets spread across four different accounts.[6] Even with these comparatively large accounts (nearly twice median family income in America), the fund industry has to deal with a large number of small accounts.

Tables 7-1 and 7-2 give a finer breakdown of the asset holdings and liabilities of U.S. families in 2007, by type of asset or liability, for all families and by position in the income distribution. These tables highlight various features of consumer financial markets. First, as noted, the median account balances for many of the cells in the bottom panels of tables 7-1 and 7-2 are indeed relatively small. Second, although transaction accounts are the most widely held asset (92 percent), one-quarter of families in the bottom decile of the income distribution do not have such accounts. These families, the so-called unbanked, rely on other mechanisms for

---

4. See Federal Reserve Board (2010). This information refers to households and nonprofit organizations, as the two are considered a single sector in the flow-of-funds calculations. As nonprofits account for only 5–7 percent of assets and liabilities, these figures are largely reflective of the household sector (Teplin 2001).

5. See www.corporate.visa.com/av/pdf/Visa_Inc_Overview.pdf and www.mastercard.com/us/company/en/newsroom/annual_report/MasterCard_2007AR.pdf. Figures represent all card transactions worldwide.

6. See www.ici.org/pdf/rpt_profile09.pdf.

Table 7-1. Financial Holdings of U.S. Families in 2007

Family characteristic	Transaction accounts	Certificates of deposit	Savings bonds	Bonds	Stocks	Pooled investment funds	Retirement accounts	Cash-value life insurance	Other managed assets	Other	Any financial asset
Percentage of families holding the asset											
All families	92.1	16.1	14.9	1.6	17.9	11.4	52.6	23.0	5.8	9.3	93.9
By income percentile											
< 20	74.9	9.4	3.6	n.a.	5.5	3.4	10.7	12.8	2.7	6.6	79.1
20 to < 40	90.1	12.7	8.5	n.a.	7.8	4.6	35.6	16.4	4.7	8.8	93.2
40 to < 60	96.4	15.4	15.2	n.a.	14.0	7.1	55.2	21.6	5.3	10.2	97.2
60 to < 80	99.3	19.3	20.9	1.4	23.2	14.6	73.3	29.4	5.7	8.4	99.7
80 to < 90	100.0	19.9	26.2	1.8	30.5	18.9	86.7	30.6	7.6	9.8	100.0
90 to < 100	100.0	27.7	26.1	8.9	47.5	35.5	89.6	38.9	13.6	15.3	100.0
Median value of holdings for families holding the asset (thousands of dollars)											
All families	4.0	20.0	1.0	80.0	17.0	56.0	45.0	8.0	70.0	6.0	28.8
By income percentile											
< 20	0.8	18.0	0.5	n.a.	3.8	30.0	6.5	2.5	100.0	1.5	1.7
20 to < 40	1.6	18.0	1.0	n.a.	10.0	30.0	12.0	5.0	86.0	3.0	7.0
40 to < 60	2.7	17.0	0.7	n.a.	5.5	37.5	23.9	5.2	59.0	4.0	18.6
60 to < 80	6.0	11.0	1.0	19.0	14.0	35.0	48.0	10.0	52.0	10.0	58.3
80 to < 90	12.9	20.0	2.0	81.0	15.0	46.0	85.0	9.0	30.0	10.0	129.9
90 to < 100	36.7	42.0	2.5	250.0	75.0	180.0	200.0	28.1	90.0	45.0	404.5

Source: Bucks and others (2009) from the 2007 Survey of Consumer Finances.
n.a. Not available.

Table 7-2. Financial Liabilities of U.S. Families in 2007

Family characteristic	Secured by residential property		Installment loans	Credit card balances	Lines of credit not secured by residential property	Other	Any debt
	Primary residence	Other					
Percentage of families holding debt							
All families	48.7	5.5	46.9	46.1	1.7	6.8	77.0
By income percentile							
< 20	14.9	1.1	27.8	25.7	n.a.	3.9	51.7
20 to < 40	29.5	1.9	42.3	39.4	1.8	6.8	70.2
40 to < 60	50.5	2.6	54.0	54.9	n.a.	6.4	83.8
60 to < 80	69.7	6.8	59.2	62.1	2.1	8.7	90.9
80 to < 90	80.8	8.5	57.4	55.8	n.a.	9.6	89.6
90 to < 100	76.4	21.9	45.0	40.6	2.1	7.0	87.6
Median value of debt for families holding debt (thousands of dollars)							
All families	107.0	100.0	13.0	3.0	3.8	5.0	67.3
By income percentile							
< 20	40.0	70.0	6.5	1.0	n.a.	3.0	9.0
20 to < 40	51.0	42.0	9.8	1.8	1.3	4.0	18.0
40 to < 60	88.7	68.9	12.8	2.4	n.a.	4.0	54.5
60 to < 80	115.0	83.0	16.3	4.0	5.1	5.3	111.3
80 to < 90	164.0	125.0	17.3	5.5	n.a.	5.0	182.2
90 to < 100	201.0	147.5	18.3	7.5	17.3	7.5	235.0

Source: Bucks and others (2009) from the 2007 Survey of Consumer Finances.
n.a. Not available.

payment services.[7] Third, asset and liability holdings vary considerably by position in the income distribution, particularly for direct holdings of equities and retirement savings accounts and for mortgage debt. This disparate incidence has led some policymakers to call for expanded access to some types of financial services.

The small sizes of accounts and transactions have several implications for retail financial services and their regulation. First, the cost of customer acquisition or asset gathering is large relative to the cost of producing actual services. Bergstresser, Chalmers, and Tufano find that distribution costs account for 39 percent of all charges paid by mutual fund investors.[8] Second, because of the sheer number of transactions, the level of contact with and information about customers may be limited. This makes full-information contracting nearly impossible and gives rise to low-cost automated solutions like credit-scoring models. Third, economies of scale and scope are often more complex than they appear in simple microeconomics models. For example, the marginal cost of a single additional account might be nearly zero, but adding many accounts might necessitate more call center operators, or even a new call center, with lumpy additions to cost. Finally, because of the joint nature of production, establishing product or activity costs can be challenging. All of these considerations should be factored into assessments of the costs and benefits of financial regulation.

The Need for Consumer Financial Regulation

Consumer advocates often make the case for consumer financial regulation on distributional grounds, arguing that unregulated markets disadvantage lower-income households. This is an important consideration, but we begin by first assessing the potential inefficiencies of consumer financial markets that might call for regulation and then turn to distributional considerations.

Several features of consumer financial markets can lead to inefficient outcomes that may justify government intervention. Most fundamentally, financial markets often involve both time and uncertainty. Many financial transactions require initial payments from one party to another, offset by payments in the opposite direction in the future that are explicitly state contingent or implicitly subject to the risk of complete or partial default. During the life of a financial transaction, the two parties involved have conflicting interests and often have asymmetric information, leading to a rich variety of problems that have been studied by contract and information theorists. It is difficult to structure contracts that handle every

---

7. Another substantial group of households (17 percent) maintain transaction accounts but are considered underbanked because they also rely on alternative financial services, such as payday lenders and pawnshops (FDIC 2009).

8. Bergstresser, Chalmers, and Tufano (2009).

possible contingency that may arise during the life of a transaction, and this contractual incompleteness can create problems.

Another set of problems arises because consumers may not behave as time-consistent, rational utility maximizers. They may, for example, have present-biased preferences, in which decisions made each period favor present consumption, even though the consumer would display greater patience if enabled to commit to a future consumption plan. Just as important, consumers may lack the cognitive capacity to optimize their financial situation, even if presented with all the information that in principle is required to do so. It is unusually difficult to learn how to optimize in certain financial markets. Many financial transactions are infrequently undertaken and have delayed outcomes that are subject to large random shocks, so personal experience is slow to accumulate and is contaminated by noise. Social learning is encumbered first by the fact that random events in financial markets often affect many people simultaneously, so that averaging outcomes across neighbors may not eliminate noise, and second by the rapid pace of financial innovation, which reduces the relevance of older cohorts' experiences. A strong social taboo on discussing personal financial matters in certain cultures further reduces the effectiveness of social learning.[9]

In order to understand the many sources of inefficiency in consumer financial markets, it is helpful to start with the traditional taxonomy of conditions that may result in market failure even with fully rational consumers.[10] We then relate these to the failures that may be caused by present-biased preferences or cognitive limitations. Finally, we consider distributional issues.

Traditional Economic Justifications for Consumer Financial Regulation

The first rationale for consumer financial regulation is to facilitate enforcement of financial contracts. Many consumer financial transactions span long time horizons or entail the transfer of wealth over considerable geographic distance. The temporal aspect of financial products creates moral hazard allowing firms to act in ways that may impede market efficiency. In markets such as those for retirement savings or life insurance, performance occurs over a long period of time, well after consumers and firms enter into a contractual commitment. Consumers are unlikely to be able to engage in continuous monitoring, and reputation may be insufficient to discipline firms that are tempted to expropriate their clients' wealth. In this case, mandatory capital requirements and other forms of ongoing

---

9. Zelizer (1994).

10. Earlier papers have presented more limited taxonomies of the economic justifications for consumer financial regulation. Hynes and Posner (2002) offer an overview of potential market failures with regard to consumer credit transactions. Carlin and Gervais (2009) and Inderst and Ottaviani (2009) present models dealing with financial advice. Bar-Gill (2008) and Wright (2007) provide differing perspectives on the behavioral economics of consumer contracts.

supervision may be needed to ensure the development of well-functioning markets. Such regulation is valuable not only for consumers, but also for firms, as it provides a commitment device that enables them to win business that would otherwise be unavailable.

A second rationale for consumer financial regulation is that of externalities: individual financial behavior may affect others in ways that are not reflected in market prices. Positive externalities from human capital accumulation and home-ownership have been used to justify government subsidies to student loans and home mortgages. Conversely, foreclosures have social costs that are not taken into account by mortgage borrowers and lenders.[11] More generally, correlated investment strategies may increase the systemic risk in financial markets and thus warrant supervisory intervention.

A third rationale for consumer financial regulation is to counter market power that is facilitated by high consumer search costs. Price dispersion is a feature of many retail markets. It can be sustained by the existence of search costs that make some consumers willing to pay higher prices than they might find elsewhere. These search costs give retailers a degree of market power, allowing them to charge prices above marginal cost. One example in the financial arena is Standard and Poor's 500 index funds—providers charge a wide range of fees for an essentially identical product.[12] Search costs can be addressed by providing information on market prices (for example, Medicare Part D prescription drug plan decision aids), by standardizing the provision of information (for example, requiring firms to quote interest rates as an annualized percentage rate or mandating uniform disclosure of fees and past returns in mutual fund prospectuses), or by directly regulating prices. More general responses to market power include limitations on the scale or scope of financial services firms or enhanced antitrust requirements.

The role of information as a public good provides yet another rationale for consumer financial regulation. To make informed decisions, consumers often need information about financial products that they cannot efficiently generate themselves and for which joint production with other consumers is not easily coordinated. Often the financial provider will be the most efficient supplier of this information. Disclosure requirements—mandates that the firm produce and disseminate certain types of information—are an example of interventions that address this type of market failure. Antifraud rules backed by judicial enforcement mechanisms serve a similar purpose, although traditionally fraud remedies were limited to intentional affirmative misrepresentations as opposed to negligent omissions or half-truths.

---

11. Campbell, Giglio, and Pathak (forthcoming) present evidence that foreclosures lower the price of nearby houses. The effect is extremely local and is stronger in low-priced neighborhoods, suggesting that the transmission mechanism may be vandalism or neighborhood deterioration.

12. Hortacsu and Syverson (2004).

There are other information failures that also provide a basis for consumer financial regulation. Indeed, consumer finance provides the textbook cases of information problems: the underprovision of insurance and consumer credit as a result of adverse selection and moral hazard. The regulatory responses to this type of market failure include mandating the purchase of insurance (for example, auto insurance), the public provision of universal insurance programs such as Social Security to mitigate adverse selection, and the subsidization of private insurance purchases through the tax system.

In some cases, the government "solution" to ill-functioning private insurance markets may itself create moral hazard that might justify further intervention. For example, the social safety net might encourage individuals to assume excessive financial risks that will result in some suffering large financial losses that qualify them for public aid. Government can mitigate this moral hazard by restricting financial risk taking, such as placing limits on employer stock holdings in retirement accounts, or by encouraging actuarially accurate, risk-based pricing.

Finally, the complexity of many consumer financial products generates both information asymmetries (firms know more about the products than consumers do) and transaction costs that make it difficult for even the most sophisticated individuals to comparison-shop. This complexity may suppress the development of robust markets for certain consumer financial products. In these circumstances, constraints on the variation in product terms may actually improve social welfare, albeit at the cost of inhibiting consumer choice.

Justifications Based on Behavioral and Cognitive Limitations of Consumers

In addition to the traditional market failures described above, recent research in behavioral economics has highlighted the potential for inefficient market outcomes that result from consumers' cognitive limitations. The division between these cognitive limitations and the neoclassical justifications for government intervention can admittedly blur at times, but there are important differences in their analytical frameworks and policy implications. Neoclassical justifications locate market failures in the structure of markets and the incentives faced by individuals and firms, whereas behavioral justifications locate the failures in the mental processes of individuals.[13] Beyond this difference in orientation, research in behavioral economics often suggests different kinds of government interventions, in particular, measures designed more to correct biases and reorient consumer decision-making than to proscribe business activities or dictate the terms of exchange.[14]

The first behavioral justification for consumer financial regulation is that consumers have preferences that are biased toward the present. These so-called

---

13. The possibility that firms might exploit these biases to enhance profits creates a further rationale for government intervention (Barr, Mullainathan, and Shafir 2008).
14. Thaler and Sunstein (2008).

present-biased preferences generate a type of externality in which the decisions of an individual today negatively affect the welfare of the same individual in the future in a way that is not internally consistent and that implies future regret.[15] This type of negative externality is sometimes referred to as an "internality." Present-biased preferences have been used to explain behaviors as diverse as failing to save for retirement and taking up smoking. The proposed policy responses to such preferences are to constrain today's self from taking actions that would be too detrimental to the future self and could include limiting early access to retirement saving or taxing consumption of cigarettes.

A second behavioral justification for consumer financial regulation is individual cognitive limitations. Recent research has documented a pervasive lack of basic financial literacy.[16] For example, consider the answers to a short set of financial literacy questions first added to the Health and Retirement Study in 2004 and subsequently incorporated into several other national and international surveys. Table 7-3 lists these questions and the answers of respondents to two such surveys. The first column for each of the two surveys lists the fraction of respondents who answered each individual question correctly. But some of the respondents could have simply guessed the correct answer, so what is more interesting is the fraction of respondents who answered multiple questions correctly. Among the older Health and Retirement Study respondents, only 56 percent correctly answered the first two questions, and only 24 percent correctly answered all three questions.[17] The younger respondents to the National Longitudinal Survey of Youth fared even worse, with only 46 percent answering the first two questions correctly and 27 percent getting all three questions right.[18]

A lack of financial literacy need not be problematic if, as Milton Friedman suggests, consumers learn to behave optimally through trial and error, much as a pool player need not have any knowledge of physics in order to play pool well.[19] But there is growing evidence that consumers make avoidable financial mistakes with nontrivial financial consequences.[20] Moreover, these mistakes are more common among consumers who have lower levels of education and income and who are less financially literate.[21] While cognitive ability is difficult to measure in a way that can be matched to financial data, there is some evidence that consumers who

15. Strotz (1955); Laibson (1997).

16. For example, see Lusardi and Mitchell (2006, 2007); Lusardi, Mitchell, and Curto (2010); Lusardi and Tufano (2009).

17. Lusardi and Mitchell (2006).

18. Lusardi, Mitchell, and Curto (2010).

19. Friedman (1953).

20. Agarwal and others (2009); Campbell (2006); Choi, Laibson, and Madrian (forthcoming).

21. On consumers with lower levels of education and income, see Calvet, Campbell, and Sodini (2007, 2009); on consumers with lower levels of financial literacy, see Kimball and Shumway (2007).

Table 7-3. *Individual Financial Literacy*

Financial literacy question	Health and Retirement Study 2004[a]			National Longitudinal Survey of Youth 2007–08[b]		
	Correct	Incorrect	Don't know or refused	Correct	Incorrect	Don't know or refused
Suppose you had $100 in a savings account and the interest rate was 2 percent a year. After five years, how much do you think you would have in the account if you left the money to grow: more than $102, exactly $102, less than $102?	67.1	22.2	10.7	79.5	14.6	5.7
Imagine that the interest rate on your savings account was 1 percent a year and inflation was 2 percent a year. After one year, would you be able to buy more than, exactly the same as, or less than today with the money in this account?	75.2	13.4	10.4	54.0	30.7	15.1
Do you think that the following statement is true or false? "Buying a single company stock usually provides a safer return than a stock mutual fund."	52.3	13.2	34.6	46.8	15.8	37.3

Source: For the Health and Retirement Study, Lusardi and Mitchell (2006); for the National Longitudinal Survey of Youth, Lusardi, Mitchell, and Curto (2010).
a. Respondents largely ages 50–69.
b. Respondents ages 23–28.

perform better on cognitive tests make better financial decisions in laboratory experiments and earn higher returns on their equity portfolio later in life.[22]

If consumers cannot maximize their own welfare, there is no reason to believe that competitive markets will be efficient. A social planner can in principle achieve better outcomes, judged using the true welfare function of consumers, than a free market that responds to the biased decisions that financially illiterate consumers make. This is true both because financially illiterate consumers may pick inappropriate financial products and because real resources may be wasted as firms seek to persuade consumers to purchase excessively expensive, and hence profitable, products. Such rent-seeking behavior creates deadweight loss.

In practice, of course, it is difficult for regulators to know the true objectives of households. But in certain cases outcomes may be improved by regulations on market conduct that reflect the presumed judgment of what most consumers would want, were they fully informed and well advised. This logic underpins the libertarian paternalism or "nudges" discussed at length by Thaler and Sunstein.[23] Other examples include mandatory capital requirements and portfolio restrictions on depository institutions, prior approval regimes regarding the integrity of personnel in many areas of the financial services industry, and many mandatory restraints on the structure of mutual funds and other financial firms.

Another behavioral justification for consumer financial regulation is the role of trust in consumer financial markets. Consumers with cognitive limitations may use rules of thumb to guide their behavior. One such rule of thumb is to avoid the use of certain financial products altogether.[24] This has been interpreted as a lack of trust in the financial system.[25] Since lack of financial market participation can be a serious mistake, there is a case for regulation to improve consumer trust through restrictions on insider trading, suitability and fiduciary requirements, and other measures that convey a sense of strong supervisory oversight.[26] There is evidence that mutual fund markets with stronger levels of investor protection are larger than those with lower levels of protection, perhaps working through this channel of trust.[27]

A final behavioral justification for consumer financial regulation is individual lack of self-knowledge. Markets may work poorly if consumers do not correctly understand their own time-inconsistent preferences or cognitive limitations, in

22. On making better financial decisions in laboratory experiments, see Benjamin, Brown, and Shapiro (2006); on earning higher returns on their equity portfolio later in life, Grinblatt, Keloharju, and Linnainmaa (2009).

23. Thaler and Sunstein (2008).

24. Christelis, Jappelli, and Padula (2010); Cole and Shastry (2009).

25. Guiso, Sapienza, and Zingales (2008).

26. Interventions to promote trust are analytically similar to traditional economic justifications of regulation as a means to facilitate long-duration financial contracts.

27. Khorana, Servaes, and Tufano (2009).

other words, if they lack self-knowledge. For example, consumers may choose a bank account with "free" checking, underestimating the extent to which they will pay penalty fees for overdrawing their account in the future. Such lack of self-knowledge leads to several problems. First, naïve consumers may purchase too many bank services because they underestimate the total cost to them. Second, banks compete away the excess profits they obtain through overdraft fees by keeping base charges low on checking accounts. This implies that naïve consumers cross-subsidize sophisticated consumers who do not overdraw their accounts. Products that allocate costs more equally across naïve and sophisticated consumers cannot be successfully brought to market, as sophisticated consumers find it attractive to retain the cross-subsidies embedded in existing products. Nor is it profitable for firms to educate naïve consumers, because educated consumers become sophisticated and then demand fewer high-cost financial services. Finally, there are troubling distributional implications because naïve consumers are likely to have lower incomes than sophisticated consumers. Gabaix and Laibson have modeled this "shrouded equilibrium."[28] Campbell presents evidence that similar phenomena are important in mortgage markets.[29]

Distributional Considerations and Consumer Financial Regulation

Even when unregulated markets are efficient, they may generate unacceptable distributional outcomes. While in principle this can be addressed by social welfare programs and progressive income taxation, distributional considerations also motivate some consumer financial regulation. As noted, consumers with high search costs are likely to pay higher prices in unregulated markets. In some contexts, search costs are higher for those with a high value of time and are likely to be positively correlated with income. Aguiar and Hurst, for example, show that middle-aged consumers pay higher prices than retired consumers because they spend less time shopping.[30] In consumer financial markets, however, search costs may be correlated more with cognitive ability and financial experience than with the value of time. Individuals of limited cognitive ability or financial expertise may have higher search costs because they lack easy access to information or the capacity to process it and thus may pay high prices for financial products even though they have low incomes. Distributional considerations thus strengthen the case for measures to reduce search costs or to limit the ability of firms to exercise market power over consumers with high search costs.

Distributional concerns also motivate regulatory restrictions on the ability of financial firms to vary pricing of certain products, even when there is variation in the underlying cost of delivering services. Current legislation about certain credit

---

28. Gabaix and Laibson (2006).
29. Campbell (2006).
30. Aguiar and Hurst (2007).

products is predicated on the logic that low-income consumers should not pay more than high-income consumers for credit. In some auto insurance markets, state laws prohibit setting insurance premiums on the basis of geography or age. In the area of consumer credit, various federal statutes, including the Equal Credit Opportunity Act and the Fair Housing Act, prohibit price discrimination based on race and various other individual characteristics. And, in the case of depository institutions, the Community Reinvestment Act of 1977 requires firms to serve the credit needs of low- and moderate-income borrowers. Other forms of this logic, framed around universality, have motivated measures to subsidize access to financial markets by lower-income consumers.

The Structure and Mechanisms of Consumer Financial Regulation

In the United States, a complex system of government agencies, statutory structures, and implementing regulations exists to regulate consumer financial markets. Both federal and state agencies play important roles, as do the courts and various private bodies. The mechanisms of regulatory interventions—that is, the regulatory requirements and supervisory techniques—are also multifaceted. In this section, we offer an overview of this legal regime.

The Regulatory Structure of Consumer Financial Markets

The core of our system of financial regulation is organized around the three traditional financial sectors of deposit taking, trading in securities or other capital market instruments, and insurance.[31] Before entering these lines of business, firms must usually obtain an operating charter or license from the appropriate authorities and then comply with required regulations, submit periodic reports, and undergo regular examinations to ensure compliance with regulatory standards. One important function of financial regulators is to enjoin the unauthorized provision of these regulated financial services.

While in other developed countries the oversight of the financial services industry has been moving toward more consolidated operations, the United States retains an idiosyncratically fragmented system of financial supervisory oversight.[32] Depository institutions, for example, can have either federal or state charters. The federal government has three chartering agencies (the Comptroller of the Currency for commercial banks, the Office of Thrift Supervision for thrifts, and the National Credit Union Administration for credit unions) as well as two other supervisory bodies (the FDIC and the Federal Reserve Board) that share jurisdiction over state-chartered banks. This fragmented system of chartering can pro-

---

31. Jackson and Symons (1999).
32. GAO (2009).

mote beneficial regulatory competition among government agencies, but it can also lead to regulatory arbitrage and lax oversight.

In the area of capital markets, two federal agencies (the SEC and the Commodity Futures Trading Commission) maintain divided jurisdiction over securities and commodities markets, with state regulators offering supplemental oversight of securities firms, smaller investment advisers, and other areas of the securities business. Self-regulatory organizations, such as the Financial Industry Regulation Association (FINRA), contribute an additional layer of consumer protection in capital markets through quasi-governmental structures that combine industry participation and public oversight.

States are the most important regulators of insurance companies, with a complex system governing various lines of insurance (for example, life and health insurance versus property and casualty) and insurance intermediaries (agents as opposed to underwriters or reinsurers). The federal government provides supervision of some important insurance products, most notably employer-provided health insurance, pensions, and retirement savings plans. Federal and state governments also directly provide many forms of social insurance, including Social Security, Medicare, Medicaid, unemployment insurance, workers compensation, and flood insurance.

Some financial statutes are cross-cutting. For example, the privacy provisions of the Financial Services Modernization Act of 1999 (the Gramm-Leach-Bliley Act) apply to all sectors of the financial services industry as well as to financial information retained by firms that do not engage in traditional financial activities. Enforcement, however, is delegated to sectoral regulators for regulated firms and the Federal Trade Commission for unregulated firms.

Other consumer financial statutes deal with specific financial functions. The Truth in Lending Act and the Equal Credit Opportunity Act, for example, apply to most forms of consumer credit. Some statutes apply more narrowly: the Real Estate Settlement Procedures Act, the Home Mortgage Disclosure Act, the Home Owners Protection Act of 1998, and the Secure and Fair Enforcement for Mortgage Licensing Act relate only to mortgages. Other statutes address different features of consumer finance, including the Electronic Funds Transfer Act, the Fair Credit Reporting Act, the Credit Repair Organization Act, the Fair Debt Collection Practices Act, and the Truth in Savings Act.

Jurisdictional authority over these statutory requirements is complex and has, at times, been inconsistent. In many areas, especially areas involving consumer credit and payments systems, the Federal Reserve Board has had the authority to establish implementing regulations, but enforcement is left to other agencies with direct oversight of regulated firms. In other cases, notably those tied to residential mortgages, the Department of Housing and Urban Development has had some rulemaking authority. In still other areas, such as the oversight of credit repair organizations—that is, firms that purport to assist consumers in improving their credit scores—the Federal Trade Commission plays a leading role. The CFPB will centralize oversight of most of these consumer finance statutes, although supervision would, in some cases, remain delegated to traditional frontline supervisory agencies in certain cases, such as small and medium depository institutions.[33]

At the state level, various consumer financial protection laws prohibit unfair and deceptive practices; additional protections against unscrupulous business practices derive from common law doctrines in contract and tort law. In addition, the states maintain a variety of licensing and oversight arrangements for non-traditional financial intermediaries, such as mortgage brokers, real estate agents, payday lenders, pawnshops, check-cashing operations, and other specialized providers of financial services. Sometimes these entities are indirectly overseen by other regulators; for example, alternative financial services providers typically need to work with regulated banking partners in order to gain access to the payment systems.

The relationship between state-based consumer financial protection systems and federal law is at times controversial, especially where state authorities have attempted to apply local standards to federally chartered commercial banks or thrifts.[34] The Dodd-Frank act includes provisions that would clarify the relationship between state and federal consumer finance regulation and expand the authority of state officials to police some aspects of the activities of federally chartered firms, areas where judicial decisions had previously limited state supervision.

State and federal bankruptcy and tax laws also affect the structure of consumer financial markets. The bankruptcy code defines the conditions under which consumers can be discharged of financial obligations. Of particular note, some types of debt (mortgages secured by a primary residence and student loans) are more difficult to restructure in bankruptcy than others, and conversely, certain assets (employer-sponsored savings plan balances and investment retirement accounts) are protected from creditor claims in bankruptcy.[35] Similarly, the tax code favors certain types of assets, expenditures, and debt. Mortgage interest is generally deductible from federal taxable income; most expenditures on employer-provided fringe benefits (notably health insurance, pensions, and retirement savings accounts) are not included in taxable income, and certain types of savings and capital accumulation receive tax preferences.[36]

Finally, the financing programs of government-sponsored enterprises such as Fannie Mae and Freddie Mac have profoundly affected the evolution of consumer credit over the past half century. This is most evident in mortgage markets, but these innovations in mortgage finance have facilitated comparable mechanisms of

---

33. Department of Treasury (2009).
34. Schiltz (2004).
35. White (2009); Jacoby (2010).
36. Bittker and Lokken (1999).

private financing for other types of consumer credit (at least until the recent market contractions).

The Mechanisms of Regulatory Intervention

To address the market failures and distributional concerns outlined above, government authorities employ a vast array of regulatory tools. In this section, we follow Jackson and consider these various regulatory options, organized loosely from less to more interventionist, and conclude with several strategies that rely more on private actions than on public oversight.[37]

These interventions do not easily or precisely map onto the economic justifications for consumer financial regulation outlined earlier. Neither legislators nor regulatory agencies routinely justify their actions in purely economic terms. Political considerations and the views of key constituencies often play a major role in shaping the choice of regulatory tools. Government officials are also sometimes subject to regulatory capture and fail to pursue policies that advance the public interest, whether defined in economic or other terms.[38]

Still, developing a catalog of regulatory options is instructive. Doing so may facilitate the formulation of preliminary hypotheses as to which approaches or combination of approaches would most suitably address the principal market failures associated with consumer financial markets. And one may also begin to develop criteria by which government authorities might ascertain which kinds of consumer financial transactions warrant the costs associated with more heavy-handed forms of intervention.[39]

CONSUMER EDUCATION AND FINANCIAL LITERACY PROGRAMS. Some of the simplest forms of government intervention in consumer financial markets are efforts to improve the financial literacy of consumers, either through curricular innovations in primary and secondary school education or through more general educational efforts.[40] Several government programs are intended to promote such educational efforts, although the evidence of their efficacy is mixed at best. The new bureau is explicitly mandated to oversee this activity, with a new Office of Financial Education mandated by the Dodd-Frank act.

ANTIFRAUD RULES. Another traditional method of consumer protection is through antifraud rules, which create a cause of action against parties that engage in intentionally deceptive selling practices. One innovation of the New Deal–era

---

37. Jackson (1999).
38. Stigler (1971).
39. A partial list of considerations might include size of potential injury (such as inappropriate mortgage versus problematic gift card); lack of consumer sophistication (education, experience with products); limited capacity of consumers to protect self; salience of market forces; availability, efficacy, and cost of disinterested advice; product complexity (for example, pricing, terms); and existence of cognitive biases or limitations (see Jackson 2007).
40. Hillman (2009).

federal securities laws was to expand the scope of antifraud rules for securities transactions to materially misleading omissions as well as misleading affirmative statements and to offer a host of procedural advantages to aggrieved purchasers or sellers of securities. Loosely analogous remedies are available under the Employee Retirement Income Security Act of 1974 (ERISA) for deceptions arising out of employer benefit plans, but such liability rules are less common for banking and insurance transactions.

DISCLOSURE REQUIREMENTS. Perhaps the most straightforward response to information asymmetries is through disclosure requirements. Such requirements differ on a variety of dimensions. Some consist of affirmative obligations to disclose specific information about a product or provider. The SEC's disclosure rules for corporate issuers, for example, specify in considerable detail the kinds of information that corporate issuers must include in their SEC filings and provide to investors under certain circumstances. Often the content of disclosures will be structured in highly prescriptive ways so as to facilitate consumer comparison across products. Examples include the annual percentage rate (APR) disclosures under the Truth in Lending Act for consumer credit and the annual, three-year, and five-year investment performance disclosure requirements for mutual funds. In some contexts, disclosures must be tailored to individual transactions, as is the case with settlement costs for home mortgages under the Real Estate Settlement Procedures Act. Finally, in contexts where it is difficult for customers to judge the significance of disclosures regarding individual transactions—for example, in securities transactions when the concern is whether a broker has achieved adequate price improvement—disclosures are required on an aggregate basis reflecting a large number of transactions over an extended period of time.[41]

FIDUCIARY DUTIES. Another important category of legal protections in consumer finance consists of fiduciary duties. Typically imposed in situations where firms or individuals have discretionary control over the financial decisions of their customers, fiduciary duties impose legal obligations on fiduciaries to safeguard their clients' interests. In consumer finance, fiduciary duties are commonly imposed where a firm is giving financial advice or is engaged in the retail distribution of financial products.[42] Similarly, ERISA imposes a wide range of fiduciary duties on the parties involved in the provision of employee benefit plans.

---

41. Jackson (2008).

42. One source of confusion among both consumers and industry experts is the variation in fiduciary duties across different sectors of the financial services industry. While securities brokers are subject to an extensive system of fiduciary duties imposed under both the Securities Exchange Act of 1934 and the FINRA requirements, much less onerous obligations are imposed on selling agents in the insurance industry and on mortgage brokers (Jackson and Burlingame 2007). The Dodd-Frank act authorized the SEC to align the fiduciary duties of securities brokers providing investment advice to retail customers with the more extensive duties imposed on investment advisers under the Investment Advisers Act of 1940.

In the words of Justice Felix Frankfurter, "To say that a man is a fiduciary only begins the analysis."[43] The scope and content of fiduciary duties can vary considerably across context.[44] In some fields, such as securities regulations, fiduciary duties are defined by elaborate regulatory guidelines with clear requirements for determining, for example, whether fiduciaries have complied with suitability requirements or satisfied duties to obtain best execution. There are also differences in whether fiduciary duties can be waived through adequate disclosure and knowing consent on the part of the party or whether the duties cannot be waived. In the former case, the fiduciary duty can become little more than an open-ended disclosure requirement where the disclosing party bears the burden of establishing that the counterparty knowingly assents to the disclosed terms. In the latter case, the duty functions more as a mandatory term of business. An example of the second category would be the FINRA markup rules, which prohibit securities firms from marking up the price of securities by too great an amount when selling securities to customers from the firm's own account.

NONBINDING STANDARDS. Another category of regulatory intervention that has become increasingly popular in recent years consists of *default rules, opt outs, opt ins,* and *safe harbor provisions,* which steer firms toward organizing their affairs in a certain way, but without imposing an outright mandate. Default rules are common in contracts and impose terms that presumptively apply unless the parties clearly choose to agree to other terms. Under federal securities laws, the default rule is that customers aggrieved with their broker-dealers can seek redress in federal courts, but firms can and typically do contract out of that regime by including an arbitration clause in agreements executed before opening new accounts.[45] With opt-out requirements, a provider can establish its own policies, but the consumer must be given the opportunity to opt out of that policy. The Gramm-Leach-Bliley act's rules for financial privacy protection are a good example.[46] With opt-in requirements, providers can only offer a service if a customer affirmatively chooses to accept it, as is the case with the Federal Reserve Board's new rules on overdraft protection for electronic transactions. With a safe harbor provision, a firm is typically insulated from potential liability under some open-ended fiduciary standard if the firm complies with specific rule-like terms. So, for example, 401(k) plan sponsors can insulate themselves from various forms of liability by offering participants a range of diversified investment choices accompanied by certain disclosures.

In certain contexts—most notably where many but not all consumers would benefit from a certain requirement regime—nonbinding standards may be

---

43. *SEC* v. *Chenery Corp.,* 318 U.S. 80, 85–86 (1943).
44. Langbein (1995).
45. Again, this is an area where the Dodd-Frank act has given the SEC new authority to restrict the capacity of securities firms to insert mandatory arbitration clauses into customer agreements.
46. Swire (2003).

preferable to mandatory requirements, which have less flexibility and may inhibit mutually beneficial transactions. Policy analysts focusing on the cognitive limitations of consumers sometimes advocate nonbinding standards as an effective means of nudging consumers toward what are assumed to be better financial decisions, while leaving latitude for those with a strong preference for other choices.[47] In devising these standards, a key concern is the degree of "stickiness" in the standard, that is, the degree of difficulty that consumers face in choosing to work outside the transaction. Also of concern is the extent to which financial services firms can steer consumers away from nonbinding standards when it would be profitable to do so.[48]

MANDATORY REQUIREMENTS. A large number of consumer financial regulations take the form of mandatory requirements imposed on service providers and products. In many areas, there are *licensing or chartering requirements* before firms or individuals can engage in regulated activities. These are meant to ensure that providers have the requisite knowledge and experience and, in some cases, to prevent individuals with records of fraudulent past behavior from assuming positions of responsibility or trust. Another set of mandatory requirements dictate the permissible structure of the balance sheet and business activities of financial intermediaries and their affiliates. These *portfolio-shaping* rules, which include capital requirements, restrictions on investments, and regulation of the form of firm liabilities, are intended to reduce the riskiness of financial intermediaries and ensure their capacity to honor their commitments when they come due.[49] In certain sectors, financial intermediaries are also required to obtain third-party guarantees of their obligations. For example, most regulated depository institutions are required to participate in government-sponsored deposit insurance programs, and other financial services providers are often required to set up private bonding arrangements before starting business.[50]

In some areas, mandatory requirements *limit the form of financial products.* For example, commercial banks are generally prohibited from offering secured deposits, lest one class of depositors obtain a priority in liquidation procedures. Similarly, the investment terms of mutual funds must include daily repricing and redemption of shares based on current market values of the underlying mutual fund portfolio. Consumer insurance products are extensively regulated, with numerous restrictions on the form of permissible contracts.

---

47. Thaler and Sunstein (2008).

48. Barr, Mullainathan, and Shafir (2008).

49. Portfolio-shaping rules are also important to prevent systemic risks from the failure of financial institutions.

50. Organizational structure is also sometimes used as a regulatory instrument, as when financial institutions are encouraged or required to organize in mutual form rather than the more familiar corporate structure in which shareholders serve as residual claimants.

Another category of mandates prevalent in consumer finance consists of *anti-conflict rules,* which are designed to prevent the managers and controlling shareholders of financial intermediaries from applying the resources of the intermediary or customer funds for their own benefit. So, for example, commercial banks are limited in their ability to extend credit or engage in other transactions with affiliates. Comparable rules govern insurance firms and investment companies. The federal securities laws include similarly spirited requirements designed to prevent broker-dealers from misusing customer funds and securities. Some anti-conflict interventions take the form of *restrictions on information flows*—so-called "Chinese walls"—designed to prevent employees dealing with customers from being pressured by other employees in ways that might be detrimental to the customers' interests. A good example is the settlements that arose out of the analysts' scandals of the late 1990s, which imposed a series of structural barriers designed to prevent the investment banking side of securities firms from influencing the recommendations of affiliated analysts.[51]

The existence of such extensive and often costly mandatory requirements for consumer financial products creates considerable incentives for parties to restructure their interactions so as to fall outside of regulatory requirements. In some areas, the law includes important explicit exemptions from regulatory requirements. For example, the Securities Act of 1933 includes the "private placement" exemption that relaxes the disclosure standards and liability for securities sold to sophisticated and wealthy investors. Similarly, the Investment Company Act of 1940 offers comparable exemptions that allow hedge funds and other alternative investment products to escape the onerous requirements imposed on mutual funds and other registered investment companies. Beyond these statutory exemptions, creative providers (and their attorneys) routinely seek to characterize their products as "mere" contracts so as to escape mandatory requirements and operate under the more liberal common law rules of "caveat emptor."

PRICE CONTROLS AND RATE REGULATION. Price controls sometimes figure into consumer financial regulation. Usury rules, which restrict interest rates, are perhaps the most familiar example of this approach. While legal developments permitting depository institutions to export interest rates from the state of their choice has greatly weakened the efficacy of usury laws, for many consumer financial transactions, including payday lending, local usury rules are still relevant. Price controls in the form of rate regulation are sometimes used in the insurance industry, and all states prohibit the use of certain risk classifications (often including gender and sometimes geography) to set prices. The federal government recently added restraints on the use of genetic information to set insurance prices. Recently enacted federal health care reform imposes new restrictions on the ability of health

---

51. Agarwal and Chen (2008).

insurers to discriminate among customers due to preexisting medical conditions. Even in the securities field, restrictions are placed on the pricing of certain consumer financial services, including distribution costs charged to mutual fund shareholders. Finally, antidiscrimination laws prohibit discrimination based on race and other suspect categories in the extension and pricing of credit.

MECHANISMS OF ENFORCEMENT. Enforcement is an important component of consumer financial regulation and consists of a variety of overlapping elements, including reporting requirements (both public and confidential); mandated internal controls (increasingly assigned to a chief compliance officer reporting to the highest levels of management); periodic examinations, including (in some sectors) examinations focused primarily on consumer protection issues; public enforcement actions ranging from informal to administrative to civil and then potentially criminal; and in some areas of consumer finance, most notably securities and employee benefit plans, robust private rights of action.

THIRD-PARTY VALIDATION. The public regulation of consumer finance is sometimes supplemented through systems of third-party validation. One familiar example of this strategy is the common requirement that independent auditors review the financial statements of regulated intermediaries on an annual basis. But financial regulations also have increasingly relied on outside credit-rating agencies as external (and, as it turns out, not particularly reliable) arbiters of permissible investments for regulated firms. In a different vein, the Investment Company Act of 1940 makes extensive use of independent directors to safeguard the interests of mutual fund shareholders, especially with respect to transactions when the interests of shareholders and investment company managers may be in conflict.

SUPPLEMENTAL PRIVATE POLICING. Finally, our system of consumer financial regulation also often depends on, and in some cases facilitates, the use of private policing. In the mutual fund industry, private vendors such as Lipper and Morningstar play an important role in digesting a massive amount of publicly available information about mutual funds and synthesizing that information for customers. Another area in which private policing plays an important role is the sharing among financial firms of information about consumer defaults and credit performance. This collection of information permits the development of individual credit scores, which allows firms to determine credit risks and develop more accurate prices for loans and other credit transactions.[52] Finally, in a variety of areas, industry groups promulgate standards of best practices, against which industry participants can assess their own practices. While these standards do not typically have formal legal standing, they often influence regulatory developments in the

---

52. This particular area of innovation has led to additional consumer financial regulation to protect consumers from errors in the creation of credit scores and abuses from firms that purport to have the capacity to improve an individual's credit score.

future and can form a sort of soft law around which many industry participants organize their operations in the short term.

OVERLAPPING STRATEGIES IN PRACTICE. One of the challenges of empirical studies of the efficacy of the different components of consumer financial regulation is that the components are rarely implemented in isolation. Rather, in most important areas of consumer finance, multiple forms of regulatory tools are used. The mutual fund industry offers a good example.[53] At the center of mutual fund regulation is the Investment Company Act of 1940, which strictly regulates the structure of mutual funds, requiring relatively simple liabilities, daily pricing of shares for sale and redemption, and substantial diversification requirements for fund assets (supplemented through further diversification requirements effected through the tax code). In addition to these stringent portfolio-shaping rules, the Investment Company Act and implementing SEC regulations mandate the creation of independent boards of directors to police many aspects of fund business. Further fiduciary duties are imposed on fund advisers and the securities firms that distribute mutual fund shares, and the amount of resources that can be spent on distribution activities is strictly constrained. In addition, extensive disclosure requirements are imposed on mutual funds (including both fund-specific information and disclosures designed to facilitate comparison across funds), and a substantial private industry of rating systems and publications digests and interprets fund disclosures for the investing public. SEC and FINRA staff members examine all mutual funds on a periodic basis and routinely bring and publicize enforcement actions against offending firms. Under a range of statutory provisions, private litigants can and do sue mutual fund companies and related parties for, among other things, misleading disclosures, excessive fees, or abusive sales practices. Finally, the Investment Company Institute and several other trade groups play important roles in developing best practices and conducting research relevant to industry participants.

The mutual fund industry is often cited as a sector of the financial services industry that has benefited from successful and effective regulation, and the growth of the sector over the past several decades is consistent with that claim. But even accepting the assumption that effective regulation played an important role in the industry's success, it is difficult to ascertain whether some particular element of the mutual fund regulation made the critical contribution or whether the full smorgasbord of mutual fund oversight was necessary for the sector's success.

A Case Study on Payday Lending

To illustrate how the themes discussed in this chapter apply to specific consumer financial markets, we turn now to a case study involving payday loans (PDLs): relatively small, short-term, generally unsecured loans that are often sold to less

53. Frankel and Kirsch (2003); Coates (2009).

well-to-do consumers, many of them at a physical point of sale. This form of lending has grown rapidly in recent years, and the industry now estimates loan volume at roughly $40 billion a year.[54]

Background

Most payday loans follow a relatively standard lending process and take a relatively standard form. Consumers visit a storefront location, request a loan, have their employment verified, and, if approved, walk out minutes later with the loan proceeds. The average payday loan is fairly small—80 percent of transactions are for less than $300.[55] The loan comes due on the borrower's next payday and is extinguished by either an explicit payment from the borrower, a prearranged ACH withdrawal from the borrower's bank account, or the cashing of a postdated check. The time until the next payday, and hence loan maturity, can range from a few days to nearly a month, but the norm is two weeks. Instead of a finance charge that varies with balance and duration of the loan, the fee is either fixed or related simply to the loan amount, typically $15 to $30 per $100 borrowed.[56]

In some states, borrowers can repay the loan (plus fee) by rolling it over to a new, higher-balance loan. Some states limit same-store rollovers to no more than four or five a year; others prohibit them entirely. Even in such states, nothing prevents a borrower from getting another loan elsewhere. According to Elliehausen, 40 percent of payday loan consumers use more than one payday lender within a twelve-month period, and of those, more than 35 percent use a payday loan from one lender to pay off another.[57]

By virtue of the product itself, PDL customers must have a checking account and be employed. Lawrence and Elliehausen find that PDL customers tend to have a moderate level of education, are disproportionately young (under age forty-five), and have children.[58] Most are from lower- and middle-income households with limited liquid assets—fewer than half report any savings.[59] Generally, they

54. The Community Financial Services Association of America is the national payday lending industry association: www.cfsa.net. Caskey (1994, 2001, 2002) provides some of the earliest research documenting this form of what he calls "fringe banking." For a more recent overview of payday loans, see Stegman (2007).
55. Stegman (2007).
56. Stegman (2007).
57. Elliehausen (2009). Many other studies also document sizable repeat use of payday loans. Stegman and Faris (2003) report that the average PDL user took out seven loans in 2000, and the Center for Responsible Lending reports that 90 percent of loans are made to borrowers with five or more transactions a year (Parrish 2008). Lawrence and Elliehausen (2008) find that 20 percent of PDL customers roll over more than eight loans in a twelve-month period. Flannery and Samolyk (2005) find that 46 percent of store PDL transactions are rollovers, accounting for 34–40 percent of total loan volume.
58. Lawrence and Elliehausen (2008).
59. Elliehausen (2009). The most-reported household income levels of PDL customers are $25,000–$39,999 (27.6 percent), $15,000–$24,999 (17.6 percent), and $50,000–$74,999 (16.7 per-

are in life stages where demand for credit is high, and although 92 percent rely on other types of credit, many have been denied credit in the past twelve months, have credit cards at the limit, have concerns about their ability to access credit, and are less likely to have home equity to tap.[60]

Payday lending grew out of the check-cashing industry of the 1990s, and the leading industry association reports almost 24,000 outlets nationally.[61] The industry is fairly dispersed with only a few large corporations holding a substantial share of the market—most payday lenders are small storefront operations.[62] The few studies on the profitability of payday lending rely on self-disclosed figures and hence may not be representative or objective, but they suggest that the business is not as profitable as critics charge. Flannery and Samolyk, for example, analyze data for 300 stores in two chains.[63] They conclude, "Fixed operating costs and loan loss rates do justify a large part of the high APRs charged on payday advance loans," and loan volume, rather than repeat borrowing per se, is a primary determinant of profitability. Tufano and Ryan, who conduct a case study of a single chain, provide consistent anecdotal evidence, as do Huckstep as well as Skiba and Tobacman, who examine the financial statements of publicly traded payday lenders.[64]

Applying the Regulatory Justifications to Payday Loans

In this section we consider the application to payday loans of several rationales for regulation of consumer financial markets.

Traditional market failures seem an unlikely basis for regulation of payday lending. There is little evidence of market power.[65] The apparent absence of abnormal profits may reflect competition, the small scale of most operations, the requirements for both local real estate and personnel, and loan losses. In some low-income communities, the number of PDL outlets far exceeds the number of banks and even fast

---

cent). Nearly all PDL borrowers have a high school diploma (91.2 percent), and many have some college (35.1 percent). See also Stegman and Faris (2003). It is also possible to characterize borrowers with regard to their larger pattern of financial services experiences. Lusardi and Tufano (2009) find that payday borrowers are more likely than others to engage in related high-cost financial transactions.

60. Elliehausen and Lawrence (2001); Lawrence and Elliehausen (2008).

61. See www.cfsa.net/about_cfsa.html.

62. Stegman (2007) estimates that six large companies control about one-fifth of all PDL activity.

63. Flannery and Samolyk (2005).

64. For a case study of a single chain, see Tufano and Ryan (2009); for an examination of the financial statements of publicly traded payday lenders, see Huckstep (2007) and Skiba and Tobacman (2007).

65. However, as Mann and Hawkins (2007) argue, the most convenient locations for customers are more expensive, which may privilege established firms, put a "natural limit on the density with which profitable locations can be established," and "hinder the effectiveness of price competition." DeYoung and Phillips (2009) conclude that loan pricing reflects strategic considerations, with fees rising to legislated ceilings and with large multiple-store firms charging higher prices than independent single-store operators.

food restaurants.[66] Given the prevalence of payday loans in select neighborhoods and the relatively standard terms in the industry, it is reasonable to suppose that consumers have low search costs. Similarly, there do not appear to be asymmetries of information or public good aspects of payday lending that would justify additional regulation of information, although standardized APR disclosures required of payday lenders under the federal Truth in Lending Act do provide a useful baseline of information, which might not be available in an entirely unregulated market.

There is mixed evidence on whether payday loans generate externalities. Some evidence suggests that they lead to financial hardship, which could give rise to greater need for public or private redistribution ex post. Other evidence suggests that they may give rise to positive externalities: Morse finds that households facing natural disasters are less likely to experience foreclosures or larcenies when payday loans are more accessible.[67] Wilson and others replicate Morse's general result using a laboratory experiment with 318 undergraduate subjects who had to manage a household budget over thirty periods.[68] They find that the addition of payday loans to a mix of credit products helped subjects to absorb expenditure shocks. Comparative evidence from Oregon, which imposes a PDL interest rate cap, and the neighboring state of Washington, which does not, shows that restricting access to payday loans causes "deterioration in the overall financial condition" of households.[69] This evidence suggests that a payday loan may be better than its alternatives.

By contrast, other studies find that payday loans are associated with increased financial hardship and thus perhaps negative community externalities. Melzer, for example, exploits geographic and temporal variation in the availability of payday loans and finds that access to payday loans leads to increased difficulty paying mortgage, rent, and utility bills; a higher rate of moving out of one's home due to financial difficulties; and delayed medical care, dental care, and prescription drug purchases.[70] There also is evidence that payday loans are associated with adverse

---

66. The geographer Graves (2003) reports that PDL stores and bank branches are inversely related, with loan stores growing in areas where banks are exiting: poorer communities with a larger fraction of minorities. Morse (2009) reports that in 2007 the number of PDL stores per zip code in California was twice as large as the number of McDonald's restaurants (1.9 and 0.95, respectively).

67. Morse (2009).

68. Wilson and others (2010).

69. Zinman (2008).

70. Melzer (2009). Using a regression-discontinuity approach applied to borrower-level data from Texas, Skiba and Tobacman (2009) conclude that loan approval for first-time PDL applicants increases the likelihood of Chapter 13 bankruptcy filings by 2.5 percent through two channels: a selection effect (higher-risk borrowers both seek payday loans and go bankrupt) and repeat borrowing. In contrast, Stoianovici and Maloney (2008) use state-level data and find no relationship between payday loans and bankruptcy filings. Morgan and Strain (2008) find that PDL restrictions increase the incidence of credit problems, such as bounced checks. However, using disaggregated data, Campbell, Martinez-Jerez, and Tufano (2008) find fewer involuntary bank account closures due to overdrafts after Georgia banned payday lending, especially for individuals farther from state borders where payday loans are available nearby.

outcomes for military borrowers, including declines in overall job performance and lower levels of retention.[71] To discourage such loans to military personnel, the 2007 National Defense Authorization Act caps the fees on payday loans to service members at an APR of 36 percent, a regulation that industry critics support for all payday lending.[72]

Behavioral considerations for PDL regulation include both cognitive limitations and present-biased preferences of borrowers. There is a limited amount of direct and indirect evidence that PDL users may have cognitive limitations. Lusardi and Tufano find that PDL borrowers and users of other forms of nontraditional credit have low levels of debt literacy (an understanding of interest compounding).[73] As part of a field experiment, Bertrand and Morse asked PDL borrowers about the interest rate charged for their loans.[74] About 40 percent claimed the APR was around 15 percent, confusing the cash charge per $100 and the APR (or misunderstanding the question). Some PDL borrowers take out loans even when they have access to lower-cost credit in the form of unused credit card borrowing capacity or savings and checking account balances.[75] While there may be a logical reason for these choices (for example, lower intra-family disclosure or avoidance of overdraft fees), to the extent that they demonstrate a failure to understand the relative costs of alternative forms of credit, the "diagnosis" might be cognitive failure. Finally, as noted earlier, there is substantial evidence of repeat or chronic borrowing.[76] In states allowing rollovers, borrowers can quickly see their borrowing balloon out of control. This could reflect cognitive limitations of PDL borrowers; it could indicate present-biased preferences (individuals underweight the future costs of taking out a payday loan today), or it could simply reflect the fragile economic state of many PDL users. Collectively this evidence is consistent with a behavioral basis for regulation, even if the empirical evidence is still rather limited.

The distributional arguments for regulating payday loans are straightforward: the poor (or poor financial managers) pay more. As noted, payday loans are used disproportionately by less well-off individuals. Critics charge that they are targeted to (and used by) lower-income consumers and racial minorities.[77] Critics further argue that PDL pricing is "predatory"—typical fees of $15–$20 per $100 borrowed

71. Carrell and Zinman (2008).

72. Center for Responsible Lending (2009).

73. Lusardi and Tufano (2009).

74. Bertrand and Morse (2009).

75. On credit card borrowing capacity, see Agarwal, Skiba, and Tobacman (2009); on savings and checking account balances, see Carter, Skiba, and Tobacman (2010).

76. A report by the Center for Responsible Lending (King, Parrish, and Tanik 2006) claims that repeat borrowers generate 90 percent of the revenue of the PDL industry. However, Veritec, a data provider for the industry, disputes these statistics in a report dated January 18, 2007. See www.cfsa.net/veritec.html.

77. Graves (2003); Stegman and Faris (2003).

imply an APR from 390 percent (if paid back at the two-week deadline) to more than 1,000 percent (if repaid within one day). In some regulations, such as the Home Ownership and Equity Protection Act of 1994, the mere existence of high APRs, defined in reference to prevailing rates, is the basis for regulation.

While detractors argue that payday loans result in the poor paying more, one must ask "more than what?" Defenders point out that other sources of short-term credit, such as overdraft protection, returned check fees, and credit card late fees, have APRs ranging from 478 to 791 percent, depending on the duration of the loan.[78] Furthermore, the costs of not having access to credit can be extraordinarily high. For example, if electricity or telephone service is shut off, the time and expense to restart service can far exceed a PDL fee.[79] Similarly, a worker lacking the funds to repair a vehicle may be unable to get to work and may lose her job as a result.

The effects of payday lending on household welfare depend on the assumed alternative to PDL usage. If payday loans were not available, some households might find less convenient but perhaps less expensive financing or might resist the temptation to engage in short-term spending. Other households, however, might use more expensive forms of short-term credit or suffer severe consequences from lack of credit. Which counterfactual one believes will inform one's view of appropriate regulation; the existing empirical evidence provides mixed answers.

Existing Regulation

In response to the efforts of several national banks attempting to establish nationwide distribution networks through local payday lenders, federal banking authorities took a series of steps starting in 2000 to discourage federally insured depository institutions from participating in payday lending.[80] As a result, payday lending is conducted and regulated largely at the state level.[81] Georgia prohibits payday lending entirely, and nine other states effectively prohibit it as a result of interest rate caps that make it unprofitable.[82] Annual interest rate caps also exist in some states with payday lending, including Ohio (28 percent), New Hampshire (36 percent), Oregon (36 percent), and Virginia (36 percent). The Truth in Lending Act requires that the loan amount, finance charges, and APR must be clearly disclosed in any contract or agreement the borrower signs. Thirty states

---

78. Consumer Reports (2005); Lehman (2005).

79. The Community Financial Services Association of America (2006) commissioned a study to document the fees of PDL alternatives. Their findings are the following: late fees for utilities, $9.92; utility reconnect fees, $36.24; insufficient funds fees, $28.34; and bank overdraft fees, $23.18.

80. Smale (2005).

81. Peterson (2008).

82. These are Connecticut, Maryland, Massachusetts, New Jersey, New York, North Carolina, Pennsylvania, Vermont, and West Virginia. See regulations by state at the National Conference of State Legislatures: www.ncsl.org/IssuesResearch/BankingInsuranceFinancialServices/PaydayLending StateStatutes/tabid/12473/Default.aspx.

have more stringent disclosure laws, requiring payday lenders to post APRs and fee schedules clearly and prominently inside their stores.[83] Many states limit the maximum loan amount, and some states, such as California, prohibit rollover loans. Thus the range of regulatory practices extends from an outright or de facto ban (through low permissible APRs) on one extreme to disclosure requirements on the other, with a middle ground of restrictions on contract terms (for example, repeat usage).

Policy Considerations

The discussion highlights the problems with crafting optimal regulation of payday lending. While distributional considerations and externalities may form the case for regulation, there is conflicting evidence about whether payday loans benefit or harm consumers. Likely they do both. Used "responsibly" as an alternative to even higher-cost borrowing or the failure to pay certain bills, they are likely beneficial, as the industry argues. But when used repeatedly, they can lead to ballooning debt and distress, as critics argue. Any regulation must address how the product is used by the borrower.

Regulation cannot deal with payday lending in isolation. Taking the functional perspective, payday loans are just one form of short-term credit. Regulation restricting one product can lead consumers to seek other, possibly even less attractive, sources of credit. That payday loans are used in conjunction with other short-term credit products reminds us that any regulation must assist consumers in making decisions that cut across various products. This "help" might come in the form of education or disclosures.

If behavioral considerations are the basis for greater regulation, then we need to know more about what drives PDL choice before we can craft more effective (and appropriate) regulation. Well-designed disclosure can in principle help consumers to make better decisions, but existing research calls into question whether it will substantially change behavior. In a recent randomized field experiment, Bertrand and Morse test different types of PDL disclosures.[84] They find that fee disclosure in dollar terms was more effective in reducing same-store PDL demand than APR disclosure[85] or messages about the likelihood of repeat borrowing or the importance of budget planning. However, the absolute reduction in subsequent borrowing was modest (5–6 percent depending on the specification), and the experiment could not assess whether reduced borrowing at the participating

---

83. Fox and Woodall (2006), however, report that three-fourths of surveyed payday lenders fail to post the APRs as required by law and 20 percent post no cost information at all.

84. Bertrand and Morse (2009).

85. The conclusion that dollar-based versus APR disclosure is most informative echoes the results of Hasting and Tejeda-Ashton (2008), who find a similar result in their study of responses to fee disclosure for investment accounts in Mexico.

payday lender was offset by borrowing from other payday lenders. Overall, these results raise questions about the efficacy of disclosure rules.[86]

To the extent that the most problematic use of payday loans relates to repeat usage, the underlying failure could be either behavioral or structural (in that people are systematically living beyond their means). If the former, it might be possible to employ other behaviorally informed regulatory changes.[87] For example, if PDL borrowing is an impulse item, then a short "cooling off" period might give people time to consider whether they really want a loan. In the market for tax refund anticipation loans, many consumers are willing to accept a wait of one or two days for payment rather than incur additional fees to access their impending tax refund on the same day as they file.[88] If the problem is structural, in that people simply cannot manage their money, barring rollovers—or payday loans altogether—will not address the basic issue that gives rise to the product.

It seems sensible that policymakers should test the likely impact of any proposed rule changes. The experiments cited above were conducted mostly by scholars, rather than by the policymakers charged with rulemaking. Most academics, however, seek to publish papers and do not have the time or the inclination to test micro-variations in rules. As a result, some form of research needs to be carried out by policymakers themselves.

While regulation may seek to protect consumers, it needs to be mindful of the economics of this business. It is difficult to make the case that most lenders are earning supernormal profits. However, pending House and Senate bills (H.R. 1608 and S. 500) would cap interest rates at a 36 percent APR, similar to the limit imposed on payday loans for military personnel in 2007. For a $300 two-week loan, a 36 percent APR rate cap would limit the lender's total revenue to $4.15 (300 * [0.36 / 26]). According to Flannery and Samolyk, average loan losses alone were $5.72 per loan for the most mature stores, before accounting for the cost of wages, buildings, advertising, or overhead.[89] A 36 percent APR ceiling would not create "affordable" payday loans, but it could simply lead to the exit of existing vendors. More generally, rate caps could lead to new products or practices that skirt the rules[90] or push payday lending underground. However, rate caps and other PDL restrictions could also spur legitimate innovation into products that are both better for consumers and profitable for firms.

Finally, the correlated use of payday loans and other short-term lending products and the growth of the PDL industry probably reflect the desire of consumers

---

86. Choi, Laibson, and Madrian (2010) and Beshears and others (forthcoming) find that mutual fund fee disclosures are similarly ineffective.

87. Barr, Mullainathan, and Shafir (2008).

88. Cole, Thompson, and Tufano (2008).

89. Flannery and Samolyk (2005).

90. Anecdotally, after a PDL interest rate cap was imposed in Ohio, lenders responded by disbursing loans as checks rather than cash and then charged separate check-cashing fees.

for access to short-term credit. A different regulatory approach would be to encourage alternatives to payday loans. Before she assumed her role as chair of the FDIC, then-academic Sheila Bair reviewed PDL alternative models.[91] Among her conclusions, she called for regulatory encouragement of low-cost, short-term loans. As FDIC chair, she launched a pilot program to demonstrate the potential for these products, although the results so far are fairly limited. While some forms of regulation can stymie innovation, they can also spur it either in the cat-and-mouse fashion of the regulatory dialectic as described by Kane or in the encouragement to pilot new ideas.[92]

Conclusion

In this chapter we have described various rationales for regulatory intervention in consumer financial markets. Some of these relate to economists' traditional concerns about asymmetric information and imperfect contracting, others to a more recent appreciation for the limits of consumer rationality.

It is important, however, to keep in mind the limitations on the ability of regulation to improve financial outcomes for consumers. Politicians and regulators can easily do more harm than good if these limitations are ignored.

First, many consumer financial products are expensive to provide because of the small size of each transaction. In the market for short-term consumer credit, for example, it is inevitable that small loans will be expensive unless they are organized through a long-term relationship that can amortize fixed costs over many related transactions. In such markets, APR ceilings therefore have the unintended effect of eliminating the provision of one form of short-term credit and potentially forcing some consumers to rely on more expensive alternatives.

Second, there is important cross-sectional variation in the financial products that are suitable for different consumers. For example, homeowners who expect to move in the near future should not pay for the expensive refinancing option embedded in a long-term nominal fixed-rate mortgage. Similarly, payday loans may be helpful for certain consumers and harmful for others. Regulators should be cautious about imposing "one size fits all" solutions.

Third, even in markets where commonly used financial products seem satisfactory, these products are often not perfect and can potentially be improved by financial innovation. In the market for retirement savings products, for example, even the best current investment solutions, such as life-cycle mutual funds, lack any mechanism for giving consumers access to less liquid asset classes that might earn them an illiquidity premium.

91. Bair (2005).
92. Kane (1981).

Fourth, regulation can easily have unintended consequences if market participants use financial innovation to circumvent clumsily designed or costly regulations.[93] A leading example is the 1974 reform of defined-benefit pension regulations, which inadvertently encouraged the growth of defined-contribution retirement savings plans. Defined-contribution plans do have some advantages relative to defined-benefit plans—for example, their greater portability as employees move from one job to the next—but they also impose a more substantial burden on households to self-manage their retirement savings, a responsibility many households appear ill suited to bear. It is not clear that the current U.S. system has achieved an optimal balance between retirement plans with defined-contribution and defined-benefit characteristics. In the case of payday lenders, the decision of regulators to exclude federally insured depository institutions from participating in payday lending may have served largely to move that activity to smaller, local firms that are both less efficient and more difficult to supervise.

Finally, all regulation is subject to the political process, which can easily capture regulation and use it to achieve short-term political goals rather than the originally intended economic goals. It appears, for example, that politicians' desire to extend credit access to lower income households contributed to the development of the subprime mortgage market, the recent housing and credit bubbles, and ultimately the financial crisis of 2007–09.

Given these potential problems, any regulatory agency, such as the recently legislated Consumer Financial Protection Bureau, should follow a disciplined process when considering new financial regulations. The first step must be to identify specific problems such as those discussed in this chapter. To that end, the Dodd-Frank act mandates that the bureau set up a research function to inform its work. The second step is to design metrics for success in addressing these problems. For example, if the problem is the wide dispersion in the fees that consumers pay for extremely similar products such as index mutual funds, metrics for success could include an increase in consumer knowledge of available low-cost options or a decrease in the dispersion of fees that consumers actually pay. The third step is to tailor interventions to the problems at hand, taking into account the wide range of regulatory mechanisms and combinations of mechanisms potentially available. The fourth step is to implement research to determine whether candidate interventions can deliver improvements in the metrics for success.

This last step is a substantial challenge in itself and will require a broad array of research methodologies. Some evidence can be gathered from aggregate data, for example, in measuring the adequacy of retirement saving from statistics on the participation rate in 401(k) plans. This type of work requires careful attention to possible crowding-out effects, for example, shifts from fully taxable to tax-favored

---

93. The fragmented structure of the U.S. system of financial oversight and the capacity of firms to use different legal forms to provide similar financial functions create additional opportunities for regulatory arbitrage on the part of the financial services industry (Jackson 1999).

retirement saving or movement from payday lenders to other sources of short-term credit. Other evidence can come from cross-country comparisons.

But aggregate research alone is unlikely to be sufficient. There is an urgent need for improved experimental data on consumer responses to and understanding of new financial products and household-level field data to reveal cross-sectional variation in financial decisionmaking. Most household-level field research uses surveys, such as the Federal Reserve's Survey of Consumer Finances, but these surveys have severe limitations, including refusals to participate (particularly among the wealthy), limited granularity, and inaccurate responses. In the future it will be important to gather accurate household-level data from a wide array of financial services providers. Such data will be much more useful if they can be merged into a comprehensive package that describes the complete financial position of households and more useful still if they can be linked with survey data on households' beliefs, stated objectives, and financial literacy.

References

Agarwal, Anup, and Mark A. Chen. 2008. "Do Analyst Conflicts Matter? Evidence from Stock Recommendations." *Journal of Law and Economics* 51, no. 3: 503–37.

Agarwal, Sumit, John C. Driscoll, Xavier Gabaix, and David Laibson. 2009. "The Age of Reason: Financial Decisions over the Life Cycle and Implications for Regulation." *BPEA* 2 (Fall): 51–117.

Agarwal, Sumit, Paige Skiba, and Jeremy Tobacman. 2009. "Payday Loans and Credit Cards: New Liquidity and Credit Scoring Puzzles?" NBER Working Paper 14659. Cambridge, Mass.: National Bureau for Economic Research.

Aguiar, Mark, and Erik Hurst. 2007. "Life-Cycle Prices and Production." *American Economic Review* 97, no. 5: 1533–59.

Bair, Sheila. 2005. "Low-Cost Payday Loans: Opportunities and Obstacles." A report prepared by the University of Massachusetts at Amherst, Isenberg School of Management, for the Annie E. Casey Foundation (June).

Bar-Gill, Oren. 2008. "The Behavioral Economics of Consumer Contracts." *Minnesota Law Review* 92, no. 3: 749–802.

Barr, Michael S., Sendhil Mullainathan, and Eldar Shafir. 2008. "Behaviorally Informed Financial Services Regulation." Sacramento: New America Foundation.

Benjamin, Daniel J., Sebastian A. Brown, and Jesse M. Shapiro. 2006. "Who Is 'Behavioral'? Cognitive Ability and Anomalous Preferences." Unpublished paper. Harvard University and University of Chicago.

Bergstresser, Daniel, J. M. R. Chalmers, and Peter Tufano. 2009. "Assessing the Costs and Benefits of Brokers: A Preliminary Analysis of the Mutual Fund Industry." *Review of Financial Studies* 22 (October): 4129–56.

Bertrand, Marianne, and Adair Morse. 2009. "Information Disclosure, Cognitive Biases, and Payday Borrowing." Working Paper 10-01. Booth School of Business, University of Chicago.

Beshears, John, James J. Choi, David Laibson, and Brigitte C. Madrian. Forthcoming. "How Does Simplified Disclosure Affect Individuals' Mutual Fund Choices?" In *Explorations in the Economics of Aging,* edited by David A. Wise. University of Chicago Press.

Bittker, Boris I., and Lawrence Lokken. 1999. *Federal Taxation of Income, Estates and Gifts.* Warren, Gorham, & Lamont.

Bucks, Brian K., Arthur B. Kennickell, Traci L. Mach, and Kevin B. Moore. 2009. "Changes in U.S. Family Finances from 2004 to 2007: Evidence from the Survey of Consumer Finances." *Federal Reserve Bulletin* 95. Washington: Federal Reserve Board. www.federal reserve.gov/pubs/bulletin/2009/articles/scf/default.htm#nl5.

Calvet, Laurent E., John Y. Campbell, and Paolo Sodini. 2007. "Down or Out: Assessing the Welfare Costs of Household Investment Mistakes." *Journal of Political Economy* 115, no. 5: 707–47.

———. 2009. "Fight or Flight? Portfolio Rebalancing by Individual Investors." *Quarterly Journal of Economics* 124, no. 1 (February): 301–48.

Campbell, Dennis, Asis Martinez-Jerez, and Peter Tufano. 2008. "Bouncing out of the Banking System: An Empirical Analysis of Involuntary Bank Account Closures." Harvard Business School. www.bos.frb.org/economic/cprc/conferences/payments2008/campbell_jerez_tufano.pdf.

Campbell, John Y. 2006. "Household Finance." *Journal of Finance* 61, no. 4: 1553–604.

Campbell, John Y., Stefano Giglio, and Parag Pathak. Forthcoming. "Forced Sales and House Prices." *American Economic Review.*

Campbell, John Y., Howell E. Jackson, Peter Tufano, and Brigitte C. Madrian. 2010. "The Regulation of Consumer Financial Products: An Introductory Essay with Four Case Studies." ssrn.com/abstract=1649647.

Carlin, Bruce I., and Simon Gervais. 2009. "Legal Protection in Retail Financial Markets." NBER Working Paper w14972. Cambridge, Mass.: National Bureau of Economic Research.

Carrell, Scott, and Jonathan Zinman. 2008. "In Harm's Way? Payday Loan Access and Military Personnel Performance." Dartmouth College. www.dartmouth.edu/~jzinman/Papers/PayDay_AirForce_aug08.pdf.

Carter, Susan Payne, Paige Marta Skiba, and Jeremy Tobacman. 2010. "Payday Borrowers: Transaction Habits, Credit Score Changes, and Pecuniary Mistakes." Unpublished manuscript. tobacman@wharton.upenn.edu.

Caskey, John. 1994. *Fringe Banking: Check-Cashing Outlets, Pawnshops, and the Poor.* New York: Russell Sage Foundation.

———. 2001. "Payday Lending." *Financial Counseling and Planning* 12, no. 2: 1–14.

———. 2002. *The Economics of Payday Lending.* Madison, Wis.: Filene Research Institute.

Center for Responsible Lending. 2009. "Congress Should Cap Interest Rates." Research Brief. Durham, N.C.: Center for Responsible Lending.

Choi, James J., David Laibson, and Brigitte C. Madrian. 2010. "Why Does the Law of One Price Fail? An Experiment on Index Mutual Funds." *Review of Financial Studies* 23, no. 4: 1405–32.

———. Forthcoming. "$100 Bills on the Sidewalk: Suboptimal Investment in 401(k) Plans." Forthcoming in *Review of Economics and Statistics.*

Christelis, Dimitris, Tullio Jappelli, and Mario Padula. 2010. "Cognitive Abilities and Portfolio Choice." *European Economic Review* 54, no. 1: 15–38.

Coates, John C. 2009. "Reforming the Taxation and Regulation of Mutual Funds." *Journal of Legal Analysis* 1, no. 2: 591–689.

Cole, Shawn, and Gauri Kartini Shastry. 2009. "If You Are So Smart, Why Aren't You Rich? The Effects of Education, Financial Literacy, and Cognitive Ability on Financial Market Participation." Working Paper 09-071. Harvard Business School.

Cole, Shawn, John Thompson, and Peter Tufano. 2008. "Where Does It Go? Spending by the Financially Constrained." Working Paper 08-083. Harvard Business School.

Community Financial Services Association of America. 2006. "National Data on Short-Term Credit Alternatives." Alexandria, Va. www.cfsa.net/downloads/National_Data_on_Short_Term_Credit_Alternatives.pdf.

Consumer Reports. 2005. "False Security Check-Bounce Protection." *Consumer Reports* 70, no. 5: 45.

Department of Treasury. 2009. *Financial Regulatory Reform: A New Foundation.* Washington.

DeYoung, Robert, and Ronnie J. Phillips. 2009. "Payday Loan Pricing." Federal Reserve Bank of Kansas City, Economic Research Department.

Elliehausen, Gregory. 2009. "An Analysis of Consumers' Use of Payday Loans." Financial Services Research Program Monograph 41. George Washington University, School of Business.

Elliehausen, Gregory, and Edward C. Lawrence. 2001. "Payday Advance Credit in America: An Analysis of Consumer Demand." Georgetown University, McDonough School of Business, Credit Research Center.

FDIC (Federal Deposit Insurance Corporation). 2009. "FDIC National Survey of Unbanked and Underbanked Households." Washington.

Federal Reserve Board. 2010. "Flow of Funds Account of the United States." Federal Reserve Statistical Release Z.1. Washington (March 11). www.federalreserve.gov/releases/z1/Current/z1.pdf.

Flannery, Mark, and Katherine Samolyk. 2005. "Payday Lending: Do the Costs Justify the Price?" Center for Financial Research Working Paper. Washington: FDIC.

Fox, Jean Anne, and Patrick Woodall. 2006. "Cashed Out: Consumers Pay Steep Premium to 'Bank' at Check-Cashing Outlets." Washington: Consumer Federation of America.

Frankel, Tamar, and Clifford E. Kirsch. 2003. *Investment Management Regulation.* 2nd ed. Anchorage: Fathom Publishing.

Friedman, Milton. 1953. "The Methodology of Positive Economics." In *Essays in Positive Economics,* pp. 3–43. University of Chicago Press.

Gabaix, Xavier, and David Laibson. 2006. "Shrouded Attributes, Consumer Myopia, and Information Suppression in Competitive Markets." *Quarterly Journal of Economics* 121, no. 2: 505–40.

GAO (Government Accountability Office). 2009. "Financial Regulation: A Framework for Crafting and Assessing Proposals to Modernize the Outdated U.S. Financial Regulatory System." GAO-09-216. Washington (January 8).

Graves, Stephen M. 2003. "Landscapes of Predation, Landscapes of Neglect: A Locational Analysis of Payday Lenders and Banks." *Professional Geographer* 55, no. 3: 303–17.

Grinblatt, Mark, Matti Keloharju, and Juhani Linnainmaa. 2009. "Do Smart Investors Outperform Dumb Investors?" Working Paper 09-33. University of Chicago Center for Research in Security Prices.

Guiso, Luigi, Paola Sapienza, and Luigi Zingales. 2008. "Trusting the Stock Market." *Journal of Finance* 63, no. 6: 2557–600.

Hastings, Justine S., and Lydia Tejeda-Ashton. 2008. "Financial Literacy, Information, and Demand Elasticity: Survey and Experimental Evidence from Mexico." NBER Working Paper 14538. Cambridge, Mass.: National Bureau of Economic Research (December).

Hillman, Richard J. 2009. "Financial Literacy and Education Commission: Progress Made in Fostering Partnerships, but National Strategy Remains Largely Descriptive Rather than Strategic." GAO-09-638T. Washington: Government Accountability Office (April 29).

Hortacsu, Ali, and Chad Syverson. 2004. "Product Differentiation, Search Costs, and Competition in the Mutual Fund Industry: A Case Study of S&P 500 Index Funds." *Quarterly Journal of Economics* 119, no. 2: 403–56.

Huckstep, Aaron. 2007. "Payday Lending: Do Outrageous Prices Necessarily Mean Outrageous Profits?" *Fordham Journal of Corporate and Financial Law* 12 (October): 203–31.

Hynes, Richard, and Eric A. Posner. 2002. "The Law and Economics of Consumer Finance." *American Law and Economics Review* 4, no. 1: 168–207.

Inderst, Roman, and Marco Ottaviani. 2009. "Misselling through Agents." *American Economic Review* 99, no. 3: 883–908.

Jackson, Howell E. 1999. "Regulation of a Multisectored Financial Services Industry: An Exploratory Essay." *Washington University Law Quarterly* 77, no. 2: 319–97.

———. 2007. "Variation in the Intensity of Financial Regulation: Preliminary Evidence and Potential Implications." *Yale Journal on Regulation* 24, no. 2: 253–91.

———. 2008. "The Trilateral Dilemma in Financial Regulation." In *Overcoming the Savings Slump: How to Increase the Effectiveness of Financial Education and Savings Programs,* edited by Annamaria Lusardi, ch. 3. University of Chicago Press.

Jackson, Howell E., and Laurie Burlingame. 2007. "Kickbacks or Compensation: The Case of Yield Spread Premiums." *Stanford Journal of Law, Business and Finance* 12, no. 2: 289–362.

Jackson, Howell E., and Edward L. Symons. 1999. *The Regulation of Financial Institutions: Cases and Materials.* St. Paul, Minn.: West Publications.

Jacoby, Melissa B. 2010. "Making Debtor Remedies More Effective." UNC Legal Studies Research Paper 1550964. University of North Carolina at Chapel Hill, School of Law. papers.ssrn.com/sol3/papers.cfm?abstract_id=1550964.

Kane, Edward J. 1981. "Accelerating Inflation, Technological Innovation, and the Decreasing Effectiveness of Banking Regulation." *Journal of Finance* 36 (May): 355–67.

Khorana, Ajay, Henri Servaes, and Peter Tufano. 2009. "Mutual Fund Fees around the World." *Review of Financial Studies* 22 (March): 1279–310.

Kimball, Miles S., and Tyler Shumway. 2007. "Investor Sophistication and the Home Bias, Diversification, and Employer Stock Puzzles." Unpublished paper. University of Michigan.

King, Uriah, Leslie Parrish, and Ozlem Tanik. 2006. "Financial Quicksand." Durham, N.C.: Center for Responsible Lending.

Laibson, David. 1997. "Golden Eggs and Hyperbolic Discounting." *Quarterly Journal of Economics* 112, no. 2: 443–77.

Langbein, John H. 1995. "The Contractarian Basis of the Law of Trusts." *Yale Law Journal* 105, no. 625: 632–43.

Lawrence, Edward C., and Gregory Elliehausen. 2008. "A Comparative Analysis of Payday Loan Customers." *Contemporary Economic Policy* 26, no. 2: 299–316.

Lehman, Thomas E. 2005. "Contrasting Payday Loans to Bounced-Check Fees." Washington: Consumer Credit Research Foundation.

Lusardi, Annamaria, and Olivia S. Mitchell. 2006. "Financial Literacy and Planning: Implications for Retirement Well-Being." Working Paper 1. Pension Research Council.

———. 2007. "Baby Boomer Retirement Security: The Roles of Planning, Financial Literacy, and Housing Wealth." *Journal of Monetary Economics* 54, no. 1: 205–24.

Lusardi, Annamaria, Olivia S. Mitchell, and Vilsa Curto. 2010. "Financial Literacy among the Young." *Journal of Consumer Affairs* 44, no. 2: 358–80.

Lusardi, Annamaria, and Peter Tufano. 2009. "Debt Literacy, Financial Experiences, and Overindebtedness." NBER Working Paper w. 14808. Cambridge, Mass.: National Bureau of Economic Research.

Mann, Ronald J., and Jim Hawkins. 2007. "Just until Payday." *UCLA Law Review* 54, no. 4: 855–912.

Melzer, Brian T. 2009. "The Real Costs of Credit Access: Evidence from the Payday Lending Market." Kellogg School of Management, Northwestern University.

Merton, Robert C., and Zvi Bodie. 1995. "A Conceptual Framework for Analyzing the Financial Environment." In *The Global Financial System: A Functional Perspective,* edited by D. B. Crane and others, ch. 1. Boston, Mass.: Harvard Business Press.

Morgan, Donald P., and Michael R. Strain. 2008. "Payday Holiday: How Households Fare after Payday Credit Bans." Staff Report no. 309. Federal Reserve Bank of New York.

Morse, Adair. 2009. "Payday Lenders: Heroes or Villains?" University of Chicago Booth. faculty.chicagobooth.edu/adair.morse/research/Morse_paydayDisaster.pdf.

Parrish, Leslie. 2008. "High-Cost Payday Lending Traps Arizona Borrowers." Durham, N.C.: Center for Responsible Lending.

Peterson, Christopher L. 2008. "Usury Law, Payday Loans, and Statutory Sleight of Hand: Salience Distortion in American Credit Pricing Limits." *Minnesota Law Review* 92, no. 4: 1110.

Schiltz, Elizabeth R. 2004. "The Amazing, Elastic, Ever-Expanding Exportation Doctrine and Its Effect on Predatory Lending Regulation." *Minnesota Law Review* 88 (February): 518–22.

Skiba, Paige, and Jeremy Tobacman. 2007. "The Profitability of Payday Loans." University of Pennsylvania, Wharton School.

———. 2009. "Do Payday Loans Cause Bankruptcy?" ssrn.com/abstract=1266215.

Smale, Pamela. 2005. "Payday Loans: Federal Regulatory Initiatives." Report CR21728. Washington: Congressional Research Service.

Stegman, Michael A. 2007. "Payday Lending." *Journal of Economic Perspectives* 21, no. 1: 169–90.

Stegman, Michael A., and Robert Faris. 2003. "Payday Lending: A Business Model That Encourages Chronic Borrowing." *Economic Development Quarterly* 17, no. 1: 8–32.

Stigler, George J. 1971. "The Theory of Economic Regulation." *Bell Journal of Economics and Management Science* 2 (Spring): 3–21.

Stoianovici, Petru S., and Michael T. Maloney. 2008. "Restrictions on Credit: A Public Policy Analysis of Payday Lending." Battle Group and Clemson University, John E. Walker, Department of Economics. ssrn.com/abstract=1291278.

Strotz, R. H. 1955. "Myopia and Inconsistency in Dynamic Utility Maximization." *Review of Economic Studies* 23, no. 3: 165–80.

Swire, Peter P. 2003. "The Surprising Virtues of the New Financial Privacy Law." *Minnesota Law Review* 86 (June): 1263–323.

Teplin, Albert M. 2001. "The U.S. Flow-of-Funds Accounts and Their Uses." *Federal Reserve Bulletin* (July): 431–41.

Thaler, Richard H., and Cass Sunstein. 2008. *Nudge: Improving Decisions about Health, Wealth, and Happiness.* Yale University Press.

Tufano, Peter. 2009. "Consumer Finance." *Annual Review of Financial Economics* 1, no. 1: 227–47.

Tufano, Peter, and Andrea Ryan. 2009. "Blue Ocean or Stormy Waters? Buying Nix Check Cashing." Case 210-012. Harvard Business School.

White, Michelle J. 2009. "Bankruptcy: Past Puzzles, Recent Reforms, and the Mortgage Crisis." *American Law and Economics Review* 11, no. 1: 1–23.

Wilson, Bart, David W. Findlay, James W. Meehan, Charissa P. Wellford, and Karl Schurter. 2010. "An Experimental Analysis of the Demand for Payday Loans." Working Paper. Chapman University, Economic Science Institute. ssrn.com/abstract=1083796.

Wright, Joshua D. 2007. "Behavioral Law and Economics, Paternalism, and Consumer Contracts: An Empirical Perspective." *NYU Journal of Law and Liberty* 2, no. 3: 470–511.

Zelizer, Viviana A. 1994. *The Social Meaning of Money: Pin Money, Paychecks, Poor Relief, and Other Currencies.* New York: Basic Books.

Zinman, Jonathan. 2008. "Restricting Consumer Credit Access: Household Survey Evidence on Effects around the Oregon Rate Cap." Working Paper 08-32. Philadelphia: Research Department, Federal Reserve Bank of Philadelphia.

Contributors

Eric S. Belsky
*Joint Center for Housing Studies
of Harvard University*

John Y. Campbell
Harvard University

Marsha J. Courchane
Charles River Associates

Ren Essene
Federal Reserve Board

Allen Fishbein
Federal Reserve Board

Howell E. Jackson
Harvard Law School

Melissa Koide
*Center for Financial Services
Innovation*

Michael Lea
San Diego State University

Eugene Ludwig
Promontory Financial Group

Brigitte C. Madrian
Harvard Kennedy School

Nicolas P. Retsinas
Harvard Business School

Nela Richardson
*Joint Center for Housing Studies
of Harvard University*

Rachel Schneider
*Center for Financial Services
Innovation*

Peter Tufano
Harvard Business School

Peter M. Zorn
Freddie Mac

Index

Page numbers followed by *f* and *t* refer to figures and tables respectively.